MODERNIZING THE MIND

Psychological Knowledge and
the Remaking of Society

Steven C. Ward

PRAEGER NEW ENGLAND INSTITUTE OF TECHNOLOGY LIBRARY

Westport, Connecticut
London

Library of Congress Cataloging-in-Publication Data

Ward, Steven C.
　　Modernizing the mind : psychological knowledge and the remaking of society /
Steven C. Ward.
　　　　p. cm.
　　Includes bibliographical references and index.
　　ISBN 0–275–97450–2 (alk. paper)
　　1. Psychology—History—20th century. 2. Psychology—Social
aspects. 3. Knowledge, Theory of. I. Title.
BF105.W35 2002
150'.9—dc21 　　　2002067933

British Library Cataloguing in Publication Data is available.

Library of Congress Catalog Card Number: 2002067933
ISBN: 0–275–97450–2

First published in 2002

Praeger Publishers, 88 Post Road West, Westport, CT 06881
An imprint of Greenwood Publishing Group, Inc.
www.praeger.com

Printed in the United States of America

The paper used in this book complies with the
Permanent Paper Standard issued by the National
Information Standards Organization (Z39.48–1984).

10 9 8 7 6 5 4 3 2 1

Copyright Acknowledgments

The author and the publisher gratefully acknowledge permission for use of the
following material:

Excerpts reprinted from Steven C. Ward, "The Making of Serious Speech: A
Social Theory of Professional Discourse," *Current Perspectives in Social Theory*,
Copyright 1995, Vol. 15, No. 1, pages 63–81, with permission from Elsevier
Science.

Excerpts reprinted from Steven C. Ward, "Filling the World with Self-Esteem: A
Social History of Truth Making," *Canadian Journal of Sociology* 21 (Winter 1996),
pages 1–23, with permission from University of Toronto Press.

To Karen, Kinsey and Kess

Contents

Acknowledgments

WORK ON THIS BOOK WAS MADE POSSIBLE IN PART BY A CSU-AAUP summer grant, a Yale/Mellon Visiting Faculty Fellowship, research release time and a sabbatical leave from Western Connecticut State University. I am grateful for the support of these organizations. I am also grateful to Stephen Sweet, Marilyn Kuruz, Aimee Newell and the anonymous reviewers for their helpful comments and assistance. Also, I would like to thank Joanne Elpern at the Haas Library for managing to track down even the most obscure source. Finally, and most importantly, I would like to thank my family—Karen, Kinsey and Kess—for their support and encouragement.

Chapter 1 had its original incarnation in my article "The Making of Serious Speech: A Social Theory of Professional Discourse," which appeared in *Current Perspectives in Social Theory*, vol. 15 (1) (1995), pp. 63–81 (Ward, 1995a). I thank Elsevier Science for permission to use it here. Also, a segment of chapter 4 is taken from my article "Filling the World with Self-Esteem: A Social History of Truth Making," which appeared in the *Canadian Journal of Sociology*, vol. 21 (1996), pp. 1–23, (Ward, 1996a). I thank the University of Toronto Press for permission to use the segment.

Introduction

THE KNOWLEDGE PRODUCED BY ACADEMIC DISCIPLINES AND professions often appears to be both natural and progressive. Such qualities allow this type of knowledge to seem as if it has always been around, yet often only recently discovered, and as if it bears witness to an inevitable march toward an ultimate and triumphant truth. Such is the case for psychological knowledge, one of the last century's most successful and prolific knowledge forms. Although the discipline of psychology may not match the public respect and governmental spending afforded physics, chemistry, or the other natural sciences, it has arguably done more than any other recent knowledge form to transform conceptualizations of the self and mind, as well as many of the routines and experiences of everyday life (see Danziger, 1990; Rose, 1990; Hacking, 1995). Today, psychological knowledge is present in such diverse places as the discourse of TV talk shows, the organization of production in factories and the self-esteem workshops in public schools. Its practitioners and representatives are found not only at traditional centers of knowledge production, such as universities and research laboratories, but also in courtrooms, at disaster scenes, in advertising agencies, in sports training camps and corporate education centers. In fact, it can be argued that psychological knowledge is so pervasive that to think and feel in the early twenty-first century inevitably means utilizing and activating its terminology, classifications and modes of understanding.

THE "HETEROGENEOUS NETWORK" OF PSYCHOLOGY

Ironically, psychology, as the modern science of the mind, has changed cognition even as it has studied it. While physicists and chemists may have filled homes with useful gadgets and products, their concepts generally have not become part of the Western "collective vocabulary" or "colonized the lifeworld" in quite the same manner as those of psychologists (see Gergen, 1991; Herman, 1995). For instance, while most people easily recognize photographs of Albert Einstein, they often have little knowledge of what his theory of general relativity means or what physicists actually do. Most people do, however, claim to know something about human psychology. As a result of this familiarity, even if directly unrelated to the more formal knowledge found in academic psychology, people have developed a complex and often contradictory relationship with psychological knowledge: they are often critical of the prevalence of "psychobabble" in everyday life, but they readily use psychological frameworks and language to explain such occurrences as their children's lack of success in school, why a relationship has failed or why they fear flying.

As with Rodney Stark's (1997: 3) historical analysis of the spread of Christianity, the proliferation of psychological knowledge over the course of the last century leads to a number of important questions. How was this accomplished? How did a once tiny and obscure movement become one of the most influential intellectual and practical programs of the twentieth and twenty-first centuries?[1] How did psychology manage to reformulate large segments of society, help remap the way people think about themselves and others, and become embedded in the decision-making processes of such social institutions as education, business and law?

Providing answers to these questions entails tracing psychology's "mobilization of the world" (Latour, 1999: 101) and its subsequent "territorialization" of everyday life (Rose, 1996b: 193). Such a journey requires returning to the early years of the discipline of psychology and to the formation of its knowledge about the self and mind. Although the discipline of psychology is only a little over a century old, the story of its proliferation and territorialization is lengthy and multifaceted. Psychological knowledge owes its current status to the work of a multitude of actors and actants over a long period of time and in numerous places. In order for psychology to establish itself as the dominant discourse on the individual and self, prodigious amounts of knowledge work had to be accomplished in many diverse areas. Previous views of the self, mind and society had to be deconstructed and reconfigured. The network of supporters that sustained past positions in theology, mental philosophy and lay knowledge had to be dismantled or transformed into the network of psychology. Knowledge competitors, such as religious leaders, folk psychotherapists, spiritualists, doctors and philosophers, had to be subdued, dismissed, persuaded or incorporated. Nonbelievers in the explanatory power of the new knowledge had to be converted or marginalized. New avenues for the spread of the knowledge had to be created and filled. In addition to these more partisan aspects of knowledge making, the discipline of psychology itself had to become organized and self-reproducing. Workspaces and work objects had to be developed; psychological instruments and measures had to be constructed and fine-tuned; test subjects, rats, graduate students, and pigeons had to be disciplined; and introductory textbooks and diagnostic manuals had to be written, published and promoted (see Danziger, 1990).

The account of the expansion of psychological knowledge, like the story of all knowledge, is not, consequently, the often-told realist story of discovery, revelation, or truth triumphing over ignorance. Rather, it is best seen as a story both of how chaos was turned into order—that is, how facts were "established, constructed, and confirmed" (Bourdieu, Chamboredon, and Passeron, 1991)—and of how other people's knowledge orders were made to look chaotic, then eroded and replaced. Over the course of a century, what began as fragile statements made by a few local and weak psychologists about the workings of the human mind or the constitution of the self turned into strong, ubiquitous facts about the conduct of life. Indeed, these facts have now become so widely known that the majority of people in Western societies are aware of them. As psychological modes of reasoning have entered and become entrenched into everyday life, they have been transformed from provisional and local opinions into seemingly natural and universal psychological facts.

The efficacy and legitimacy of these "natural psychological facts" are supported by a large number of self-perpetuating "psy" organizations and institutions that are specifically fitted for the dissemination of psychological knowledge. For instance, today the field of education is filled with an array of psychological concepts and methods that are used to manage students, train teachers and direct pedagogy. Likewise, courts are dependent on psychological experts to provide personality appraisals and assessments of "pain and suffering" damages. As these examples illustrate, psychological knowledge has become embedded in various institutional mechanisms of decision making that, like its popularization, serve to create, legitimate and sustain its integrity. In this sense, contemporary psychology can be thought of as less a coherent body of knowledge than as, in Nikolas Rose's terminology, a "heterogeneous network of agents, sites, practices, and techniques for the production, dissemination, legitimation, and utilization of psychological truths" (Rose, 1996a: 114). This psychological network is so vast that it now extends well beyond the domain of the discipline of psychology.

In this book I examine a small segment of the elaborate history of the "heterogeneous network" of American psychology. I explore a few of the ways and places where psychological knowledge slowly came to permeate, (re)enframe and transform everyday experience. As such, this work is intended to be a case study of some of the intricate processes involved in knowledge production, circulation and incorporation. I am, however, interested in much more than how psychological knowledge moved into everyday life and produced different conceptualizations of personhood, mind, and self; I am also interested in how psychology and its particular way of conceptualizing minds and selves contributed to the production of a new version of society.

Through a complex mobilization and (re) arrangement of people and things, psychology was able to forge and spread not only new conceptualizations of the mind and self and a host of what might be termed "personal psychological practices" but also became an important means through which a new version of society was constructed— although this accomplishment was certainly produced neither alone, in isolation, nor without resistance. When this rearrangement of people and things was complete, society no longer contained mysterious souls but knowable minds. There were no longer unruly and fidgety children but children suffering from attention-deficit/hyperactivity disorder. People were no longer afraid but paranoid. Society no longer had bad people, but psychopaths. People were no longer caring but had "emotional intelligence." No longer were there shy people but those with low levels of self-esteem. The flow of psychological knowledge from the relative isolation of laboratories and universities into the activities of various professions, institutions and the practices of everyday life fundamentally changed society. In this process intelligence became measurable, selves transformable, behavior correctable, and mental states diagnosable. In short, the discipline of psychology, much like the natural sciences it often sought to emulate, modernized the mind and, as a result, remolded both the organization of society and even the concept of society itself. This book seeks to provide a small part of the complex social history of this important cultural and epistemological reformation.

PRIMARY OBJECTIVES—OR, WHAT THIS BOOK IS NOT ABOUT

With the above discussion in mind, it is possible to identify the three central objectives of this work. First, I wish to explore some of the specific practices and links that enabled the discipline of psychology to establish itself as the most important institutional authority on the individual, self, mind and their dysfunctions in the twentieth and twenty-first centuries. Second, I want to follow psychological knowledge as it moved from early disciplinary isolation in the laboratory and university and formed alliances with a number of groups and organizations throughout the United States. Third, I wish to use this history to assess how the spread of psychological knowledge was partially responsible for reconfiguring the meaning and contours of what we call "modernity."

As such, this work is intended to be neither a traditional history nor a critique of the field of psychology. Despite using numerous primary sources from the history of American psychology, I make no attempt to provide a sequenced or periodized narrative of the history of the field or an assessment of its theoretical or empirical successes or failures.[2] I am also not interested in providing a critique of psychology as a "great modern ideological system" (Williams, 1978: 128–129), a "defender of the status quo" (Prilleltensky, 1994), a form of "discipline" (Foucault, 1979) or a disseminator of "instrumental rationality." Such tasks have been readily accomplished by a host of historians of psychology and by cultural critics. Rather, my intent is to provide what Nikolas Rose (1996a: 104) has referred to as a "critical history" of psychology. Such a critical history enables us to "think against the present," by providing an account of how today's taken-for-granted psychological truths and reality came to be (Rose, 1996b: 18). This book is, consequently, best seen as a thematic or topical approach to explaining some of the ways psychological knowledge interrupted and reformulated large segments of contemporary society. As such, my treatment is far short of a comprehensive or linear history of the development of the discipline or its various branches. Rather, it is a series of historical snapshots of some of the struggles, compromises and alliances that were responsible for transforming psychology and its knowledge form from a marginal moral philosophy at the turn of the twentieth century, to a household word by the middle of the century, to an intuitive part of the cultural and institutional landscape in our own time. This is, consequently, a "theory-driven" work, in which various examples from the history of psychology are drawn upon to illustrate the various confluences of knowledge and society. It is situated somewhere between the sociology of knowledge and science, on one hand, and the history of psychology, on the other. For the empirically minded historian it may contain too few historical details on the development of the discipline and knowledge form; for the more theoretically oriented sociologist of knowledge and science, it may be overly historically descriptive.[3]

It is also important to point out that this work is primarily concerned with the *type* or *style* of psychological knowledge produced within the discipline of psychology rather than of that contained in the more general "psychological individualism" associated with modernity. As we shall see, however, such a demarcation is difficult to sustain for long, because psychology was one of the means through which this individualistic orientation was created and spread. While the central focus of this book is on the knowledge produced by academic and professional psychologists, psychological knowledge itself is perhaps better seen as the convergence of a number of epistemic and social "psy" movements in the nineteenth and twentieth centuries. The psychological knowledge produced within the discipline of psychology both borrowed from these existing "folk psychologies" and was often disseminated by their already established support networks. I argue that the merger and interchange of professional psychology and folk psychologies partially explains the ubiquity and naturalness of psychological knowledge today.

In this work I also make no attempt to sort psychological knowledge into various schools of thought or theoretical camps or to compare the knowledge contributions of those camps. It is quite evident that psychology is a loosely organized discipline—or to put it more kindly, a "multiparadigmatic field" with dozens of experimental and clinical subspecialties and numerous theoretical camps. Perhaps so general a term as "psychological knowledge" is much too unifying a concept. However, I am less interested in the theoretical arguments of the vying groups within the discipline of psychology than in the broader framework of knowledge produced by its various camps. Consequently, I place less emphasis on the specific ideas and theories of psychologists than on the various "intellectual technologies" or "technologies of the self" (Foucault, 1988) that they and their allies introduced. In this sense, I am interested in outlining some of the political and practical activities that made "visible and intelligible certain features of persons, their conduct, and the relations with one another" (Rose, 1996b: 11).

Finally, reference is made throughout this work to psychological knowledge as having its own internal logic. Psychological knowledge is treated here as a collective accomplishment—in Martin Kusch's (1999) term, a "social institution"—and not just as another professional form of truth, rhetoric or discourse. Such absence of human agency is not intended as an anthropomorphism of social systems theory or an overly macro conception of human action; rather, it is an attempt to show that psychological knowledge has reality sui generis that stretches beyond the boundaries of its individual creators. This is not to deny that psychological knowledge flows through the actions of its practitioners but to recognize that all knowledge, specifically expert knowledge, also has a "validity independent of the practitioners and clients who make use of it" (Giddens, 1991: 18). It is also meant to remind us that knowledge making is always and everywhere a coordinated activity that under certain special conditions may congeal into a self-reproducing organization, network, discipline or social form. In fact, it is through these activities that organizations, disciplines and societies are continuously made and remade.

NOTES

1. In contrast to Stark, however, this work is not intended as a traditional microsociological, exchange account of the growth of a movement (see Stark, 1999).

2. This book concerns itself with examples drawn primarily from the history of American psychology. For a listing of a few important dates and events in the history of American psychology, see the appendix.

3. Such a dichotomy seems to run through most works in the history and sociology of science. Most works are either "heavy" on theory and "light" on history or "light" on theory and "heavy" on history. Throughout this work I have tried to chart a middle path between theoretical explanation and historical detail.

1

How Truth Travels: Knowledge, Networks and the Organization of Society

ONE OF THE WAYS IN WHICH MODERN SOCIETIES HAVE BEEN distinguished from traditional or "premodern" societies is by the particular way in which they organize the production and circulation of knowledge. Whereas traditional societies are typified by local and diffuse knowledge forms, modern societies are characterized by the proliferation of a variety of centralized and interconnected "expert knowledge systems" (see Giddens, 1991). Such "knowledge societies," in the words of Karin Knorr-Cetina (1999: 1), "run on expert processes and expert systems that are epitomized by science but are structured into all areas of social life." They concentrate the production of what might be called "official" or "hard" knowledge in discrete organizations and institutions whose task it is to produce knowledge and disseminate it to those "who know less" or who simply lack the ability to create their own knowledge. Furthermore, within the confines of modern society, knowledge increasingly becomes an important part of the feedback mechanisms that various social institutions use to adjust to changing circumstances (see Beck, 1992). In this instance, knowledge is not just produced for its own sake but is actively employed to correct and realign institutions' approach to the various problems confronting them.

In modern societies, topics as far-ranging as where to construct power plants, how to have more gratifying sex or, ironically, how expertise affects social life have slowly come to be the dominion of these expert knowledge systems. Everyday examples of the proliferation of expertly crafted knowledge and language abound: a mass murder is profiled by a university criminologist, a woman is diagnosed with a case of "fear of success" by a clinical psychologist, China foreign policy is assessed by a spokesperson for the Center for Strategic and International Studies, and a new welfare plan is analyzed by a poverty researcher at the Ford Foundation. In each of these examples, the knowledge, terminology and classifications of the expert are designed to convey the true meaning of an event or process. Their purpose is to transform amorphous and uncertain stories into coherent and meaningful truths. Usually the authority of scientific or professionally based knowledge backs these descriptions and interpretations. These statements are made by groups and institutions with the power and resources to transform the abstract, ill defined, and unknown into the concrete, systematic, and understood. Furthermore, these statements are made by groups that are thought to have the power to delineate reality and appearance, fact and fiction and authenticity and simulation. They are, in essence, designed to substitute the soft belief of lay and local opinion with the hard and universal knowledge of expertly produced knowledge.

Yet, the knowledge produced by experts does much more than provide a particular language and cognitive framework for describing or redescribing the world. It also demarcates and stratifies the legitimacy of a claim to know. Expert knowledge serves as a means to segregate everyday speech and understanding from serious speech and hard knowledge. Within this context, everyday descriptions of objects and events are often presented as theoretically underdetermined, empirically imprecise or, in some cases, out-and-out distortions. Everyday understanding is portrayed as lacking the full explanatory power or logical precision contained in expert knowledge; knowledge specialists are seen as able to capture more accurately what is truly going on in the physical world, the body, society or within the psyche. Over time, the authorized knowledge of the expert often becomes integrated into the lexicon and knowledge form of daily life. In this instance it becomes part of the epistemic material one needs in order to be considered a competent citizen—or simply to negotiate one's way through the narratives and public encounters of everyday life (see Bourdieu, 1984).

Before examining psychology as a particular form or style of contemporary expert knowledge, it is necessary to offer a more general theoretical account of how knowledge is crafted and translated, how it travels, enlists others and reproduces itself. In this first chapter I sketch a rather broad theory of how knowledge travels via organizations and networks. The position I advance here looks to neither of the traditional sources of explanation—nature (i.e., the way things are) and society (the way culture makes them to be)—as the ultimate cause of knowledge but instead focuses on the specific links and practices that must be established if claims are to become truthful. This approach explores how, over time, "truth happens" as these links and practices congeal into specific organizational patterns, networks and social forms. As this occurs, not only do older notions of self, nature and society become recast and experiences change in fundamental ways, but the actual composition of such categories are (re)constituted and (re)enforced. For example, such terms as "psyche" or "society" should not be seen as referring to some original ontological ordering of things but as categories that themselves must be made, defended and enforced. In the approach advanced here, the things called "nature" or "society" are the final outcomes of the congealing of networks of actors and actants rather than the causes (see Latour, 1993; 1996). In other words, knowledge, nature and society are simultaneous coproductions and not isolated, atomistic "causes of things."

Borrowing from works in science and technology studies, I treat the knowledge forms and products of different groups as epistemologically symmetrical yet associationally asymmetrical. In other words, while no knowledge-producing group is seen as having the ability to reflect an absolute reality, at least not the version of reality and truth described in traditional epistemology, some are in better positions to produce hard knowledge than others. Certain individuals or groups are thought to represent and speak more precisely or accurately; consequently, they are more listened to and believed. Their knowledge, classification systems and discourse come to be recognized as more authoritative, scientific, rational, powerful and serious. Because of the extensive networks and organization of these groups, their knowledge becomes an important reference that one must have in order to be "educated," "informed" or merely an accepted member of a particular group. However, this is an instance not just of the power of power to coerce but of the formation of completely new "ecological niches" (Hacking, 1998) social formations and networks that enable such understandings to exist and flourish. As Foucault put it, "We must cease to always describe effects of power in negative terms: it 'excludes,' it 'represses,' it 'buries,' it 'censors,' it 'abstracts,' it 'masks,' it 'hides.' In fact power produces; it produces the real; it produces domains of objects and rituals of truth" (Foucault quoted in Gomart and Hennion, 1999: 221).

KNOWING ABOUT KNOWING: THE CONDITION OF KNOWLEDGE IN THE EARLY TWENTY-FIRST CENTURY

A book written about psychological knowledge (or any knowledge form) cannot help but encounter the reflexive paradox of the "postmodern condition of knowledge" (see Lyotard, 1984). Recently, knowing about knowing became an alluring fascination of the fin de siècle West. It was responsible for launching the "science wars" between the sciences and the humanities in the mid-1990s and spawned numerous debates within various academic disciplines over the relationship between representation and reality (see Gross and Levitt, 1994; Ward, 1995b). There appears to be no clear-cut winner in these various epistemic and cultural wars (see Latour, 1999). For every claim of an accurate representation of reality in the realists' corner comes an equally plausible counter-claim of its linguistic or social construction in the relativists' alcove.

To some extent this quandary over the status of knowledge has resulted from the epistemological landscape left by traditional epistemology and by various philosophies of science since the seventeenth century. In such an epistemological landscape it is possible to identify three prevalent, general frameworks for understanding knowledge acquisition: progressive, critical and social constructionist.[1] These three frameworks are dependent, at least to some extent, on their understandings of the role of society and politics in the production of knowledge. Progressive theories often utilize positivist and scientific realist philosophies of science. They picture contemporary knowledge, particularly the type produced under the confines of scientific methodology, as always better than its predecessors or cross-cultural rivals (see Leplin, 1984; Kitcher, 1993).[2] Within this model, knowledge is discovered rather than created. The immutable laws of nature, society or human nature have ordered the world in such a way that knowledge producers are capable of extracting and conceptualizing the essential order or classification system contained in reality. However, from this perspective, reality will not unlock its conceptual secrets to just anyone, or under just any circumstance. The "mirroring of reality" will occur if, and only if, proper methodology has been followed, mind and matter are in alignment, supporting evidence is available for inspection and peer scrutiny and the findings are open to replication. For progressivists, the specialized conceptual language of science and other professional knowledge forms is merely a neutral, although sometimes problematic, instrument for conveying what is already there. Here knowledge accumulates, and truth triumphs, as practitioners hone their methodology, learn from their mistakes and further approach the reality of what is given. In these theories society and politics have no constructive roles to play in the production of knowledge; they are, as Bacon warned in the seventeenth century, contaminating influences on truth that must be kept at bay in order for reality to be uncovered and unbiased knowledge to prevail.

Whereas progressive theories hail the evolutionary and teleological aspects of knowledge making, critical accounts view most contemporary knowledge, except often their own, as largely regressive or repressive. These accounts may employ social theory from middle and late nineteenth-century philosophy or sociology, or they may rely on more recent versions of poststructuralist or essentialistic feminist or postcolonialist theories. Critical theorists treat contemporary knowledge as either the erosion of traditional, and allegedly more genuine and authentic, forms of knowing or as instrumentalist outcomes of increasingly oppressive forms of social control.

From the critical perspective, the pursuit of knowledge is defined by the intrusion of instrumental rationality, the domination of the Apollonian over the Dionysian spirit, "the violence of the letter," masculinist assumptions secretly posing as human universals, Western logocentrism, the expansion of "technologies of the self" or capitalist ideology's one-dimensional emphasis on profit and efficiency, to name but a few. In these theories society also contaminates knowledge; however, it is the instrumentalist, ideological, masculinist, logocentric or Eurocentric knowledge produced in the modern West that most corrupts and threatens our understanding of how the world actually works. As such, it becomes necessary to clear away these forms of oppression before a more complete understanding of events and phenomena can emerge.

Social and textual constructionism is at the opposite end of the epistemological spectrum from the above frameworks. This approach shares critical theories' emphasis on the cultural and historical situatedness of knowledge. Constructionists are, however, generally much less normative about the implications of recognizing that knowledge is socially and linguistically produced. They utilize a num-

ber of influences, ranging from phenomenology and symbolic inter-
actionism to postmodern textual deconstruction. For constructionists,
society always and everywhere provides the material for building
knowledge: meaning must always pass through society. All representation is, therefore, affected by language and culture. Linguistic
practices and the acts of nomination and signification are always key
processes in the creation of reality. In this understanding of knowledge, language is not, as the progressivists contend, the "neutral instrument of a triumphant content" (Barthes, 1976: 10) that merely
aggravates truth finding; nor is it, as the critical theorists see it, the
misrepresentations of modernists; rather, it is the central ingredient
in the constitution of all reality states. Discourse is not to be seen as
merely a group of referential signs but, as Foucault (1972: 49) put it,
as "practices that systematically form the objects of which they speak."

One result of establishing language and rhetoric as primary elements in knowledge making is that there is considered to be nothing
beyond the text (Derrida, 1976). There is no unmediated reality waiting to be unlocked by accurate conceptualization or representation,
only more and more signification (see Rorty, 1991). All attempts to
escape or subdue language, such as in scientific knowledge or critical
assessments of scientific knowledge, ultimately feed back on themselves and "engender the repetition and continuation of literature"
(de Man, 1971: 162). As a result, constructionists conclude that all
truth is to be seen exclusively as a discursive creation, backed by the
prevailing power configurations of a society. Knowledge can never be
free from the power dynamics, conceptual hierarchies or cultural material of a given society. Consequently, modernity does not necessarily
contaminate knowledge any more than occurs at other times and
places, but neither does it provide the conditions necessary for the
realization of knowledge. The task of constructionists is to show how
culture and society everywhere and always shapes both the form and
content of knowledge. Understanding the elaborate social history of
a prolific knowledge form, such as psychology, makes it necessary to
rethink all three of these current epistemic frameworks. The progressivists' present an otherworldly view of knowledge production—
a place where there are no political disputes, alternative representations, historical accidents or even meaningful human and nonhuman
actors. In the words of Hilary Putnam (1994: 452), it proposes reality
as "a single super thing, instead of looking at the ways in which we
endlessly renegotiate—and are forced to renegotiate—our notions of
realty as our language and our life develops." In contrast, the banal-

ized society of critical theories lacks an appreciation of the intricate struggles and craft work involved in the process of knowledge making in all times and places. Their efforts at unmasking truth force them to see knowledge as raw power and nothing else (see Hacking, 1999). However, by treating knowledge always as an outcome of confining social forces and oppressive power operations, they are ironically wedded to the very epistemology they seek to overthrow. Critical theorists are as guilty as progressivists of providing an a priori, epistemological treatment of knowledge; however, this time the enlightenment's grand narrative of knowledge making is simply told in reverse.

The other prevailing theory of knowledge, social and textual constructionism, has provided a valuable and often-used contemporary technique for rethinking the meaning of reality, truth and knowledge. Constructionists, however, employ what Ian Hacking (1998: 101) has referred to as a "lazy terminology" that establishes vague links between social context and knowledge. While many of these accounts concur that the ideas, truths, concepts, and theories are to be seen as social or textual constructs rather than as reflections of reality, few provide detailed descriptions of the various associations that make up the elaborate networks of knowledge. As such, they often utilize a type of "cultural ether" to explain the social construction of reality (Michael, 1996: 157). Constructionists are, consequently, guilty of utilizing ambiguous, circumstantial evidence to link knowledge and context. They treat culture and society as already constructed entities rather than as works that are themselves in process. In this sense constructionism "is adequate only if it can explain why some constructs appear unconstructed" (Fuchs, 2001: 338).

Many social and textual constructionist accounts also suffer from the classic problem of reflexivity that accompanies discussions of the relationship between knowledge and society (see Lawson, 1985; Ashmore, 1989). Within this problem the arguments of constructionists can easily be turned on their own accounts. For instance, if a concept or knowledge form is seen as the result of prevailing social forces, the idea that social forces are the cause of the concept or knowledge must be the result of social forces. In most cases, this problem creates a reflexivistic spiral that either renders the constructionist's arguments about the social constitution of knowledge paradoxical and ineffective or ends in a familiar deadlock between realist and relativist epistemic factions (see Woolgar, 1988; 1992; Ward, 1995b).

A social history of knowledge, like the one of psychology described here, requires the adoption of a new epistemic attitude and method (see Latour, 1993). First, it is necessary to become "amodernistic" (Latour, 1993) by abandoning the distinctions between modern and premodern, Western and non-Western and professional and lay practices or forms of knowledge—a distinction that in some manner supports all three of the above theories of knowledge. Modernistic approaches allow for the classification of knowledge along a developmental time line. Knowledge produced under the modern, scientific conditions of experimentation and replication is said to be of a special and higher variety than that produced in other times and places. Being amodernistic requires treating knowledge as a pragmatic and contingent accomplishment. In this approach there are no qualitative cognitive or methodological differences between the modern and the premodern, Western and non-Western or professional and lay ways of knowing, only variations in the types, size and resilience of the networks that different groups are able to forge at different times and places (see Latour, 1987). What separates an Azande witch doctor and a MIT physicist is not the level of individual freedom, the correct methodology, the degree of cognitive complexity or finally getting the terminology right, as most progressivists argue. Rather, it is the ability to establish strong and heterogeneous associations, mobilize resources and forge truth. With this move the focus is now placed on the ability of knowledge producers to persuade and convert others into accepting their designations—to construct elaborate, meaningful and powerful networks of the truthful. Consequently, the processes that explain the growth of knowledge are fundamentally no different from those that explain the expansion of religions, pop music or artistic styles. All must establish networks in order to spread the word.

Second, as the strong programme in the sociology of scientific knowledge suggested a few decades ago, it is important to treat both truth and lie symmetrically (see Bloor, 1976). Separating the wheat of knowledge "from the chaff of ideology" (Latour, 1993: 35), as both progressivist and critical theorists of knowledge attempt, often ends in a confusing and contradictory normative task of cleansing or defending certain knowledge styles and strategies. While clarifying methodology may be a valuable undertaking in certain instances, it does not allow for an understanding of the varied and heterogeneous processes involved in the production of truth or lie. All groups battle over what is true or false; however, deciding in favor of one faction over another, particularly before truth has "settled," is beyond the scope of an empirically focused sociology of knowledge. Finally, it becomes important to rethink the concept of society and its role in shaping knowledge. Instead of seeing society as a ready-made entity, which then effects some knowledge form, as social and textual constructionists have it, it is important to explore how knowledge and society are coproduced (see Latour, 1993; 1996). Both society and knowledge are to be conceptualized as works in process. Only when networks are stabilized and alliances are gelled into self-perpetuating organizations do we have things fixed enough to be called "knowledge" or "society," and even then this solidity exists only within the networks that are doing the naming. Until this occurs, we do not have absolute truth but "truth in the making." Nor do we have societies but "societies in production." In this sense, ways of knowing and social formations are constantly being made and remade. This, then, makes problems of knowledge essentially problems of social order, and vice versa (see Shapin, 1994).

In order to provide a social history of knowledge in the making, it is necessary to de-epistemologize, or "de-essentialize," knowledge (see Fuchs, 2001)—to dispense with both the progressivists' and critical theorists' attempts to sort truth neatly from lie, and with the constructionists' confounding of them. This de-epistemologicalization requires us to follow knowledge as it travels the long road from fragile beginnings to an indisputable and widespread truth—or perhaps, in many cases, to collapse. In this process it is important to take note of the various objects and people the knowledge network pulls into its ever-expanding system of knowing, and how this network then begins to take on a reality of its own. When progressive, critical and constructionist accounts of knowledge are abandoned, it becomes possible to conceptualize knowledge as neither the asocial triumph of nature, the power-ridden decline of Western civilization, nor as an oversocialized sociological assemblage. In the following pages I elaborate on how such a theory requires new ways of approaching the production and dissemination of knowledge.

GETTING TO THE TRUTH: THE PRODUCTION OF KNOWLEDGE

The making of knowledge, like the making of a breakfast cereal or an automobile, requires a centralized site of production—a "center of calculation" (Latour, 1987), or a "heterotopia" (Foucault, 1986). In order for knowledge to happen, significant capital must be appropriated, equipment must be constructed, data must be collected and stored, artifacts must be produced, allies must be recruited and a network of knowledge makers must be forged. The ability to make the knowledge of one group that of another requires a concentrated and sustained effort that only organizations specifically fitted for the production of hard knowledge can perform. It is only at such sites that documents and artifacts can be made to "represent reality" and "speak the truth." It is here where a collective and sustained effort can provide the practical opportunities for a truth claim to be established. In these centers of calculation, human and nonhuman resources can be rallied to transform localized practices into documents or artifacts that are capable of traveling beyond the confines of sites of production (Law, 1986).

Since expert knowledge production requires a centralized site of production, it is most often located at universities, corporate headquarters, research institutes, think tanks, military command centers or bureaucratic agencies. These interlocking centers have the dense organization and financial capital needed to mobilize the human and nonhuman resources necessary for the production of hard knowledge. Creating professional, scientific knowledge is an expensive undertaking, and "only a few people, nations, institutions or professions are able to sustain it" (Latour 1987: 179). This is why most modern knowledge is made within disciplines. These are some of the only groups organized enough to make knowledge happen.

In modern societies, one of the prime sites for the production of hard knowledge is the research institute. These reality centers rarely operate as described in methodological accounts, logic textbooks or valiant reports of scientific discovery (see Latour and Woolgar, 1986). For example, social studies of science have shown that scientists reason more like ordinary sense makers than logisticians, and that their knowledge is more of a contingent interpretive accomplishment than a fixed representation of reality (see Fuchs, 1992; 1993, Knorr-Cetina, 1981; Knorr-Cetina and Mulkay, 1983; Lynch, 1985; Collins, 1985). However, while these empirical studies of science reveal scientists to be "undercover hermeneuticians," this does not lessen their ability to define the real and speak the truth—that is, if we drop the epistemological distinction between true and false knowledge forms discussed earlier. What determines reality and truth is not the cognitive supremacy of the producer or a more refined methodology but a "trial of strength" (Latour, 1987; 1988).

In this trial of strength, most statements begin as fragile opinions about the nature of an object, event or phenomenon. As such, these statements are often weak, lonely and unsupported. In order for a weak and isolated opinion to become a strong fact, it must recruit and attach itself to a heterogeneous array of allies. Essentially, a position must be tried and acquitted before it can obtain the status of truth (Fuchs and Ward, 1995). This is accomplished not by showing that a particular position corresponds with the real, as in traditional epistemology, but by establishing strong allies and associational networks that are capable of resolving disputes over data interpretation, ending controversies, resisting the deconstructionist tactics of adversaries and spreading the word. The more encompassing the network, the truer, or harder, a position becomes. In those rare instances when a position is solidified and the "black boxes" of knowledge have been sealed, people do not "live in a world of fiction, approximation, convention; they are simply right" (Latour, 1987: 206). In other words, if a position has been successful in recruiting a large number of allies (some human and some nonhuman) and can sustain those alliances in the face of the efforts of adversaries to unravel it, the network becomes strong, and the position becomes true. In such situations a position becomes difficult to challenge, since all legitimate threats have been convinced, incorporated or neutralized. There is neither magic nor an epistemological miracle involved in this process of closure: the practical activities of knowledge workers and their elaborate networks have forged the true out of the materials at their disposal.

As a consequence of strong associational linkages, the products of these professional knowledge-producing organizations are more likely to become truthful. Their knowledge differs from ordinary knowledge not because it is more accurate but because it is embedded in networks that are stronger or harder (i.e., ones that are larger, more encompassing and more resilient). In turn, the soft facts of everyday life differ from the hard facts of science not by their respective degrees of logic or empirical precision but by the type of "sociologic" required for their construction (Latour, 1987). Millions of dollars have gone into the creation and maintenance of hard-knowledge institutions and their discursive products; hundreds of papers and articles have been published, computers have been filled with data, experimental hardware has been fine-tuned and strong links have been forged among participants and allied groups. In the face of so many "officially sanctioned props" (Mehan et al., 1986: 130) and so much coordinated and sustained effort among participants, ordinary knowledge becomes secondary, irrational, inaccurate, primitive or imprecise. These are less clear-cut epistemological distinctions than cries of a winner (Latour, 1988b).

Like all manufactured products, hard knowledge must travel from sites of production to localized markets. The process by which this occurs is crucial for understanding the ways in which hard, expert knowledge comes to challenge and often replace ordinary knowledge in everyday life.

GETTING THE TRUTH OUT: THE DISSEMINATION OF KNOWLEDGE

Once hard knowledge has been produced at a center of calculation, it is ready to be disseminated. Often the legitimacy and financial integrity of the knowledge-making institution is linked with its ability to attract knowing converts outside of its organizational and professional confines (see Amsterdamska, 1987). However, while all knowledge-making groups need some degree of outside support and acquiescence, dissemination does not occur through the same avenues or at the same rate in all areas. Some knowledge-making institutions are very protective of their epistemic products, for fear of contamination or distortion by "outsiders," while others actively and openly seek public recognition, acceptance and conversion.[3]

Depending on the type of knowledge-producing institution involved, there are several means through which knowledge can travel from one place to another. In one strategy, a knowledge-producing group can directly appeal to outsiders through information offices or through such large media organizations as the U.S.-based group Media Resource Service. Information offices play a key role in dissemination, because they are often involved in the critical task of reinscribing or visually representing the hard, insider knowledge of the institution. Knowledge that is not reinscribed risks being unduly isolated by its own abstruseness. Often few outside of the knowledge-producing site are able to decipher the cryptic symbolism of the profession. In the reinscription process, the hard, insider knowledge of the institution is replaced with more "novel and docile elements" that are easily transportable beyond the walls of the research site (Law and Whittaker, 1988: 160). Reinscription allows the knowledge product of professional producers to be translated into a more palatable form that can be more easily disseminated. Although translated during the process of reinscription, the knowledge must still maintain an "impression of rationality" for the receiver (Lynch, 1985; 1991). It must convey "the impression of precise distinctions, bounded cognitive fields, and delimited causal forces" (Lynch, 1991: 13). Reinscription covers over any interpretative scratches and gives the knowledge product the accessibility it needs in order to be efficiently disseminated. It also increases the chances that the knowledge will be accepted by other individuals and groups, particularly in applied wings of a field or related fields.

Another means of direct dissemination can be identified in science service groups, such as the Media Resource Service (MRS). Established in the United States during the Three Mile Island incident, the MRS links the media with scientists in particular fields (Jerome, 1986). Reporters wanting to know about a particular scientific issue can call the service, which puts them in contact with specialists in the field. Such direct contact with the public, either in the form of information offices or groups like the Media Resource Service, is usually reserved for knowledge-making institutions and individuals that are already well established and respected. Knowledge-making institutions without the proper credentials are usually not involved in this type of direct dissemination.

A second, and more common, type of dissemination can also be identified. Here, knowledge is first disseminated to lower-ranking professionals within a hard-knowledge field before it is disseminated to a certain strata of the general public. In this instance, knowledge "trickles down" from the truth-making institution through lower-echelon professionals to the general public. The lower-echelon professionals can be thought of as the foot soldiers of the knowledge-making centers. Like traveling salespeople, they go door to door peddling their intellectual wares. The lower-echelon professionals' conversion to official knowledge occurs not through direct exposure to hard-knowledge production but through secondary sources, such as books, journals, annual conventions and conferences and informal informational networks. These second-order disseminators often have relatively low reputational status within their own professions. Often these individuals are on the periphery of their professions and hard-knowledge production. In some cases they are academics at second-tier institutions, in other cases applied practitioners. These individuals usually lack the centers of calculation and formal reputational networks necessary to produce their own hard knowledge. Consequently, they are obliged to adhere to the products of the institutions or professions of which they are members in order to maintain their credentials and increase their prospects of becoming part of the larger formal reputational network of the hard knowledge-making centers—although they rarely do.[4]

Once hard knowledge has been disseminated to lower-echelon professionals, it can be spread through direct contact to certain segments of the public. This second-order dissemination and reproduction occurs in doctors' offices, in counseling groups, at corporate training centers, in classrooms, at seminars, over local-television air waves and at countless other sites. Patients listen to doctors telling them of "chronic fatigue syndrome," clients listen to counselors describing a "dependent personality disorder," office workers listen to managers lauding "total quality management," and students listen to professors extolling the details of "cosmological natural selection." In turn, these listeners return to their homes, offices or classrooms and further spread the word. First, however, these listening groups must have certain credentials to be in the position of listening. Listening to the truth, like producing it, does not come cheaply.

The proceeding discussion provides an explanation of how hard knowledge is disseminated. However, it does not tell us why people accept it. How does hard, professional knowledge come to be dominant? Also, and most importantly, why do some convert, while others are left with the "imprecision" of ordinary knowledge?

BEING IN THE TRUTH: THE INCOPORATION OF KNOWLEDGE

It has been shown that in hospital settings over time patients adopt the medical language of the health professionals with whom they are in contact. On the other hand, doctors rarely seek to communicate in the everyday language of their patients (Bourhis, Roth and MacQueen, 1989). Other discursive studies reveal that professionals are much less likely to be interrupted or to be asked for clarification in speech events than are nonprofessionals (Mehan, 1986). It has also been shown that defendants in court proceedings who are able to act and speak in accordance with the dominant strategies and values of the courtroom (i.e., middle-class defendants) are more likely to be viewed positively by judges. Those who do not are often viewed negatively and asked for clarification (Wodak-Engel, 1984).

The "code switching" apparent in these localized settings is similar to the dynamics involved in the acceptance of hard knowledge. Expertly produced knowledge comes to be recognized as having the most symbolic and moral power, and consequently the largest exchange value. Those who are able to communicate with the knowledge and in the language of the powerful (e.g., doctors, psychologists, scientists or judges) are more likely to be perceived as possessing the status of the organization and people doing the speaking. Speaking in accordance with these codes will allow one to be admitted to universities, do well on standardized exams, understand public discourse and fit in with professional groups. Those who do not acquire these forms of speech or knowledge are often considered not only linguistically inferior but socially inferior as well. For instance, people who lack the psychological vocabulary to express emotions are sometimes viewed as possessing impoverished vocabularies and outlooks. The terminology, taxonomy and classification schemes of serious, professionalized knowledge are the recognized exemplars of appropriate patterns and styles of communication. Collectively, they become the way the competent and correct are supposed to communicate.

Pierre Bourdieu (1977: 652) has remarked that "when one language dominates the market, it becomes the norm against which the prices of the other modes of expression . . . are defined." Hard knowledge, like "high fashion" or "fine wine," serves to demarcate the sophisticated from the unsophisticated, the learned from the ignorant or the correct from the misinformed. Just as one could recognize fifteenth-century European nobility by the quantity of velvet in their hats (see Ewen, 1988), it is possible to tell who is "educated" and "in the truth" by the forms of knowledge and speech they employ to represent and talk about the world. Since hard knowledge is the most expensive to produce and disseminate, contains the most encompassing networks, and has the backing of the most important and powerful allies, it sets the criteria of epistemic competence. Hard knowledge supplies the dominant code for the discussion of "important matters" (e.g., affairs of the state, economy, health, etc.) by providing the framework through which things are properly represented. It becomes the standard against which all epistemic currencies are measured, as well as the raw material for the construction of moral and symbolic boundaries between groups with varying levels of "epistemic competence." In Durkheimian terms, those who use the same terminology and knowledge forms as we do are part of our correct epistemic tribe. Speaking this language becomes a way of further enacting and sustaining membership.

Since the procession of hard knowledge is inevitably caught up within, and contributes to, stratification, some groups are better able than others to enhance their positions by employing the terminology of hard knowledge in both professional and everyday interactions. These groups are often the central consumers and promoters of hard knowledge and of insider/outsider knowledge boundaries in everyday life. In this instance, the newly established fact serves as a moral weapon, to be used to fend off transgressors of the group's normative order or to convert the remaining isolated pockets of conceptual atheists or heathens.

An individual's knowledge style becomes an aspect of his or her symbolic capital, much as does the design of his or her car or home. In such a situation a technical vocabulary "implies a superiority and a special knowledge" (Mehan et al., 1986: 130). A person may give the impression of increased competence and status through the use of serious knowledge products. Like hospital patients attempting to converse in "doctorese," the lay reasoner recognizes the privileges to be acquired through the use of the hard knowledge, at least in certain settings. Groups who are exposed to hard knowledge due to their economic and cultural position are more likely to promote it as a marker of status and as a means for separating themselves from other, "less knowledgeable" people.

There are, of course, sites where the use of hard, expertly produced knowledge is detrimental. However, these sites are usually outside the prevailing patterns of epistemic power; they do not impact upon matters of economics, health and governance. Being in the truth or compelling people to speak the truth is certainly not something that everyone has the ability to do, however. The discursive acts of some groups, while perhaps important for establishing group membership and solidarity, seldom extend beyond the boundaries of a particular collectivity. These "lesser" discursive acts remain internal to the group and are not generally involved in mobilizing or commanding the resources of an institution, state or economy.

The acceptance of hard knowledge, consequently, can be seen as a moral or associational imperative. The user of ordinary knowledge incorporates hard knowledge in order to increase his or her cultural capital and status, and to distinguish him or herself from others in close and competitive social groups. The possession of hard knowledge can then serve as a collective symbol or label through which an individual can identify and define him or herself in relation to others. It becomes a measure by which people can socialize and resocialize themselves (see Bowker and Star, 1999: 230). As Mary Douglas (1986: 108) describes the process, "first the people are tempted out of their niches by new possibilities of exercising or evading control. Then they make new kinds of institutions, and the institutions make new labels, and the label makes new kinds of people." Like the religious conversion described by Stark and Bainbridge (1980), accepting expert knowledge becomes a means of bringing one's own beliefs and actions into alignment with those of others who possess them. As such, it becomes part of an individual's structure of meaning, thereby directing future cognitive and practical activities. Consequently, hard knowledge is not utilized in everyday life because it is more rational or closer to the real than are ordinary ways of knowing. Rather, it is mobilized to acquire and sustain status in the epistemic and moral landscapes, hierarchies and networks of modern life.

REPRODUCING TRUTH: HOW KNOWLEDGE IS SOCIALLY ORGANIZED

If knowledge is to become a well-known and indisputable matter of fact, it is not enough for it to be produced, disseminated and incorporated into everyday use. Without an organized core, knowledge risks being misinterpreted and co-opted by other knowledge-producing groups. Successful knowledge, consequently, requires organizational mechanisms for its reproduction, protection and evolution into new knowledge. Knowledge, like a musical or artistic style, will persevere only if there are new, like-minded individuals and groups to perpetuate it (see Becker, 1982). This means that knowledge, at least in the modern context, must become disciplinary (see Abbott, 2001; Lenoir, 1997). It must organize itself into self-reproducing disciplinary, or quasi-disciplinary, organizations in order to withstand incorporation or extinction. In this context, disciplines serve to "demarcate areas of academic territory, allocate privileges and responsibilities of expertise, and structure claims on resources" (Lenoir, 1997: 58). If they are particularly well organized, academic disciplines, like bureaucracies, "restructure" and "renormalize" the objects they study using their own internal rules (Fuchs, 2001: 236). In doing so, disciplines inevitably reduce and simplify variation by lifting an object of study "out of a natural habitat and inserting it into a model or a theory or a poetic account of it" (Feyerabend, 1999: 12). Hence, disciplines provide the mold for selecting and fashioning the raw data of observation and immediate experience into a nicely packaged and delineated form.

Implicit within this disciplinary organization is a realization that knowledge cannot survive merely by being inscribed in texts or by "personality." Knowledge must be embedded within a self-reproducing professional culture and in a specific form of institutionalized practice in order to socialize the next generation of knowledge makers, or it faces extinction. Such knowledge and skill transference can only be accomplished as knowledge becomes arranged into autonomous, self-reproducing organizations replete with insider vocabularies, students, unique skills, publication outlets, formal connections to other professional knowledge-producing organizations and, in some cases, specialized equipment and techniques.

The reproduction of hard knowledge is also made possible by its institutionalization in such diverse forms as professional organizations, graduate programs and professional journals. Like disciplines, professional organizations serve to set the standards and the rules of the knowledge-making group. They also help keep knowledge from "becoming too abstract or overwhelming" by chopping up and delimiting the knowable (Abbott, 2001: 130). In this process organizations often develop criteria for distinguishing between legitimate practitioners on the inside and illegitimate "quacks" on the outside. Often these organizations are also instrumental in seeking legal acceptance of the knowledge-making group through special licensure and certification from the state. These efforts, if successful, mark off the group's domain and insulate it from unwelcome outside influence and contamination.

Graduate programs perform a somewhat different task. They inculcate in students the cognitive standards and interpretative limits of the knowledge-making group, thus ensuring that "specialists are produced from amateurs in the same way soldiers are made out of civilians" (Latour, 1999: 102). They also provide the central myths of the field—the stories of heroic individuals struggling against the odds to discover a basic truth or rebels defying an established paradigm to establish a new way of knowing (see Collins, 1999). Graduate programs may also furnish the skill for utilizing the specialized equipment of the group and the practical rules for "doing things right" to the new recruits. Without such enculturation efforts, the knowledge of the organization would soon splinter into "mini-logues," or splintered dialogues filled with varying forms of knowing and individualistic methodologies. If this occurs, the knowledge form risks becoming fractured to the point that entirely new and independent lines of knowledge develop.

Journals and other publication outlets also lend themselves to the reproduction of professional knowledge-making fields. Editors, editorial boards and journal reviewers serve not only as outlets for the flow of expert knowledge but also establish prevailing standards of competence and acceptability. Contributors to journals or books series are forced to come to terms with the classic literature of the field, accepted methodologies, key knowledge contributions and the citations of the core practitioners, who often sit on the editorial boards or are series editors. This ensures that the knowledge of the group retains a degree of internal coherence and historical consistency. It also guarantees that only those "in the truth" are capable of generating the group's knowledge, for only long exposure to the groups "interaction rituals" can make one a legitimate member (Fuchs and Ward, 1994; Collins, 1999).

Finally, laboratory equipment, experimental hardware, measures, computers and related instruments must also be seen as providing for the reproduction of expert knowledge, particularly in scientific and quasi-scientific fields (see Bijker, Hughes and Pinch, 1987; Hirschauer, 1991). They are, therefore, not passive objects of their creators but active players in the construction and maintenance of a discipline and its knowledge. In addition to requiring specialized skills and languages to operate, laboratory equipment and measures serve to objectify and "black-box" a group's knowledge. Often they erase all traces of human agency and replace it with the systematic and repetitious precision of the machine, or the standardized outcome of the measure. As the hardware obtains similar readings over time, the knowledge often takes on a transhuman mathematical or graphical character. In turn, quantification and graphical representation relocates a claim from the realm of the speculative to that of hard knowledge. It also removes the knowledge from the domain of one individual and places it in the control of the larger knowledge-making collective.

The successful construction of a knowledge-producing organization, complete with professional organizations, graduate programs, publications outlets and experimental hardware, allows "normal science" (Kuhn, 1962) to proceed. The knowledge-making organization is now able to establish newly crafted facts as collective representations of the group. These collective representations serve to routinize the practical activities of the organization, establish the range of cognition, economize on decision making, establish internal hierarchical and group boundaries and ritualize the further establishment of facts (Wynne, 1982; Fuchs, 1992). Furthermore, these representations help new participants acquire a "naturalized familiarity" with the group and its knowledge-seeking objectives (Bowker and Star, 1999: 35). Without these maneuvers, the group and its knowledge would soon whither away or lose out to other knowledge-making groups wishing to establish and expand their own representations. If these requirements manage to fall into place, knowledge becomes automated by becoming situated in a set of institutionalized rules, regulations and rituals rather than in an individual or group of individuals. When this happens, as Mary Douglas (1986: 83) put it, "the burden of thinking is transferred to institutions." As in a classic bureaucratic organization, where power is everywhere but nowhere, no one in a well-organized knowledge field is capable of taking sole credit or responsibility for the creation of knowledge. This ensures that the entry into or departure from the knowledge field of any given person will not dramatically affect its production of knowledge.[5] Likewise, the automation of knowledge guarantees that power will not be concentrated in the hands of a few actors, who could remake the knowledge in any way they choose, but is instead housed in the larger, self-directed and increasingly bureaucratic rules of the knowledge-making field. This, in turn, makes objectivity possible by investing "power in rules rather than persons" (Porter, 1994: 227).

CONCLUSION: THE STATUS OF KNOWING

There are a limited number of ways by which the initially weak and fragile knowledge of the few can become the strong and encompassing knowledge of the many (see Miller and Rose, 1994: 34–35). In one method, people are coerced and regulated by formal authority. In this instance, prevailing power holders force people, through formal sanctions and rewards, to speak, and "be in," the truth. Another common strategy involves "educating" others. Here, people are persuaded to give up voluntarily their own conceptualizations and modes of reasoning for the presumably more accurate ones provided by experts. However, the most effective strategy involves a total and complete conversion of personhood and society. In this strategy, self and society are changed so dramatically that people "understand and explain the meaning and nature of life-conduct in fundamentally new ways" (see Miller and Rose, 1994: 35).

Often the successful expert knowledge of the twentieth century followed this latter route. To the present, people have not just been coerced or trained to recite the particular terminology and representations of expertly produced knowledge; rather, their lives and experiences have been thoroughly transformed through their encounters with it. Like religious conversion, this epistemic transmutation creates a new "ecological niche" (Hacking, 1998) that provides a new ethical and practical regime for understanding and conducting life. In doing so, it obliterates other, more "localized" notions of self and society and replaces them with the more "universal" constructions provided by a larger professional knowledge field. New intellectual techniques emerge that enable the world to be thought of, enframed and acted toward in radically different ways. As a result, "new people" are made up (Hacking, 1986), and these "new people behave differently than they ever did before" (Douglas, 1986: 100).

In the end, however, the knowledge and terminology produced by the expert can be said to "mirror reality" (Rorty, 1979) no more than do the colloquialisms of the lay reasoner. Having a child with an "attention deficit disorder" may sound more precise and correct than having an "unruly child," but neither terminology corresponds to an objective condition out in the world. It is a representation of reality, not reality itself. However, this does not mean that these representations do not work pragmatically or that they are meaningless, professional textual verbiage. While neither professional nor lay knowledge makers can lay claim to a privileged epistemic position that more closely mirrors the real, or to the proper grammar of reality, certain knowledge forms and discursive acts are nevertheless recognized as more legitimate than others. For instance, the knowledge of the astronomer, the pediatrician or the foreign policy expert is "stronger" than that of the astrologer, midwife or local bureaucrat. The former groups are more likely to appear in the media, write textbooks, give lectures, testify at congressional hearings and be involved in the formulation of social, health or economic policy. Notwithstanding of the inability of any group to capture reality epistemologically, the knowledge of the former group becomes harder than that of the latter associationally. This is so because such knowledge has the backing of a larger and more heterogeneous network of allies, who work to sustain its integrity and objectivity. In this epistemic struggle, lay knowledge is often relegated to the ranks of the "primitive," "misinformed," "irrational," "mythical" or of "belief." Conversely, the utterances of the hard knowledge producers are elevated to the levels of the "modern," "accurate," "rational," "scientific" or of "knowledge." As a result of this, an epistemic hierarchy is formed that raises the representations of one group above another and then justifies this stratification through its own demarcations.

Individuals who learn and speak of "co-dependency" or that they suffer from a dehabilitating "fear of success" are no closer to the true story about themselves than they would be using the terminology, discursive form or world picture provided by ordinary knowledge. They are enmeshed within, and participating in, the proper grammar of a particular network of knowing.[6] They are converting to telling and being in a particular order of truth. In this process certain knowledge-making groups have imparted a particular meaning to events or to the self and have provided the official language and cognitive style in which to express these issues. Professional knowledge-making groups have made their conceptualizations so appealing and irresistible that all (or most) begin to speak, represent and understand the world as they do.

While it is always difficult to draw clear, epistemologically verifiable distinctions between different ways of knowing, there remain other important pragmatic distinctions of importance. The distinction between science and literature, knowledge or belief or fact and fiction are not, nor arguably have they ever been, pure epistemic distinctions. Both are carefully forged categories, distinctions, and symbolic boundaries backed by varying networks of support and types of organization. Contrary to the postmodernists' and constructionists' accounts described earlier, deconstructing the biased philosophical hierarchies of the hard knowledge of the expert or "big science" (Price, 1986) in no way alters its power to define the real and speak the truth—for this ability to speak the truth derives from the accumulated authority of a network of knowing, not from its unique methods or the characteristics of the words themselves. Only shutting down the various centers of knowledge production and severing the links of the network, not textual or social deconstruction alone, would eliminate such knowledge. Consequently, critics of traditional conceptualization of knowledge "are right in saying that all languages are linguistically equal; they are wrong in thinking they are socially equal" (Bourdieu, 1977: 652). The central question is not that of who has the language of reality and the proper conceptual apparatus, but "What body of persons shall decide the proper pattern of these concepts?" (Bloor 1983: 80).

Finally, to reveal that knowledge is shaped by texts and language games does not mean, as certain deconstructionist epistemological critics seem to argue, that the world is composed exclusively of texts, language games, or chains of signs (see Fuchs and Ward, 1994). As Latour (1988b: 169) puts it, "If all discourse appears to be equivalent, if there seems to be 'language games' and nothing more, then someone has been unconvincing." Some arguments are simply stronger than others. This is not because they capture the real but because they are located in networks that are well organized and encompassing. As we shall see in the coming chapters, a more fruitful and perhaps less nihilistic route is to recognize that science and expertise are merely labels we apply to the successful actions and practices of certain knowledge-making groups under particular circumstances. Likewise, society is merely the label we apply to the coalition of these and other networks. Claiming epistemic superiority is not the result of good methodology, cognitive superiority or a manifestation of naked power but the cry of a strong and successful coalition (Latour, 1988b). Knowledge and society are, consequently, a series of continually changing and often overlapping networks of people and things.

In the chapters ahead we will see how this theoretical sketch of "knowledge on the move" can be used to understand the development and expansion of the vast network that now supports psychological knowledge.

NOTES

1. There are obviously other means of organizing and labeling these theories of knowledge. Some have grouped them along methodological lines. Others have organized them in terms of modern versus postmodern, realist versus relativist, rationalists versus pragmatist, etc.

2. Such progressive accounts are most often found in disciplinary histories. Often written by insiders, these histories usually focus on the progress of the discipline's body of knowledge, the heroic efforts of its founders, or the discipline's general conquest of myth and ignorance.

3. For example, the *New England Journal of Medicine* has what is called the "Ingelfinger Rule." Named for a former editor, this rule declares, "Any research receiving substantial attention from the medical trade publications or the popular media runs the risk of being rejected out of hand by the journal's editors" (Dunwoody and Ryan, 1985: 28).

4. For example, it has been shown that higher-status scientists are more likely than lower-status scientists to be in direct contact with the media (Dunwoody and Scott, 1982).

5. Although much is often made of "intellectual stars" in academia, unless they are attached to networks or can form their own, their knowledge products are usually short-lived (see Collins, 1999; Abbott, 2001).

6. As P. Bourdieu (1977: 649) has put it, "The power of words is never anything other than the power to mobilize the authority accumulated within a field." The power of words to explain is a reflection of the power of particular social fields or groups and not an intrinsic characteristic of the words themselves, the cognitive

2

From a Moral Philosophy to a Science: The Struggle to Construct and Defend the "New Psychology"

A SCIENCE OF PSYCHOLOGY WAS NOT SUPPOSED TO HAVE BEEN possible (see Buchner, 1903). In 1786 Immanuel Kant ([1786] 1970) wrote a forceful and influential epistemological dismissal of the possibility of psychology and the human sciences in general, in his *Metaphysical Foundation of Natural Science*. For Kant, a reflective science of consciousness or "science of the soul" could never obtain mathematical exactness like the natural sciences, because exact precision could not be applied to something as fundamental and amorphous as internal sense perception. The self, as a unique organization of experience, was the transcendental prerequisites for all sciences but could never be the material for a science in itself. Kant further maintained that it was impossible to achieve accurate experimentation with mental phenomenon because observations always alters the observed subject (see Leary, 1982). As Georges Canguilhem (1980: 43) put it two centuries later, it is impossible to "experiment on ourselves or on others." As such, psychology could never be more "than a historical (and as such, as much as possible) systematic doctrine of the internal sense, i.e., a natural description of the soul, but not a science of the soul" (Kant, [1786] 1970: 8). However, as the discipline of psychology would show over the course of the twentieth century, Kant's epistemological critique ignored the fact that sciences are never really based on epistemologically prerequisites. They are, instead, disciplinary entities, crafted and sustained from the various materials at their creators' disposal.[1]

Understanding the elaborate practices and processes that enabled psychology to overcome such influential Kantian epistemological objections and to reshape dramatically the twentieth century's knowledge of the mind and self requires returning to the formative years of the discipline and the establishment of its form of knowledge. This was a period when the discipline's fate had not been sealed, when its statements were still provisional and contested, when it had few supporters or allies, and when its claims often fell on deaf ears among peers and the public. This was an early stage of the formation of its professional journals and organizations, separate academic departments, graduate programs, disciplinary histories and public attention, and before the development of its now-familiar concepts.

In this chapter I explore a few of the knowledge-making practices found in the early history of what advocates often called the "new psychology." The phrase the "new psychology" was given by late-nineteenth-century advocates both to demarcate the discipline from mental and moral philosophy and to denote the discipline's new emphasis on scientific procedures and experimental methodology.[2] It signified an attempt by proponents to make psychology as scientific and rigorous as the natural sciences and to carve out a specific domain of things that was inherently "psychological" in nature. Along the way to disciplinary formation and solidification, psychology would have to endure what Andrew Abbott (2001: 137) has called the "chaos of disciplines" and all the processes associated with group ecology, such as competition, accommodation, alliance and absorption. From psychology's inauspicious beginnings I want to follow some of the early links the fledgling discipline made and some of the battles it had to fight as it sought to establish itself within the university, the scientific community and already existing professions.

In the first section of this chapter, I outline some of the initial attempts to make the "new psychology" special and extraordinary. Here, I look at some of the rhetoric of early advocates of the discipline as they sought to show competing fields the novelty of their approach and construct particular notions of mind, psyche, self, behavior and cognition. I also explore how early psychologists sought to show competing fields that psychological knowledge did not pose a threat to their established domains. In the next section, I examine some of the initial efforts of psychologists to forge alliances with the "stronger fields" of the natural sciences and to distance themselves from some of the relatively "weaker fields" in the humanities and the fledgling social sciences. Next, I examine some of the early efforts of psychologists to draw boundaries between legitimate and illegitimate psychological knowledge and practitioners through membership in the American Psychological Association and through professional certification. Following this section, I survey the friction between psychology and psychiatry as the disciplines crossed into each other's domain and vied for intellectual territory and influence. Finally, I will use this brief examination of the history of psychology to list some of the prerequisites that are necessary for the development and growth of new knowledge, particularly new knowledge that "wants" to become recognized as a scientific discipline.

CARVING OUT INTELLECTUAL AND ORGANIZATIONAL SPACE: THE "EXCEPTIONAL CHARACTER" OF THE NEW PSYCHOLOGY

People seeking to establish a new area of knowledge or significantly reconfigure an old one are often faced with the "newcomer's dilemma of conformity versus differentiation" (Camic and Xie, 1994: 797). As part of this dilemma, they must simultaneously legitimate their knowledge by conforming to practices and procedures established by other related fields, while distinguishing their novel knowledge wares from those of other knowledge-producing groups (see Ben-David and Collins, 1966). In this process, new knowledge forms often face the scrutiny of colleagues in related fields, or within a field they seek to occupy, who contend that the new knowledge is not that special after all or that another field has already adequately reduced and explained what the new field is examining. In some cases, they also may face the scorn of members of the general public or university deans and presidents who are cautious or ambivalent about the benefits of such a new knowledge endeavor, particularly as a course of academic research and study. If the individuals seeking to establish a new knowledge form are successful, they become the intellectual heroes of the new field. They will appear in textbooks, often with "brief biographical boxes," and become the moral and epistemic standard bearers of the discipline, complete with special awards and honors in their names. If they fail, they collectively become just another footnote in the history of ideas or are, as in most cases, simply forgotten altogether.

Advocates of a new knowledge, therefore, often utilize a number of different, but nevertheless convergent, rhetorical and practical strategies directed toward showing other knowledge makers that their new knowledge is special and extraordinary. These strategies are often aimed at specific knowledge-producing groups who may prove to be potential competitors, adversaries or perhaps allies. Often one of the first targets for the promotion of new professional knowledge is colleagues in other related fields who may be suspicious of and hostile toward the new discipline. One common way of convincing them of a new knowledge's special status is to reinterpret and incorporate past writings in other fields—to make the familiar and respected works of the past part of the new knowledge's conceptual repertoire. In the case of psychology, this meant retranslating material in philosophy, theology and physiology as precursors of psychological thought (see, for example, Strong, 1891). Past knowledge, particularly that found in mental and moral philosophy, was often identified by early psychologists as but a milestone on the inevitable path toward the development of the discipline. In other cases, as in physiology, past knowledge was viewed as a necessary precursor to the germination of psychology's own contemporary theories and findings.

In the early 1890s, William James (1962 [1899]: 3) argued that a new psychology did not exist—only "the old psychology which began in Locke's time." Later, in his 1895 presidential address to the American Psychological Association (APA), James McKeen Cattell located the origins of the new psychology with the Greeks: "While the recent progress of our science has been great, we do not admit that psychology is a new science. . . . If science is to date from the year of 'the master of those who know,' then we may take pride in the beginnings of psychology whose foundation were more securely laid by Aristotle than those of any other science" (Cattell, 1978 [1895]: 54–55).

Cattell's (1978 [1895]: 55) APA address also identified the poet Shelley as having provided the "explicit formulation of the problems of experimental psychology." In his view, both Aristotle and Shelley had provided the basic material for the germination of psychology; it was now the task of his contemporaries to transform it into a fully developed experimental science.[3]

Admitting that new knowledge is actually old knowledge or asserting that such prominent intellectual figures as Aristotle, Locke and Shelley had merely set the stage for psychology's inevitable emergence may be seen as an attempt to show skeptics in other fields that the new knowledge of psychology was an inevitable extension and refinement of a long, well-established line of investigation. Alone, however, such a move would be insufficient to convince skeptics of the new knowledge's uniqueness or even of its right to exist. Knowledge legitimation also requires that knowledge makers provide evidence that their new knowledge has a distinct focus and specific object of analysis and therefore, that it is not significantly treading on the territory of other fields. It may also prove important to show these other fields that the new knowledge will be a useful supplement to and collaborator for their own disciplinary or applied endeavors.

Some of the best efforts in this regard lie not just in the programmatic statements of the founding figures of the new psychology but also in the pages of some of the early psychology textbooks. In the late nineteenth century, the status demarcation between those who produced textbooks for students and those who wrote primarily for their colleagues was not as clearly defined as it was to become in the twentieth century. It was, thus, common to find leading intellectual figures of the discipline writing textbooks for a wider, more general audience. These textbooks provided pertinent examples of the "front stage talk" of psychologists as they tried to convince an audience, in this case captive students and in some cases skeptical practitioners in other fields, the unique lessons and findings of their discipline.

John Dewey, in his seminal 1887 work *Psychology*, contended that psychological investigation had languished too long under a metaphysical philosophy associated with the American mental philosophers. It was time psychology had "a treatment of its own," a treatment that was "scientific and up to the times" (Dewey 1887: v–vi). Psychology was, however, conceived of as more than simply another science, alongside chemistry, physiology or physics. It was, in Dewey's terminology, a "central science." For Dewey (1887: 4), "all the other sciences deal only with facts or events which are known; but the fact of knowledge thus involved in all of them no one of them has said anything about. . . . This science is accordingly something more than one science by the side of others; it is a central science, for its subject-matter, knowledge, is involved in them all." While psychology shared the method and scientific outlook of other sciences, it was unique, in that its subject matter included even the causes of those other sciences' knowledge. Dewey felt that psychology ultimately would unite the sciences under the umbrella of one general, overarching discipline.

Like Dewey, William James was also concerned with showing skeptics the unique properties of the new psychology. In his landmark 1890 work *The Principles of Psychology* (1952 [1890]: 120), James sought to establish the idea that "psychology is a natural science."[4] James employed a careful strategy of borrowing from other sciences, particularly the relatively powerful field of physiology, while maintaining that psychology should leave all but certain "cerebral issues" to those disciplines. Describing the content and delimitations of *The Principles*, he wrote, "Many nervous performances will therefore be unmentioned, as being purely physiological. Nor will the anatomy of the nervous system and organs of sense be described anew . . . of the functions of the cerebral hemisphere, however, since they directly subserve consciousness, it will be well to give some little account" (James, 1952 [1890]: 7).

James made it clear that psychology should join the ranks of the natural sciences; however, these sciences need not fear the encroachment of psychology into their domain. Instead, psychology would be strictly limited to "cerebral processes." The study of the rest of the body would be left in the hands of biologists, chemists, anatomists and physiologists.

Another important effort at making psychological knowledge special can be found in James Baldwin's 1893 work *Elements of Psychology*. Here, Baldwin sought to outline some of the concepts and findings of early psychology and also to show how psychology was capable of answering questions that had hitherto eluded other sciences, particularly physiology. "There is, first of all, in consciousness a kind of activity which affords at once the necessity and the justification of a higher science, inductive, internal, descriptive, and analytical. . . . [T]he science can never reach completion, or its laws attain their widest generality, until all mental facts are interpreted in the light of this connection with body or shown to be independent of it" (Baldwin, 1893: 18).

Baldwin (1893: 2) concluded that physiology's confusing of "organic and vital fact" was misconceived. While psychology was similar to physiology in its methodology, its focus on the unique qualities of consciousness required a distinct empirical science. The ontological division between the somatic and mental required "two distinct sciences—equally sciences of fact or natural sciences" (Baldwin, 1893: 4).

These early rhetorical attempts to demarcate psychological knowledge from other related fields and to show its special qualities and objects of analysis were not unlike those found in the prehistories of most other disciplines (see Ward, 1996b: 1–16). In the new psychology, care was taken to illustrate both that its knowledge was distinct and rigorous enough to merit the label of a new science and that it would not be a threat to other disciplines, particularly the powerful and influential field of physiology. Only with such declarations would it be possible to appease those within the university and elsewhere who might block the attempt to forge ahead with the new knowledge.

ALLIES AND ENEMIES: EARLY PSYCHOLOGY'S RELATIONSHIP WITH THE NATURAL SCIENCES AND PHILOSOPHY

Early psychology, like many of the developing social sciences of the time, was divided between those who, following the lead of Wilhelm Wundt, wanted it to be modeled after the natural sciences and those who, following William James, sought to develop it as a hybrid of the humanities and the natural sciences (see Bird, 1991). This internal methodological and political division within early psychology would have important implications for the direction of the discipline in the twentieth century. In some sense, this internal division and tension within the discipline has never been resolved (see Hilgard, 1987: 791–792; Kantor, 1979).[5] Despite important epistemological and theoretical differences between early psychologists, there was, however, a unified attempt to illustrate that psychological knowledge was in league with other fields that espoused the use and expansion of the scientific method and spirit (see James, 1892). In this endeavor, it proved important to pick friends and enemies carefully.

Building new knowledge often requires a careful strategy of conformity and differentiation. First, it is crucial to select and emulate powerful allies who can further one's knowledge. It is equally important for new fields to be aware of the possibility that these allies will attempt to incorporate the newcomer, replacing the emerging field's conceptual reductions with its own (see DiMaggio and Powell, 1983; S. Fuchs, 1996: 310). Second, it is important for new fields to keep competing fields that are perceived as being weaker out of the way, by dismissing their knowledge as "gibberish," antiquated, or as simply insufficient reconfigurations of their own knowledge.

Such attachments and disengagements in the new psychology can be found as early as 1860, in the work of Gustav Fechner (1966 [1860]). Trained as a physicist and philosopher, Fechner sought to unite the study of the psychical with basic physical principles from physics and chemistry into a discipline he referred to as "psychophysics." In his view, "psychophysics, already related to psychology and physics by name, must on the one hand be based on psychology, and on the other hand promises to give psychology a mathematical foundation. From physics outer psychophysics borrows aids and methodology; inner psychophysics leans more to physiology and anatomy" (Fechner, 1966 [1860]: 10). For Fechner (1966 [1860]: 1) until this point the study of mind and matter had "remained merely a field for philosophical argument without solid foundation and without sure principles and methods for the progress of inquiry." With the basic insights from physiology, physics and chemistry, some of the central and long-standing questions regarding the mind and consciousness would finally be answered. The speculation of past philosophical systems would become passé as they were replaced by the scientific findings of psychophysics.

Psychology's close affinity to physiology and the natural science was also a prominent theme in the work of Wundt, one of the central founding figures of the discipline (see Danziger, 1979; Leary, 1979). In the preface to his 1874 work *Principles of Physiological Psychology*, Wundt (1969 [1902]: v) described his mission as "an attempt to mark out a new domain of science." This domain was recognized as having its foundation in anatomy and physiology, but it was unique enough to require a distinct scientific line of inquiry. Wundt (1969 [1902]: 10) wrote,

Now physiology and psychology, as we said just now, are auxiliary disciplines, and neither can advance without assistance from the other. Physiology, in its analysis of the physiological functions of the sense organs, must use results of subjective observation of sensations; and psychology, in its turn, needs to know the physiological aspects of sensory function, in order rightly to appreciate the psychological.

Physiology was capable only of providing knowledge about "bodily processes," while psychology offered a broader understanding of the interconnection of consciousness and bodily life (Wundt, 1969 [1902]: 1). Wundt argued that the two disciplines should work together to solve the long-standing problems associated with mind/body interaction.

There is perhaps no more fitting example of the rhetoric of engagement and dismissal than Cattell's 1895 presidential address to the APA (also see Ladd, 1894). In the address, he carefully utilized a tactic of joining hands with the natural sciences while putting distance between psychology and the relatively weaker fields of philosophy and sociology. In his discussion of the natural sciences, Cattell employed a vocabulary of unity of purpose, emphasizing goals that linked psychology and the natural sciences in a common quest for truth. In this endeavor he tried to convince members of the more powerful fields that they were obliged to join with psychology to further the goals of science.[6] On the relationship between physics and psychology, Cattell (1978 [1895]: 63) maintained that "the treatment of certain subjects in common with physics has set for the psychologist a higher scientific standard, whereas it may be hoped that the physicist has learned that processes of perception and thought are part of the real world which science as a whole must take into account." Earlier Cattell (1947 [1888]: 131) had held that just as "the physicist counts, and he measures time, space and energy" the psychologist "measures time, space and intensity in mental magnitudes." As for physiology, Cattell (1978 [1895]: 63) argued that "the treatment of certain subjects in common must ultimately result in mutual benefit." In the case of biology, he asserted that the two disciplines "cannot advance excepting hand in hand" (Cattell, 1978 [1895]: 63).

Despite the amiable and cooperative words directed toward the natural sciences, Cattell had less generous things to say about the disciplines of sociology and philosophy. He attempted to distance psychology from these knowledge forms while simultaneously offering a helping hand. He folded sociology under the wing of psychology by referring to it as "simply collective psychology" (Cattell, 1978 [1895]: 63). That is, he claimed sociology as but a variant of group or ethnic psychology. It lacked a focus unique enough to distinguish it from the investigations being performed by psychologists.

His most critical remarks, however, were reserved for philosophy and its more speculative approach to knowledge. This resentment may be attributed, at least in part, to Kant's strong and influential dismissal of the possibility of psychology (and of the human sciences in general) a century earlier. In Cattell's view, the days of speculative philosophy were over. Philosophical systems developed prior to the advent of modern science "may receive our admiration as poetry, but they cannot claim our adherence as truth" (Cattell, 1978 [1895]: 64). In his account, all the traditional domains of philosophy—such as epistemology, logic, aesthetics and ethics—rested more and more on the foundations provided by the new knowledge of psychology (see Cattell, 1978 [1895]: 64). Philosophy was in a dismally unscientific state, but psychology was in a position to rescue it from speculation and poetics. Cattell (1978 [1895]: 64) contended that "the twilight of philosophy can be changed to its dawn only by the light of science, and psychology can contribute more light than any other science." However, this was achievable only if psychology could finally "divorce itself from literature" and become a mature science (Reed, 1997: xv).

Despite such dismissive rhetoric, the new psychologists were in an awkward political position with respect to the discipline of philosophy, particularly the mental and moral schools found in American departments of philosophy. The new psychologists wanted to replace the mental philosophers, whose "mere schooling as minister[s]" (Ladd, 1899: 125), as well as their religious and metaphysical approach to the mind, stood in their way of establishing psychology as a science. Psychologists however, required their acceptance if they were to gain positions within academic departments of philosophy— homes of many early psychologists (see A. Fuchs, 2000). An implicit compromise resulted, as the new psychologists used the existing concerns of the mental philosophers and added their own experimental approach and apparatuses. Despite their rhetoric to the contrary, the new psychologists did not so much replace mental philosophy as add "laboratory experimental procedures to what was already defined as an empirical, inductive science" (A. Fuchs, 2000: 11).

Despite the resistance of mental and moral philosophy, the new psychologists managed over time to gain control, at least publicly, over the discourse on the mind and self in the United States. In 1908 J. MacBride Sterrett, the president of the Southern Society for Philosophy and Psychology, concluded that most psychologists favored affiliation with the natural sciences (Smith, 1981: 29; Sterrett, 1909). By the time of his remarks, psychology had received recognition and had established ties with the American Society of Naturalists and the American Association for the Advancement of Science (Camfield, 1973: 68). In addition, by 1908 the American Psychological Association no longer held its meetings in conjunction with the American Philosophical Association. Most "philosophers" had voluntarily withdrawn from the APA, and the Library of Congress had begun listing experimental works in psychology under physiology rather than philosophy (Smith, 1981: 29; Camfield, 1973: 69).

By the 1940s, the separation of psychology and philosophy was essentially complete. Psychology had, according to Clifford T. Morgan (in Leahey, 2000: 450), "shortened its hair, left its alleged ivory tower and gone to work." It had done this by severing almost completely its links from the "long haired" philosophers of the past. The encounter between followers of Wundt and James had seemingly been decided in Wundt's favor, at least for the time being (see Bruner and Allport, 1940).[7] Psychology was not to become a new branch of philosophy or a separate humanities discipline, as could have happened. Rather, it was to join with the natural sciences and utilize their methods, epistemology and experimental apparatuses, while maintaining its uniquely constructed object of investigation. Later this development would set into motion a number of internal conflicts that would fragment the discipline from within.

EXCLUDING "CHARLATANS, QUACKS AND IGNORAMUSES": MAKING OTHER PEOPLE'S KNOWLEDGE IRRATIONAL

A new knowledge form cannot direct all its efforts outward toward skeptics or potential allies. As I argued in the first chapter, new knowledge must also be concerned with its own organization and with keeping its members in line. Like social and religious movements, emerging knowledge-producing groups face the dilemma of how and where to draw the boundary between members and nonmembers (see, for example, Abbott, 1988; Starr, 198). Again like these movements, they must also create guidelines for determining who is legitimate and who is not, and whose statements can be trusted and whose cannot. At stake in this boundary division in knowledge production is not just the monopolization of a particular domain of knowledge or skill but the validity and relevance of the discipline's own knowledge creations or specialized expertise. If just anyone can practice or produce the knowledge of the new discipline, or the numbers of its practitioners greatly outstrip demand, its value, integrity and potential influence will be greatly diminished (see Whitley, 1984). Disciplines with an overly portable and commodified knowledge form can quickly lose power to professionals outside its confines (Abbott, 2001: 147). Consequently, knowledge-producing groups often utilize a number of means for controlling their ranks and enforcing guidelines distinguishing between the rational and competent practitioner on the inside and the irrational and incompetent imposter on the outside.

In the United States, early psychologists sought to control their ranks primarily via their professional arm, the American Psychological Association. The APA set itself up as an alternative to the already existing American Society for Psychical Research (ASPR), which had been organized in 1884. Following the model set by British Society for Psychical Research, the ASPR had rather loose standards of membership and had received substantial coverage in the popular press for research on paranormal phenomena and the spirit world (see Leary, 1987: 321). Such publicity obviously had limited appeal for members who wanted to develop psychology as a university-centered, experimental science. Consequently, members such as G. Stanley Hall, William James, Joseph Jastrow, Morton Prince and James Jackson Putnam, who wanted to establish psychology as a science, left the ASPR in 1892 to form the APA (see Moore, 1977: 143). In departing, however, they sought to take with them many of the focal concerns that had made psychical research popular with the public (Leary, 1987: 322).

The founding group of the APA that met at Clark University was composed of thirty-seven individuals who simply wanted to discuss "psychological matters" (Fernberger, 1932: 3).[8] During this early period the APA had relatively loose standards for membership; however, its central administration was tightly controlled by the seven founding figures of the discipline (Camfield, 1973: 67). Membership in the organization was determined by nominations and majority vote of the associates. Anyone from any field who was interested in the general area of psychology could join (Fernberger, 1932: 8; see Dennis and Boring, 1952). Training in a German university proved to be a particularly important symbol for the new psychologists; it served as proof that a practitioner was trained in the new experimental methods and valued the goal of making psychology a respected science.

After 1906, as membership grew to over two hundred, the APA began to formulate more stringent guidelines for official inclusion. Criteria for membership changed from anyone who wanted to discuss "psychological matters" to individuals "who are engaged in the advancement of Psychology as Science" (Fernberger, 1932: 9).[9] Such a move barred people in nonresearch-oriented fields, such as education and philosophy, from full membership. It also limited membership to those with a Ph.D. Such a move may also be seen as an attempt to limit further the influence of mental philosophy within the field, by essentially removing scholars with religious training from the ranks of psychologists (see A. Fuchs, 2000: 9). In 1911, membership in the APA was further restricted when applicants for membership were required to provide copies of their published research (American Psychological Association, 1912). In 1916, membership criteria were even further tightened to exclude candidates who lacked "acceptable publications of a psychological character, or a permanent position in psychology" (Fernberger, 1932: 10).

By 1920, the discipline of psychology could claim at least limited success in its relatively short history. Although it still held a rather low academic standing and a muddled professional and public position, the initial skepticism of related disciplines had significantly declined (see Ruckmich, 1912). Evidence of psychology's success can be found in the facts that psychology classes were increasing in number and locations, the number of new Ph.D.s was at an all-time high and membership in the APA had grown to almost four hundred (Napoli, 1981: 14). Despite this success, however psychology was beginning to face a new, and somewhat unique, problem associated with its growing popularity—how to exclude the growing number of people who were practicing what APA members called "pseudo-psychology."

Despite the closing of ranks through APA membership, psychologists had not succeeded at eliminating people they considered undesirable from producing psychological knowledge or claiming to practice psychology. Membership in the APA indicated a generalized competence to those within the organization, but with people outside APA criteria had little weight. With the growth in the popularity of psychology in the 1920s and 1930s, psychologists began to complain openly about the spread of pseudo-psychology by "charlatans, "quacks," and other "ignoramuses." Donald Paterson (1923: 101) of the University of Minnesota bitterly protested the proliferation of pseudo-psychology in the "quack infected Northwest." He criticized the "various charlatans who invade our larger cities, advertise extensively in the newspapers and on the bill boards, give free lectures in the best hotels or theaters and then conduct large classes for four or six weeks at so much per head" (Patterson, 1923: 101). Likewise, Henry Garrett (1932: 5) of Columbia University warned a radio audience on Walter Bingham's program *Psychology Today* that "psychology has progressed too rapidly and has aroused so much popular interest that many well-intentioned novices and less sincere persons have come into prominence, peddling a decidedly inferior and often misleading brand." The Psychological Corporation, organized by Cattell to provide consultation and testing materials to corporations, went so far as to develop a blacklist of "charlatans and ignoramuses, and a gray list of camp followers" to distinguish between reputable and disreputable psychologists offering applied psychological services (Cattell, 1923: 166). Only those who met the corporation's guidelines for acceptable psychology were permitted to be members of the organization.

In a 1932 book Dorothy Yates warned the public of the dangers of what she referred to as "psychological racketeers." Yates (1932:

194) worried about the effect of these psychological impostors on the real, scientific psychology: "When these popular inspires call themselves 'scientific psychologists,' they are either deliberate frauds or self-deluded. A very few, the least dishonest, are, I think, self-deluded—and usually not above indulging in a certain amount of hocus-pocus and highly colored assertions to help themselves along" (Yates, 1932: 190).

Yates feared that the standing of reputable psychologists and their emerging science were jeopardized by the proliferation of such quacks. She urged her readers to contact the APA and the Psychological Corporation in New York to find out the location of reputable psychologists who always will be "modest in [their] charges and [are] likely to do a good deal for nothing" (Yates, 1932: 202).

Introductory psychology books of this period also warned of the dangers to unsuspecting students of pseudo-psychologists. Students were instructed to avoid such charlatans as character analysts, spiritualists, health experts, mystics, success specialists and sex experts (see Powers, McConnell, Trow, Moore and Skinner, 1938: 25–29). Describing the dangers, Powers et al. (1938: 28–29) wrote of such a mystic:

He claims to come from far lands and be the master of wonderful and ancient lore. For a consideration, he is willing to share this vast background of knowledge. Oriental names, flowing robes, red turbans, and incense are part of their stock-in-trade. Usually their antecedents can be found in Indiana rather than India, and in New York rather than New Guinea.

A well-publicized 1953 report of the American Psychological Association estimated that there were as many as twenty-five thousand charlatans operating in the United States. The report also estimated that the activities of these charlatans cost the public close to four million dollars annually (Steiner, 1953: 708).

The fear of contamination and distortion by "quacks" and outsiders also prompted movements to gain both state licensure and a formal certification process for psychologists. In this movement psychologists faced an important dilemma, brought about by a growing division between experimental psychologists, with their emphasis on making the discipline a "pure science," and their more clinical counterparts, who advocated the application of psychological knowledge to everyday affairs, such as education and mental health. In universities and colleges the Ph.D. had effectively distinguished between the legitimate and the illegitimate psychologists. However, in the growing applied subfields, clinicians sometimes saw the Ph.D. as too limiting for their applied work; for many it seemed unnecessary. However, in certain applied settings, such as mental facilities, many feared the psychologist without the Ph.D. would always be seen as inferior to the medically trained psychiatrist (see Napoli, 1981: 45).

It was not until the end of World War II that the push for certification that began in the 1920s finally came to fruition. The first law of certification went into effect in Connecticut on July 1, 1945 (Miles, Bousfield and Bills, 1953). The Connecticut law listed "a Ph.D. in psychology or education from a recognized institution, one year's experience in the practice of psychology, and passing of an examination in a chosen field" as requirements for certification as a psychologist (Miles, Bousefield and Bills, 1953: 572). The state established a board of examiners to process applications and award certifications. Other states slowly began to join the movement to certify psychologists. Many of these state legislative efforts provided legal definitions of the term "psychologist" and delineated the duties he or she could perform. By the late 1950s, some fifteen states had passed legislation certifying psychologists (Reisman, 1991: 293). By the late 1980s, clinical psychologists could obtain certification or licensure in all fifty states (Reisman, 1991: 377).

Impatient for the legal process to move through the various states, the APA launched its own certifying authority in 1946, the American Board of Examiners in Professional Psychology. Fear of potential lawsuits forced the group to become a separate corporation in 1947 (Reisman, 1991: 252). The Board of Examiners required the doctorate, five years of experience and the passing of written and oral examinations for certification as an applied psychologist. By the late 1950s, of the now nearly seven thousand members of the APA, about one thousand were in the clinical division (Reisman, 1991: 253). By the mid-1960s, psychology had become one of the fastest-growing professions in the United States (Garfield, 1966). By the mid-1990s, of the eighty-three thousand members of the APA, some thirty-five thousand (42 percent) identified themselves as clinical psychologists (American Psychological Association, 1995a).

In the course of a few decades psychology had managed to separate itself from outsiders through professional membership and certification. However, debates within the discipline over the very symbols of science and experimentalism used to subdue these outsiders had shattered it into numerous distinct specialties, many with unique and irreconcilable methods, theories and interests.

THE CONTESTED MIND: THE BATTLE BETWEEN PSYCHOLOGY AND PSYCHIATRY

During the period in which psychology was solidifying its disciplinary organization and developing and attracting new allies in applied settings, the field of psychiatry was also seeking to expand its domain and influence. In the nineteenth century, most of psychiatry's impact had been limited to mental hospitals and asylums (see Burnham, 1974: 94). However, in the early twentieth century, as clinical psychologist began to also move into those areas and as psychiatrists began to gain control over psychotherapy and move into more public settings, a confrontation—sometimes open, sometimes hidden—began to develop between the fields over who was truly in charge and who had the more effective treatment strategy. Psychiatrists, their history and political support rooted in physiology and medicine, were generally on stronger ground than psychologists; thus they were able to gain control over the emerging mental hygiene movement, psychotherapy and the growing popular concern over mental health and illness.

Some of the first hints of a conflict between psychology and psychiatry began to emerge in 1916, when the New York Psychiatrical Society forwarded a letter to the APA protesting its advocacy of psychologists as experts in the certification of people for commitment to mental facilities. For psychiatrists, issues of mental illness and retardation were solely medical problems and required the judgment of medically trained personnel exclusively. Even the practice of psychotherapy, they contended, should be the sole preserve of psychiatry. In the letter the society expressed discontentment with the intrusion of psychologists into their domain: "We have observed with much distrust, however, the growing tendency of some psychologists, more often, unfortunately, those with the least amount of scientific training, to deal with the problem of diagnosis, social management and institutional disposal of persons suffering from abnormal mental conditions" (New York Psychiatrical Society, 1917: 225).

The New York Psychiatric Society (1917: 225) made three central recommendations in its letter to the APA: (1) that the sick, whether in mind or body, be treated only by the medically trained, (2) that the work of clinical psychologists be restricted and occur only under the direction of a physician, and (3) that psychologists be barred from passing judgment on abnormality or mental illness.

Sensing the urgency of the growing conflict between the two fields, the National Research Council sponsored a symposium in 1920 on the relationship between psychology and psychiatry. However, the psychologists and psychiatrists who participated in the symposium failed to find much common ground. They disagreed over the most fundamental definitions, including even the terms "psychiatrist" and "clinical psychologist" (see Napoli, 1981: 53). One of the participants, the psychologist Carl Seashore (1942: 128), described the meetings as an "intensive war," where "both sides were contesting living space" and "each considered the other an intruder." In 1925 psychiatrists in New York won this first skirmish; they succeeded in making non-medical, lay analysis illegal. The New York Psychiatric Society issued a warning to its members not to cooperate with anyone doing lay analysis, including clinical psychologists (see Reisman, 1991: 159).

The early success of psychiatry in fighting off clinical psychologists' efforts at certification in state legislatures largely relegated clinical psychologists to the role of diagnosis and testing. Legally banished to secondary status in psychotherapy, psychologists began to complain openly about the lack of respect afforded them by psychiatrists and the medical community in general (see O'Donnell, 1979: 13). As one private clinical psychologist in Los Angeles put it, "It is my belief that every clinical psychologist in private practice has experienced and continues to experience the unpleasant situation of the medical practitioner ignoring the clinical function of the psychologist in favor of the psychiatric handling of the case" (Freeman, 1953: 88). Psychiatrists responded by criticizing the "invasion of the field" by "psychologists with a smattering of analytic knowledge" and by other "poorly equipped and untrained" analysts (Everhard in Burnham, 1974: 103). Some also castigated the founding of the Association of Consulting Psychologists and the establishment of psychological clinics in schools. In their view, these developments were further evidence of the infringement of psychologists into their own domain (see May in Russell, 1932).

Psychologists also met considerable resistance from psychiatrists in their move for state certification in the 1940s and 1950s. In states such as Indiana, Illinois and North Carolina, initial certification efforts by psychologists were defeated by well-organized state psychiatric societies (see O'Shea, 1953). Two of the best-publicized attempts to block certification occurred in Michigan and New York.

In Michigan, psychiatrists used the "Medical Practices Act of the State of Michigan" to restrict the use of psychotherapy to persons with medical licenses (McKeach, 1953). The law essentially made the term "psychotherapy" the exclusive property of psychiatry. It also made clinical psychology illegal (no one was prosecuted under the law). In New York, both houses passed a certification bill for psychologists, but the governor vetoed it after consulting with the state's powerful psychiatric association (May, 1953: 579). Later, a bill was introduced, with the backing of the New York Psychiatric Association, that would have limited the practice of psychotherapy to those with medical degrees. The Committee on Mental Health of the American Medical Association argued that clinical psychologists "cannot in any way be qualified by training and experience to function independently as psychotherapists" (quoted in American Psychological Association, 1954: 160). Psychiatrists warned that if the law was not amended and psychologists received state certification, "they will be the ones who will be licensed to practice and not you or I" (Sands quoted in American Psychological Association, 1954: 160). After pressure from groups such as the American Association of Social Workers and the American School Counselors Association, as well as the American Psychological Association, the bill was eventually tabled in committee (May, 1953). In 1952 the Council of the American Psychiatric Association appeared to acquiesce to the efforts of clinical psychologists when it voted to support the efforts of clinical psychologists for certification. Five years later, however, the association rescinded this support and reaffirmed its earlier position that mental health and diagnosis was the exclusive domain of medicine (see *Joint Report on Relations between Psychology and Psychiatry*, 1960).

By the time of the *Joint Report*, however, the battle between psychologists and psychiatrists had already begun to subside, due primarily to the proliferation of available patients.[10] When the Veterans Administration (VA) mandated that all former members of the armed forces were eligible for psychiatric and psychological services, a massive supply of patients suddenly became available—a demand that psychiatry alone could never meet (see Menninger, 1947). The demand for psychologists and psychiatrists became so great that graduate schools in psychology began to revise their clinical programs in order to produce doctorates at a faster rate (see American Psychological Association, 1947). Soon the VA became the single largest employer of clinical psychologists (Moskowitz, 2001: 150). The VA mandate resulted in the overwhelming of psychiatry by psychology in numbers of practitioners. By the late 1950s psychologists belonging to the American Psychological Association outnumbered psychiatrists belonging to the American Psychiatric Association by almost eight thousand (*Joint Report on Relations between Psychology and Psychiatry*, 1960). Psychologists were fast becoming cheaper and more flexible alternatives to psychiatrists.

Another factor leading to the decline in the hostilities between psychologists and psychiatrists was a mutually agreed upon division of labor. In order to reduce the resistance by psychiatrists to the certification efforts of psychologists, some state psychological societies called for clauses that required a medical examination and consultation by a licensed physician before a psychologist could begin work (see Schnack, 1953: 594). Echoing this conciliatory tone, Frank Volle (1953: 595) wrote,

It would appear that psychology is in a poor bargaining position in relation to medicine—the medical tradition of "healing arts" is much older than psychology, and their legislative lobbies larger and more powerful. Perhaps psychology must make some concessions in terms of letting the medical men set up or be instrumental in training this "intruder" in the field of healing.

From the vantage point of many psychiatrists, it was psychologists who were the quacks and charlatans and who, consequently, needed to be barred from contact with the public. In their view, it was the psychologists who sought to overstep the medical boundary and "practice psychiatry without a license" (Jenkins, 1954: 617–620). It was they who sought to "practice psychotherapy on people suffering from well-defined nervous ailments" (Parker quoted in American Psychological Association, 1954: 162). The division of labor that was forged between the two sides essentially divided up the mental health caseload, with the most severe cases generally going to psychiatrists and less severe ones being assigned to psychologists.

CONCLUSION: SOME PREREQUISITES FOR THE AUTONOMIZATION OF A NEW SCIENCE

As Mary Douglas (1986: 45) has pointed out, the story of "how a system of knowledge gets off the ground is the same as the problem of how any collective good is created." Both require the labor of interconnected individuals working in concert to create and sustain a particular moral vision in the face of an opposition that wants to do the same with respect to its own vision. The tremendous moral labor put forth in the late nineteenth and early twentieth centuries to transform psychology from an obscure branch of mental and moral philosophy into an influential, although sometimes maligned and problematic, discipline illustrates a number of obvious points about the formation and growth of a new system of knowledge.

First, it is quite evident that the establishment of new knowledge requires concentrated and sustained effort. New knowledge never appears because it is simply "time for it," or as the result of an outflow of some universal, Hegelian human spirit. Without the coordinated practical action and political maneuvering of supporters, a niche for the germination of new knowledge can never be carved out. Second, it is evident that knowledge in its infancy is quite fragile. It is always in danger of being toppled before it has the opportunity to develop, expand and coagulate. This explains why such care is taken to make a case for the special status of the new knowledge, create alliances that may prove useful, resist encroachment from outsiders and export the knowledge to untapped domains. Without these maneuvers the new knowledge risks being isolated and forgotten.

More importantly, the early history of psychology also reveals that certain conditions are necessary for a new and provisional knowledge form to survive and then to become accepted and autonomous. It is possible to identify four general prerequisites for the autonomization of a new knowledge form. First, new knowledge must accomplish the processes of differentiation and hierarchicalization. It must be able both to distinguish itself from other competing knowledge forms, usually by illustrating its extraordinary character, and to elevate itself above other types of knowledge, often by showing how it solves problems other disciplines cannot or have not. In the case of the new psychology, this process involved a reinterpretation of existing bodies of knowledge as precursors to its own knowledge and a distinct strategy to illustrate the unique qualities of its new knowledge products.

As part of this process, new knowledge makers must also show that their products are of a higher order and a better quality than those they seek to replace. This entails pointing out the inherent weaknesses of past approaches to knowledge, such as how they languished or proved to be mythically, metaphysically or religiously based. This helps explain why most early psychologists were enthralled with the experimentation of the natural sciences. Experimentation provided a means of illustrating to established scientific fields that the new knowledge was a significant improvement over prior, more speculative forms of psychology. It also signaled that psychology was in league with the "scientific spirit" sweeping other knowledge fields. It is also important for new knowledge to reassure disciplines that fear encroachment that it is not a threat. It must show that its knowledge products do not seriously infringe on the boundaries of established knowledge and that it will make a loyal ally and supporter of the already established knowledge forms. This explains why such care was taken by advocates of the new psychology to show that the knowledge domain it wished to establish did not infringe on the relatively powerful fields of medicine and physiology. Had these fields objected to the formation of the discipline of psychology, the new field might have been stopped in its infancy. Fortunately for psychology, however, such criticism was defused by the fact that many of its early supporters had extensive training in these areas.

A second general prerequisites for autonomization is that new knowledge must both develop alliances with stronger forms of knowledge that may be able to provide assistance and support, and distance itself from weaker fields that may contaminate it by association and thereby thwart its efforts to become respected. Most new social movements "fail to keep forming and sustaining attachments to outsiders and thereby lose their capacity to grow" (Stark, 1997: 20). In the case of psychology, the theories and methods of powerful fields in the natural sciences and medicine were used to bolster the claims of the new knowledge and to protect it from nonscientific outsiders. Psychology was presented as being more than just another branch of the humanities or mental philosophy, but as an extension of the method and spirit of the natural sciences into the new and largely untapped domain of the mind and self. New knowledge producers must, however, be wary of being absorbed into and reduced by these other allied disciplines. They must draw from these disciplines' strengths while resisting incorporation and reduction. This explains why psychologists emphasized that the study of the mind could not occur under the domain of the other sciences. An independent science of psychology was the only means for explaining the irreducible workings of a mind.

The history of psychology shows that it is important to place distance between one's knowledge and that of weaker fields, or at least fields that are perceived as weaker. With psychology, this involved demeaning the fields of sociology and philosophy. Sociology was said to be but a yet unrecognized branch of the new psychology—or, in the words of the industrial psychologist Edgar Swift (1930: 19), "an array of interesting but confused facts." Likewise, philosophy was portrayed as dwelling in the darkness of speculation. Its reliance on speculative methods and armchair theorizing was ill suited to establishing empirically how the mind actually works. Psychological knowledge would ultimately provide philosophy the impetus it needed to redirect its misguided, metaphysical epistemic tradition. Early psychologists contended that the experimental rigor of their knowledge could reenergize the "lost disciplines" of sociology and philosophy.

Third, a new knowledge form must develop strategies for controlling and patrolling its insider/outsider boundary. Internally, it must develop standards and guidelines for membership. These standards and guidelines can then serve to generalize trust among members and economize interactions between members (see Shapin, 1994). They also can serve as moral codes that direct and focus the intellectual and practical activities of a field's members and its new recruits (see Ward, 1997). Without these codes, the core of the discipline would eventually splinter into a deafening chorus of competing and irreconcilable voices, as each member pursued his or her own knowledge work. In addition, without these codes the discipline would have no means of transforming its amateur students into specialists. This helps explain the efforts of the new psychologists to break with the ill-defined and loosely organized American Society of Psychical Research and to restrict APA membership rigidly. These endeavors defined, at least initially, what psychologists were to be, what types of knowledge they were to produce and what types of procedures they were to use.

Externally, a new knowledge form must use its organizational cohesiveness and any accumulated allies to condemn and exclude elements deemed undesirable. Without this external boundary there would be no way to distinguish between legitimate advocates of the new knowledge and imposters, and no moral order to rally around. This explains the outrage most early psychologists felt toward spiritualists, New Thought practitioners, Mesmerists and the like. These so-called pseudo-psychologists represented pollution of the discipline's internal/external boundary. They were, to use the terminology of Mary Douglas (1984), "monsters," who had to be barred from contaminating the order, solidarity and purity on the inside; they were matter out of place (see also Bloor, 1978). Ironically, however, throughout the twentieth century psychology was to be "a magnet for cultural anxieties about the hazy borderline between science and pseudoscience, between the natural and the supernatural" (Coon, 1992: 143).

The final prerequisite for a new knowledge form is that its producers must find ways to resist groups that may thwart its efforts at expansion or impinge on its freshly staked out domain. In this sense, as Latour (1987) defines it, reality can be seen as that which resists. In the early twentieth century, the primary obstacle for psychology's expansion into applied domains was the field of psychiatry. During this time, it seemed as if psychiatry was in a position to foil psychology's efforts to expand. After some initial victories, however, psychiatrists lost the battle to contain clinical psychology, although they managed to limit and shape its development. This can be attributed, at least in part, to psychology's success in infiltrating the domain of psychiatry; its ability to outproduce psychiatry in the number of practitioners; its ability to provide a cheaper, more flexible and more readily available product; and its eventual legal protection provided by state legislatures. It is also attributable to an implicit compromise that divided up the growing legions of people seeking psychological and psychiatric services.

Traditionally, the existence of a science is said to be an outcome of a particular ontological ordering of things. Within this way of thinking, science is possible only in realms that deal with inanimate natural objects—objects that cannot talk back. Conversely, realms that deal with self-interpreting humans are capable only of exegesis and discourse. The central problem with this accepted neo-Kantian division between *Naturwissenschaften* and *Geisteswissenschaften*, or the natural and cultural sciences, is that it conceptualizes knowledge development on purely epistemological and essentialistic grounds. Knowledge, it holds, is possible only with a proper philosophy of science to support and legitimate it. The history of psychology, however, illustrates that such an ontologically based understanding of the uniqueness of scientific knowledge is highly problematic. Kant's *Erkenntnistheorie* argued that psychology and the human sciences in general were impossible because they lacked the metaphysical foundations for a science. Yet, while psychology may have not fulfilled the Kantian epistemological prerequisites for a science, it did fulfill some of the central practical prerequisites, if never as completely as some of the other sciences. With the fulfillment of these prerequisites, the discipline of psychology not only solidified into a self-reproducing organization but transformed its knowledge products from the provisional and shaky "rhetoric" of the newcomer to the established and patterned "logic" of the well-established and bureaucratic discipline (see S. Fuchs, 2001: 54). That is, today's psychological truths are dependent upon the maturity of psychology's network of support rather than on the maturity of its knowledge.

It is tempting to conclude that the attachments psychology has made throughout its history with the strong fields of physics, chemistry and physiology have been the results of natural affinities between these disciplines. On this view, psychology was attracted to those fields because they all had a similar concern with solving problems associated with the relationship between mind and matter, and with using the best available experimental methods. Such a stance, however, ignores the fact that there were already disciplines—such as "medicine, physiology and even science journalism"—that had similar concerns and their own methodologies (see Reed, 1997: 13). Certainly philosophy, not to mention some of the emerging social sciences, also shared an interest in the intersection of environment and consciousness. What the new psychology's attachments to physics, chemistry, and physiology reveal is not an inherent connectedness of the fields but a strategy to incorporate the accumulated influence of the natural sciences. Incorporating such artifacts as statistics, measurements and experimental methods served as proof that psychology was indeed an explanatory science on the same level as the natural sciences (see Camic and Xie, 1994).

The disciplinary development of psychology could, of course have been very different. It could have become part of the humanities—as indeed some of its branches have, complete with chalk and lots of texts—or it could have become purely professional, with conference rooms and clients, as has happened in other branches. Under different circumstances, with other alliances and allies and different types of exportation sites, psychology could have become a part of the humanities, social sciences or medicine, or it could have disappeared altogether. However, joining the humanities during the late nineteenth and early twentieth centuries would have meant either linking it to disciplines that were already weakened by two centuries of assault by the natural sciences or attaching itself to the fledgling and unproven social sciences. Politically, it makes no sense to attach oneself to fields that are weak. Such a linkage can only make for another weak or discursive field; it can never produce a science (see S. Fuchs, 1992; 1993).

NOTES

1. In 1903 the experimentalist George Stratton (1903: 34) remarked that Kant "lived under the old dispensation before our psychological laboratories had shown what was the range of possibilities in the case."

2. Throughout the twentieth century many historians of psychology would also comment that the so-called new psychology that began in the late nineteenth century was but a refinement or advancement of knowledge that had existed since the Greeks.

3. The connection of psychology with past writers can also be found in many contemporary works in the history of psychology. For an example see Hearnshaw (1987).

4. James was, however, extremely critical of Wundt's version of experimentalism. He argued that such a method "could hardly have arisen in a country whose natives could be bored" (James, 1952 [1890]: 126).

5. All disciplines seem to need their founding figures—their Francis Bacon, Franz Boaz, Emile Durkheim or Margaret Mead—to serve as moral totems. One of the lessons that Wundt's and James's founding status reveals is that the establishment of a new field requires the status of someone who is already well known and respected. Young Ph.D.'s and other newcomers are not usually the ones politically or practically equipped to develop new and innovative knowledge fields.

6. It is important to note that until 1914 the APA held its annual meeting with the American Association for the Advancement of Science (Hilgard, 1978: 6).

7. James eventually moved back to the Philosophy Department at Harvard and once again accepted the label "philosopher." Part of the victory of Wundt's experimentalism over James's introspection can be attributed to the number of American students who studied with Wundt in Germany during the late nineteenth century. In contrast, James had only a handful of psychology graduate students. It was Wundt's student/mentor ties that account for his emphasis on experimentation and the enthusiasm for setting up laboratories. As Leary (1987: 319) has pointed out, in the late nineteenth century even a brief stay in Germany could greatly increase a scholar's academic standing.

8. It is interesting to note that William James was in Europe when the APA was formed. According to Taylor (1994), this was not accidental but emblematic of the struggle between James and G. Stanley Hall over the type of discipline psychology should be.

9. This membership criterion was changed in 1944, when clinical psychologists pressured the APA to adopt as its objective the advancement of "psychology as a science and as a means of promoting human welfare" (Reisman, 1991: 248).

10. The battle between psychologists and psychiatrists is now heating up again as clinical psychologists push for prescription privileges (see Moyer, 1995; and Bell, Digman and McKenna, 1995).

3

For the Children: The Alliance of Psychology and Education

IN 1892, WILLIAM JAMES PREDICTED THAT THE FUTURE SUC-cess of psychology would be determined less by its ability to provide scientific laws of the mind than by its potential to furnish "practical rules" of behavior for people in their daily lives.

What every educator, every jail-warden, every doctor, every clergyman, every asylum-superintendent, asks of psychology is practical rules. Such men care little or nothing about the ultimate philosophic grounds of mental phenomena, but they do care immensely about improving the ideas, dispositions, and conduct of the particular individuals in their charge (James, 1892: 148).

The pragmatist in James forced him to recognize that the fragile knowledge of the new psychology could not simply sit around the library or laboratory after being developed. Rather, it was imperative that advocates go out and make the world "psychological." To do this they had to problematize and reconfigure issues and phenomena in such a way as to invite the infusion of psychological knowledge into new domains (see Rose, 1996b: 60). They had to convince others that psychology had something they wanted and needed.[1] Psychologists had to show other groups that the new discipline could supply the material they required to change behavior and to remold personality in accordance with their own professional goals. In this endeavor, there proved to be no more suitable a place to showcase psychology's practicality than the field of education.

In the late nineteenth century, primary and secondary educators in Europe and America often lacked the respect of many academics and professionals (see Danziger, 1990: 102–103; Lagemann, 2000). Although teachers had earlier assembled into their own professional organizations, they were still often viewed as underprofessionalized amateurs with little chance of alternative employment. This underappreciation of schools and teachers was coupled with an explosion in the number of children attending school. From 1890 to 1930 the number of students attending public schools in the United States doubled, from 12.7 to 25.7 million students (Snyder, Hoffman and Geddes, 1997). With such a rapid expansion, educators yearned to obtain professional status, public respect and a means for managing the onslaught of new students. Psychologists were in the unique position of being able to offer assistance in all three of these objectives. At the same time, teachers and school administrators were able to provide psychologists with what the burgeoning science needed most, an established "proving ground" to illustrate the explanatory power of its new science. It was here that psychologists could show academic skeptics and the public the new discipline's resourcefulness in providing solutions to some of the central problems and issues facing teachers and school administrators in the new age of mandatory mass education. As a result of this alliance a "trading zone" (see Galison, 1997) between psychology and education was established, an interaction that would have a profound effect on children throughout the twentieth century.

In this chapter I focus on how this trading zone between psychology and education was established by examining three areas where psychological knowledge reshaped many twentieth-century educational practices, as well as children's experiences in schools. After a brief discussion of early attempts by psychologists to establish an alliance with education in the United States, I explore the introduction of psychological clinics, research bureaus and school psychologists into the public schools. Specifically, I survey a few of the tactics that enabled these groups slowly to become standard fixtures of most public schools in the United States. I also examine how, once established, these groups served as conduits for the flow of psychologically based solutions, discursive styles and modes of analysis to teachers and school administrators. Following this section, I survey the intelligence testing movement in education, from its origins in late- nineteenth-century psychology to the development and refinement of the label "learning disabled" in the 1960s and 1970s. Specifically, I look at the introduction and expansion of intelligence tests and at their role in sorting children into appropriate slots for learning and in further "modernizing" education. Next, I consider the role of developmental theory in the organization of public schools and how this contributed to the "psychologizing" of childhood in the twentieth century. Finally, in the conclusion, I discuss why the relationship between psychology and education developed in the manner it did.

AS PHYSIOLOGY IS TO MEDICINE: FORGING THE LINKS BETWEEN PSYCHOLOGY AND EDUCATION

In 1892 William James (1962 [1899]) gave a series of public lectures to teachers in Cambridge, Massachusetts on the growing importance of psychology to pedagogy.[2] At the time of his remarks, the relationship between psychology and education was in its infancy: The subfield of educational psychology was still in development, the first textbook on educational psychology had only recently been published (by James Sully in 1885) and only a handful of teacher training schools and departments had begun to offer courses in psychology (Walberg and Haertel, 1992: 7). In the lectures James argued that the new psychology promised "radical help" for classroom teachers (James, 1962 [1899]: 2). In James's (1962 [1899]: 2) words, "No one has profited more by the fermentation of which I speak, in pedagogical circles, than we psychologists. The desire of the school-teachers for a completer professional training, and their aspiration toward the 'professional' spirit in their work, have led them more and more to turn to us for light on fundamental issues." For James, psychology could, under the right circumstances, provide both the conceptual tools for systemization of educational theory and practice and the impetus for educational reform. It would also contribute to the professionalization and scientific orientation necessary if education was to become a more respected profession. Psychological research on topics such as motivation, learning, attention span and child development would finally enable teachers to implement effective, modern strategies for instructing children. By doing so, teachers could also prove to the public that they were well-informed, up-to-date professionals, deserving of both respect and higher salaries.

A year after James's influential lectures in Cambridge, G. Stanley Hall, one of the founders and the first president of the APA, formed the National Association for the Study of Children (Claparede, 1911: 14).[3] Hall (1891: 121) saw the association as a way of preventing "the mutilation which so powerful an engine as the modern school may inflict upon the tender souls and bodies of our children, and thus upon our entire national future." To accomplish this preservation, teachers and parents were encouraged to keep daily observational journals of their children's behavior. When completed, the journals would be analyzed to identify patterns in child development and provide advice on problem children.[4] Hall also circulated surveys to hundreds of teachers and parents to find out about children's appetites, toy collections, reactions to light and darkness, dreams and a host of other characteristics (see Wooldridge, 1994: 28–29). In 1894 Hall persuaded the National Education Association to establish a Child Study Department to serve as a center to facilititate communications between teachers and psychologists on teaching methods and problem children (see Hall, 1894).

John Dewey was another who, like James and Hall, devoted considerable effort to forging a close relationship between the new psychology and education. In his view, "The school is an especially favorable place in which to study the availability of psychology for social practice" (Dewey in Leahey, 2000: 362). In his 1899 presidential address to the APA Dewey claimed, "The school practice of today has a definite psychological basis" (Dewey, 1978 [1899]: 66). For Dewey, the central problem facing contemporary education was the provisional and unscientific character of the pedagogical practices of teachers. Teachers were in desperate need of an awareness of "the correct educational psychology" (Dewey 1978 [1899]: 68). The existing folk psychology of teachers was, in his view, "paralyzed, partly distorted, and partly rendered futile from the fact that they are in such immediate contact with sheer, unanalyzed personality" (Dewey 1978 [1899]: 70). Educators needed the assistance of psychologically trained experts who could step back from the fray of the classroom and offer detached scientific advice on how best to teach. For Dewey (1978 [1899]: 68), "the rank and file, just because they are person dealing with persons, must have a sufficient grounding in the psychology of the matter to realize the necessity and the significance of what they are doing." He, however, did not allow educators the right to construct their own scientifically based educational psychology. That was to be left to the "educational theorist," who would serve as a type of "middleman between the psychologist and the educational practitioners" (Dewey 1978 [1899]: 68). Trained in psychology, these theorists would export the emerging findings of psychological experimentation and observation to the schools.

Edward Thorndike (1962: 60), another leading early educational psychologist, also strongly advocated the exportation of psychological knowledge to education. Thorndike, the author of the influential works *The Principles of Teaching Based on Psychology* (1906) and the three-volume *Educational Psychology*, founded the *Journal of Educational Psychology* in 1910 to link research in the new psychology with the practice of teaching.[5] He saw psychology as providing "the laws of changes in intellect and character." It was up to the teacher to "apply psychology to teaching" (Thorndike, 1962: 60). He wrote,

> The efficiency of any profession depends in large measure upon the degree to which it becomes scientific. The profession of teaching will improve (1) in proportion as its members direct their daily work by the scientific sport and methods, that is by honest, open-minded consideration of facts, by freedom from superstitions, fancies or unverified guesses, and (2) in proportion as the leader in education direct their choices of methods by the results of scientific investigation rather than by general opinion (Thorndike, 1962: 63).

For Thorndike, psychology provided the scientific knowledge necessary to correct everything from the teaching of math to the problems of the adult learner (see Thorndike, 1921). He, like Dewey, believed that once such knowledge was incorporated into the everyday practices of the teacher, education would finally emerge as both a scientifically based endeavor and a respected profession.

Psychologists' attempt to move their knowledge into education was not limited to rhetorical remarks about the inherent affinity between the two fields, however. Psychologists also began to move into positions in university departments of education. In these positions, they often acquired the label of "professor of education" but nevertheless maintained APA membership and continued to consider themselves psychologists, performing psychological research on educational issues. Over time, such involvement helped blur the distinction between educational theorists and educational psychologists, as well as educational and psychological practice. Psychologists also obtained important decision-making positions within such groups as the National Educational Association. Of these early linkages, few were perhaps more important that Thorndike's connection with Teachers College and the establishment of its Department of Educational Psychology in 1902. Under Thorndike's direction, educational psychology courses became mainstays of teacher education and mandatory parts of the college's doctoral program in education. By the 1920s, Teachers College had become the largest school of education and teacher training in the world. Its graduates "filled twelve of the eighteen full (university) professorships of education in California, and students of Teachers College graduates filled another four. In addition, of the 145 professors or heads of departments of education in the California normal schools, fifty-five were Teachers College graduates, and eighty were students of Teachers College graduates" (Lagemann, 2000: 65–66).

In these teacher training programs psychologists instructed teachers on how to make their classrooms more interesting, challenging and motivational by using the latest techniques discovered by experimental psychology. In particular, teachers were given advice on developing the power of concentration and interest in their students, an area of inquiry that would later become known as motivational psychology (see Weiner, 1990). Herman Horne (1904: 191) argued that "interest is the oil which lubricates the wheels of the classroom machinery" (Horne, 1904: 191). Dewey (1926: 576) recommended that teachers make material palatable by presenting it "in such a way as to enable the child to appreciate its bearings, its relationships, its necessity for him." Psychologists advised teachers to follow a three-part strategy. First they were to "get the activity going with zest." Next, they should see that "success attends." Finally, they should provide strong praise for the child's ensuing success (see Kilpatrick, 1922: 236).

By early in the twentieth century, most psychologists and teachers saw psychology as a prerequisite for teacher qualification. Within a few decades this initial linkage became a requirement for teacher training at all levels. Many argued that education, and consequently students, would never progress or develop properly unless it was tied to the experimental knowledge being discovered in psychology. Psychology should have, as James Cattell declared (1898: 413), "the same relation to the profession of the teacher as physiology has to medicine." It should be the foundational science guiding the daily practice of education. With this new relationship, the concepts of psychology also became those of education.

CLINICS AND SCHOOL COUNSELORS

The intimate coupling of psychology and education envisioned by James, Hall, Dewey, Thorndike and Cattell came to further realization in 1896 when Lightner Witmer opened the first psychological clinic in the United States, at the University of Pennsylvania (see Levine and Levine, 1970: 51).[6] Witmer, a former student of both Wilhelm Wundt and James Cattell, sought to use the newly established clinic as a means to address a number of educational problems facing the schools, such as truancy, low motivation, lack of concentration and poor academic performance. Like many of the other early psychologists, Witmer (1996: 249) believed that "the progress of psychology will be determined by the value and mount of its contributions to the advancement of the human race." The application of psychology to educational practices, he was convinced, would further aid "the development of the individual and the progress of the race" (Witmer, 1908: 1).

Witmer saw his clinic as serving as a liaison between the schools and psychology. To realize this vision, he organized his clinic to serve four central functions: (1) to investigate mental development in children; (2) to provide treatment for retardation and physical defects that affect school work; (3) to offer practical experience to professionals, such as doctors and social workers; and (4) to train students for psychological careers in school systems (see Brotemarkle, 1931: 344–346). At the clinic Witmer established an annual "Schoolman's Week," where teachers from Philadelphia area schools were invited to visit the university and his laboratory. Here they could view first-hand the contributions psychology was making to the progress of education (see Levine and Wishner, 1977).

At the clinic, Witmer (1996: 248) began to see school referrals who were unable "to progress as rapidly as other children" and who were "difficult to manage under ordinary discipline." At the clinic, Witmer administered a host of psychological and medical tests, including rudimentary tests of intelligence. He also began to use experimental evaluation to test variations between different types of students. Witmer's first publicized success came when he determined that a local student referred to the clinic because of his bad spelling was simply in need of glasses (O'Donnell, 1979: 5).

Among Witmer's more enduring proposals was one for the assignment of trained psychologists to serve the needs of schools. These psychological experts would find their "career[s] in connection with the school system, through the examination and treatment of mentally and morally retarded children, or in connection with the practice of medicine" (Witmer, 1907: 5). Another of Witmer's notable proposals was for the development of special educational classes for students who were found to be "backward" or "physically defective." Witmer insisted that all public school teachers receive training in child and development psychology in order to be able to assist psychologists and other professionals in drawing distinctions between the different typologies of children in their classrooms (see Witmer, 1897).

Other leading educational psychologists of the time, such as J.E.W. Wallin, echoed Witmer's call for the need for special classes for "feeble minded" or "defective" children.

The only effective method of dealing with defective children is to segregate them into special groups and to provide special treatment, care, training or restraint. Not only will this policy tend to remove dead weights and irritating impediments from regular classes, so that the typical, hopeful, progressive children may receive their just dues, but in the long run it will prove the only way in which the deviating child can be saved to society from a life of idleness or crime (Wallin, 1911: 192).

Wallin (1911: 203), like Witmer, recommended that all children "retarded pedagogically two years or over" undergo a battery of tests in the laboratory, or by trained assistants in the schools to examine their motor skills and physical growth, and also to take a "selected standardized test of fundamental intellectual traits."

Witmer's success in Philadelphia led to the establishment of other clinics and research stations, such as at the Iowa Child Research Station and the clinic at the University of Minnesota. The Iowa Research Station, initially funded by state legislature and the Women's Christian Temperance Union, ran a nursery school "which served both as a demonstration center and a laboratory in which to study 'normal' children" (Lagemann, 2000: 134). Witmer's accomplishments also paved the way for the creation of a series of research bureaus within large, mostly urban, schools. By the early 1920s school districts in St. Louis, Chicago, Detroit and Los Angeles had opened research bureaus or departments of child study and guidance, staffed by psychologists and social workers (see Ashbaugh, 1919). One of the largest of such clinics, Chicago Public Schools' Department of Scientific Pedagogy and Child Study, served as a research laboratory for studying child development, mental deficiencies, and learning problems, and also as a conduit for administering psychological advice and testing services to teachers and students.

The introduction of research bureaus proved to be useful for introducing psychology's concepts and methods into large, mostly urban schools. Smaller school districts, however, could not afford the expense of staffing and equipping entire research centers. This dilemma saw its resolution in the multifaceted profession of the "school psychologist," a term first used by R.B.W. Hutt (1923). In its early incarnation, the school psychologist's primary responsibilities were the administration of psychological tests and general child guidance and motivation. By the end of the decade, psychologists were proclaiming that the presence of such psychological services in schools was "evidence of progressive practice in education" (Hildreth, 1930: 17).[7] It provided the standard for determining which schools were still stuck in the past and which were attempting to use approaches more in tune with the demands of the "modern world."

Throughout the 1930s and '40s the testing role of school psychologists slowly expanded into other areas (see Gray, 1963; Sandoval, 1993). Psychologists began to assist teachers and administrators in such areas as student discipline, developing student schedules, counseling and parent/school relations. They also began to serve as liaisons between teachers and parents, and between students and other professionals, such as social workers and psychiatrists. This expanded role caused the demand for school psychologists and counselors to grow steadily. By the end of World War II, the production of school psychologists and counselors was not keeping pace with demand. At the time, there were more than fifteen hundred positions needed but only about one thousand school counselors and psychologists in the entire country (Reisman, 1991: 250). The American Psychological Association responded to this shortage by instigating a massive campaign to expand the number and size of graduate programs.

Accompanying the growth of the school psychology industry was an ever-expanding role for school psychologists in classroom curriculum development. No longer relegated to the supporting fringe of academics, the school counselor was now required to take part in designing and implementing curricular programs that addressed the emotional and self-actualization needs of students. School psychologists have now become key players in the designation of students as "learning disabled" and "mentally retarded" (see Mercer, 1973). Some states, such as Missouri, mandate that school counselors spend 30–35 percent of their time in "curriculum delivery" of the classroom (Nolan, 1999: 109). Other states, such as South Carolina, require that school counselors "infuse counseling content into the regular education curriculum" (Nolan, 1999: 109). The expanded role of psychologists in the schools has recently led to the establishment of what are sometimes referred to as "full-service," or "community," schools. These "one-stop-shopping centers" serve students, families and communities in their respective mental health needs. States such as California, Florida, Kentucky, Missouri, New Jersey, Oregon and Washington have developed statewide initiatives to develop such programs (Adelman and Taylor, 2000: 50). Advocates claim these community schools help foster family and community well-being "by providing social-support networks for new students and families, teaching each other coping skills, participating in school governance, helping create a psychological sense of community, and so forth" (Adelman and Taylor, 2000: 50–51).

The growing number of school psychologists in the 1940s and '50s proved to be both a blessing and a curse for the discipline of psychology. On the one hand, it provided a large new occupation for the employment of psychology students and widened avenues for the flow of the discipline's knowledge. However, the massive growth also provided the opportunity for a new and somewhat autonomous professional to emerge. By the 1960s there were indications that school psychology had begun to strike out on its own (see Graff and Clair, 1973). In 1962, the *Journal of School Psychology* was launched; by the late 1960s; separate doctoral training programs were developed to handle the increased demand for school psychologists and counselors (Phillips, 1990: xi). In the course of a few decades school psychology had gone from one training program, in 1930, to over two hundred by the mid-1980s (see Fagan, 1986: 15). In fact, in the fifteen years from the late 1960s through the early 1980s, the number of school psychology programs doubled. Although still shaped by the knowledge being produced in psychology, school psychology had in many respects become a profession in its own right by the 1980s. Today there are over two hundred training programs in school psychology and some twenty-five thousand school psychologists in the United States (see Phillips, 1990: xi). Psychology had managed to carve out a new area where its knowledge could be applied, but it had not been able to control fully the direction of its own innovation (Danziger, 1997: 85). This was perhaps unfortunate for the discipline of psychology, but it was ultimately beneficial for the expansion of its knowledge.

FINDING THE FEEBLEMINDED: PSYCHOLOGICAL
TESTS OF INTELLIGENCE

Witmer's Philadelphia laboratory and the school psychology and child-guidance movements had partially fulfilled James's requirement that psychological knowledge would need to provide "practical rules" to professionals in their daily activities in order to become successful. Specifically, these activities had demonstrated that the psychological assessment of children could provide a useful means for school administrators to organize and sort children into different learning groups. Such a reorganization of the educational process allowed teachers to manage and control the classroom more effectively, and administrators to reallocate resources to areas where they felt they were most needed. In these efforts, no aspect of psychological knowledge proved more valuable than "mental tests," or tests of intelligence.

The first mention of the term "mental test" in American psychology appeared in an article by James Cattell in 1890. Cattell had borrowed the general concept of mental testing from the work of the British eugenicist Francis Galton at his Anthropometric Laboratory at the South Kensington Museum (Sokal, 1987: 26). Cattell's first mental test was conducted on students in an experimental psychology class and on "all who present themselves" at the Psychology Laboratory at the University of Pennsylvania (Cattell, 1890: 371). The examination consisted of ten distinct tests, ranging from reaction time to a sound, to repeating letters. The results were then used to rank-order participants in terms of their general mental abilities.

In 1894, Cattell received permission from the president of Columbia College to begin using his now-revised test to examine every entering student in the college and the Columbia School of Mines. In a letter to the college's president, Cattell (in Sokal, 1987: 32) contended that the tests would be used "to determine the condition and progress of students [and] the relative value of different courses of study." However, by the late 1890s Cattell judged his test to be largely a disappointment and began to question the validity of his intelligence test and its findings. Primarily, he felt that the test had failed to distinguish between those who would perform well in college and those who would not.

In France, however, intelligence tests were beginning to show more useful outcomes. Ten years after Cattell initiated his mental and physical tests in Philadelphia and four years after the opening of Witmer's

laboratory, Alfred Binet and Ferdinand Buisson established the So-
ciété libre pour l'Étude psychologique de l'Enfant to study the mental
adjustment of students in French schools (Pollack and Brenner, 1969:
x). Four years later, in 1904, Binet was appointed to a commission to
improve the teaching of "backward children." Binet and his associate
Theodore Simon established a laboratory in a Parisian primary school
in order to develop a test to identify students who would not benefit
from a regular classroom environment (Gray, 1963: 30). In 1905 Binet and Simon published the first results of their new test in an article
entitled "Méthodes nouvelles pour le Diagnostic du Niveau intellec-
tuel des Anormaus" (Pollack and Brenner, 1969: x). The scale they
devised, later named the Binet-Simon Test, was revised in 1908 and
again in 1911. Binet and Simon (1916: 273) believed that their new
test of intelligence would help psychology finally become "a science
of great social utility."

The original 1905 Binet-Simon scale contained thirty items of increasing difficulty. The more influential 1908 version expanded the
test and provided age-specific guidelines for comparing levels of intelligence. The 1908 test contained yearly measures of intelligence
between the ages of three and thirteen. According to the criteria of
the test, a child at the age of three should be able to point to his or
her nose, eyes, and mouth, repeat sentences, react to pictures and
identify his or her family name (Binet and Simon, 1916: 184–195).
By the age of seven children should be able to complete unfinished
pictures, know how many fingers he or she had, copy a written model,
copy a diamond shape, repeat five figures, describe pictures, count up
to thirteen different objects and give the names of the four common
coins (Binet and Simon, 1916: 207–211). The reading test, conducted
at the age of eight, held special importance in the overall tests. For
Binet and Simon (1916: 211) this test "serves as a borderline between
imbecility and moronity." Children who were able only to "read with
two memories" (i.e., recall at least two points from a reading passage)
were considered to have reached the level of a "moron" (Simon and
Binet, 1916: 211). The Binet-Simon Test was to be graded on the
basis of the age or maturity level the student could obtain. Children
who scored above their age level were considered advanced, while
those who scored below their level were considered backward or feebleminded.

In the United States, the first to use Binet and Simon's test of
intelligence was Henry H. Goddard, a student of G. Stanley Hall's
at Clark University and the director of psychological research at the

New Jersey Training School for Feebleminded Boys and Girls at Vineland. Goddard (1910: 19) contended that the tests "come amazingly near what we feel to be the truth in regard to the mental status of any child tested." With Goddard's advocacy, particularly in the mental hygiene movement, doctors at Vineland and elsewhere began to accept the Binet-Simon Test as the most reliable method to date for determining the mental status of feebleminded children (Zenderland, 1987: 46).

At roughly the time Goddard was using the Binet-Simon Test at Vineland, Lewis Terman, another student of G. Stanley Hall at Clark and now a professor of psychology and education at Stanford University, began to work on revisions. While at Clark, Terman had used some of Binet and Simon's early work in his dissertation, entitled *Genius and Stupidity: A Study of Some of the Intellectual Processes of Seven Bright and Seven Stupid Boys* (Dunn, 1980: vii). In 1910 and 1911 Terman and an associate used the Binet-Simon Test to examine the intelligence of 396 children. In 1913, based on their study's findings and in response to growing criticism among psychologists that the existing test lacked adequate comparison data, particularly for adults and the very young, Terman began working on a revision (Dunn, 1980: vii). In 1916 the Stanford revision of the Binet-Simon Test was complete (see Terman, 1916). The Stanford revision contained ninety items, thirty-six more than Binet and Simon's 1911 version. Like its French counterpart, the Stanford revision had subjects perform a series of tasks and then compared the results with statistical norms for their age groups.

Like Binet and Simon before him, Terman considered intelligence to be defined in terms of an individual's ability "to carry on abstract thinking" (Terman, 1921: 128). It was, he believed, "the races which excel in abstract thinking that eat while others starve" (Terman, 1921: 128). Terman asserted that these "abstract thinking races" could, if they desired, "quickly exterminate or enslave all the races notably their inferiors in this respect" (Terman, 1921: 128). Accordingly, his test contained various measures he believed captured the concept of abstract reasoning. These measures ranged from determining the difference between terms—such as "laziness" and "idleness," or "evolution" and "revolution"—to interpreting the meaning of fables (see Terman, 1916: 324). Subjects who could reason using abstract concepts and principles were considered to possess higher mental ages than those whose intelligence relied only on rudimentary, skill-based processes.

For Terman and other supporters, intelligence testing's primary contribution was that it offered an efficient means for organizing children into appropriate slots for learning.[8] He wrote,

We are beginning to realize that the school must take into account, more seriously than it has yet done, the existence and significance of these differences in endowment. Instead of wasting energy in the vain attempt to hold mentally slow and defective children up to a level of progress which is normal to the average child, it will be wiser to take account of the inequalities of children in original endowment and to differentiate the course of study in such a way that each child will be allowed to progress at the rate which is normal to him, whether that rate be rapid or slow. (Terman, 1916: 4)

Terman (1916: 6) argued that the use of intelligence testing would eventually bring "the high grade defectives under the surveillance and protection of society." This would aid in "curtailing the reproduction of feeble-mindedness and in the elimination of an enormous amount of crime, pauperism, and industrial inefficiency" (Terman, 1916: 7).

About the time Terman was completing work on his revision of the Benet-Simon Test, superintendents around the country were beginning to warm to the general idea of using widespread intelligence testing in schools. Between 1905 and 1908 a host of other standardized psychological tests became available to educators, such as the Thorndike-McCall Reading Scale, the Hillegas Composition Scale, the Woody Arithmetic Test and the Morrison-McCall Spelling Scale (see Grinder, 1981: 357). The success of these tests in sorting students led some superintendents to consider the possible advantages of broad-based tests of intelligence. After years of resistance, superintendents at a 1915 national meeting agreed to accept the tests as part of their regular academic testing efforts. Reflecting on the council meeting, the educator Charles Judd (1925: 806–807) later wrote, "There can be no doubt as we look back on that council meeting that one of the revolutions in American education was accomplished by that discussion. Since that day tests and measures have gone quietly on their way, as conquerors should. Tests and measures are to be found in every progressive school in the land."

The victory of 1915, slowly prepared during the preceding twenty years, was decisive. With this formal acceptance, intelligence and other aptitude testing took an important step toward becoming a standard fixture of most public schools. Four years after the meeting, in 1919, Edward Thorndike reported to the National Society of the Study of Education that over one million school children had been given group intelligence tests within the last year (Joncich, 1968). In 1921, M.E. Haggerty (1921: 215) predicted that "the time will come when all progressive schools will record the intelligence score of a pupil with same care that it records his chronological age." Bolstered by the success of new techniques of group testing, particularly with American soldiers during World War I, intelligence testing had by the mid-1920s found its way into many large school systems throughout the United States (see Courtis, 1925; Carson, 1993). As Terman had suggested, the tests were now being used to segregate children into particular classes on the basis of their performance. Most psychologists and educators concluded that these tests were an overwhelming success.[9] As one researcher concluded, "When mental age and brightness are used as a basis for classification, it is possible to separate the dull and feeble-minded children from the average and superior individuals, so that each may compete with others of his own mental caliber" (Lowell, 1922: 289).

By the late 1920s, Henry Goddard (1928) had proclaimed that the scientific classification of students based on intelligence measures had been the most noteworthy accomplishment to date of clinical psychology. Gertrude Hildreth (1930: 8) argued that "before the introduction of psychological measurement there was little effective classification of school pupils, little provision of real value for educational needs, and scarcely any educational guidance worthy of the name. Tests have helped appreciably both to reveal and to solve educational problems." Between 1927 and 1948 almost 1,300 various achievement tests were developed and put to use (Monroe, 1950: 1461). Terman's Stanford Achievement Tests alone had annual sales of over 1.5 million by the mid-1920s (Chapman, 1988: 101). Psychology could claim over sixty measures for testing intelligence and mental development (see Hildreth, 1930: 282–285). A few decades later, in the 1950s, the number of achievement tests had grown to nearly 2,400, and the number of intelligence tests had climbed to nearly eight hundred (see Buros, 1953); by the mid-1980s there were some three thousand (see Sweetland and Keyser, 1986).

In the late 1950s and early 1960s, psychological tests of intelligence began to enter a new, more elaborated phase. Whereas previously intelligence testing had been used to rank students into specific IQ slots, the new version sought to sort children's abilities into emotional, cultural and intellectual categories. During the 1950s many educational psychologists began to question the logic of using intelligence as the only criterion for classifying and subsequently tracking children. Many psychologists and educators argued that a child's cultural and emotional background should be included in the overall assessment of her or his abilities and potentials. This new assessment procedure placed children who performed poorly on intelligence measures or in class in the newly developed categories of "slow learners," the "mentally retarded," "emotionally disturbed," "culturally deprived," and "learning disabled" (Sleeter, 1986: 49). As with earlier intelligence testing, psychologists and educators claimed that sorting children based on these more intricate criteria would aid both administrators in their organization of education and teachers in their classroom instruction.

The appropriate classification of the "underachieving child" was ascertained through both tests of intelligence and consideration of the student's background. Students who fell below an IQ of 75 were considered "retarded," while those scoring between 75 and 90 were labeled "slow learners" (Sleeter, 1986: 49; see Mercer, 1973). Those who performed poorly and were also discipline problems were given the label "emotionally disturbed." Poorly performing children who were from specific cultural backgrounds—such as poor white, African American and Mexican-American—were labeled as "culturally deprived." The category of "learning disabled" was reserved for those who came from "normal family stock" but who nevertheless performed poorly in class and on intelligence tests (Strauss and Lehtinen, 1963: 112). The causes of a learning disability were said to reside in a host of biological conditions, ranging from minimal brain damage (Strauss and Kephart, 1955) to problems in neurological development (Delcato, 1959).

By the 1980s, pressure from groups who argued that the labels "culturally deprived" and "slow learners" were racist and class-based led to the collapse of the five categories of the 1960s into the two primary labels of "mentally retarded" and "learning disabled" (Sleeter, 1986). The learning-disabled category became a catchall for children who performed poorly in class but tested above the "mentally retarded" cutoff score on intelligence tests. Meanwhile, children who performed well on these tests came to be labeled "gifted" or "exceptional" and were placed on a different educational track. In some cases, however, they too were seen as problematic and were said to be prone to "overachiever syndrome" and in need of counseling to deal with victimization brought by their success in school and on achievement tests (Dineen, 1996: 17).

By the early twenty-first century, the long, strange story of intel-

ligence testing had entered a new phase. What had begun as an uncertain and fragile attempt to aid administrators in their efforts to
rationalize education at the turn of the century had been transformed
into a reliable and resilient means for organizing and streamlining all
educational practices. Today one hundred to two hundred million
psychological tests are administered to students every year, an average
of 2.5 to 5 tests per student per year (Hanson, 1993: 10). The presence of these tests on the educational landscape has become as normal
and seemingly as necessary as that of desks and books. The monopolization of intelligent testing served to ensure that psychologists'
conceptualizations and standards of learning and intelligence would
be the benchmarks by which all students were judged.

SCHOOLS AND THE DEVELOPMENTAL IMPERATIVE

In 1901, G. Stanley Hall presented to the National Education Association a model of the ideal school, based on the early findings of
his child study project. Hall (1926: 713) divided his ideal school program into four intervals, based on his understanding of the distinct
stages of child development. During the first stage, kindergarten age,
the child "needs more mother, and less teacher; more of the educated
nurse, and less the metaphysician" (Hall, 1926: 713). During this
phase the primary educational emphasis should be on developing the
body and hygiene of the child. Hall (1926: 714) described the next
stage, at ages seven or eight, as a transitory stage, one that was "of
the greatest interest for science." The third stage, at ages eight or
nine, "should be devoted to drill, habituation and mechanism" (Hall,
1926: 714). During this stage children should be taught reading, writing and other skills that disciplined the mind through memorization
and recitation. During the final stage, which Hall labeled adolescence,
the drilling of the previous stage should be replaced with an emphasis
on individuality, exploration, and freedom. In the adolescent stage,
"we can no longer coerce and break, but must lead and inspire" (Hall,
1926: 714). Teachers needed to realize that during this critical stage
of development "each individual must be studied and made a special
problem if his personality is to come to full maturity" (Hall, 1926:
714).

For Hall, adolescence was the most important stage for the creation
of a successful, psychologically fit adult. This period, situated at the
intersection of childhood and adulthood, heralded "the birthday of
the imagination" (Hall, 1969 [1904]: 313). As such, it required par-

ticular attention and care on the part of teachers and parents if it was to unfold properly. Hall believed that this period of "storm and stress" marked both a tension between larger societal struggles (between the primitive and the civilized) and individual tensions between childhood and adulthood (Hall, 1969 [1904]). In Hall's view, the stage of adolescence was like the premodern phase in the history of humankind. Without enlightenment and rational guidance, the adolescent, much like premodern Western society, would never reach full potential.

Although reconfigured to fit a more gradualist understanding of child development over the ensuing decades, Hall's designations and classifications of distinct developmental stages and unique modes of educational treatment are still retained in most contemporary systems of educational theory and practice. In this developmental imperative, schoolchildren are expected to move through various levels of socio-cognitive development and more advanced modes of reasoning until they reach the apex of adult abstract thinking. Corresponding to these developmental stages are distinct methods of learning and teaching. Educators must direct their pedagogy in accordance with the developmental demands of particular stages of childhood. Likewise, children are required slowly to relinquish their more "primitive callings" in order to take on the rules and regulations of the larger civilized society. In this process the developing child became an "object premised on the location of certain capacities within the child" and therefore within the domain of psychology (Walkerdine, 1984: 154).

In Hall's writings, along with those of other educational psychologists, we find the forging of an influential twentieth-century definition of the child, a view that would have far-reaching implications for both schools and children. For Hall's and other early psychologists, "the child is literally a different creature from the adult" (Burnham, 1926: 2). The child is a "young barbarian" in need of the civilizing hand of an ameliorative parent, teacher and school system (Hall, 1926: 303; also see Johnson, 1995). For some psychologists, such as Herman Horne (1906: 267), "the wild life of the world is caged in the cerebrospinal nervous system of the veriest child." To be on guard against the dangers of this unchecked wild life, teachers needed to be trained to "cultivate children like flowers" (Burbank, 1905: 457). They needed to "know something about all the new movements, and not only about feeble-mindedness, intelligence tests, standard scales and the like, but also psychoanalysis, the Freudian mechanisms, social and antisocial attitudes, the principles of sociology, if not those of psychiatry" (Burnham, 1926: 205).

Likewise, schools needed to be organized in such a manner as to transform the undomesticated child into a responsible adult, as well as sort out those who were capable of being domesticated from those who were not, by using intelligence and aptitude tests. Such transformation required fervent dedication on the part of school administrators and teachers to understanding the way children's minds work. It was not enough "just to command inanimate nature[;] we must constantly study, love, obey her, so to control child nature we must first, and perhaps still more piously, study, love, obey it" (Hall, 1965: 51). As Hall and Dewey tried to show, schools were not just places where lessons were taught; they were to be laboratories of psychological development.

Today, children are aided in their journey to "modernization" by scores of school psychologists, counselors and teachers, all of whom are trained, in varying degrees, in the methods, discourse, concepts and theories of psychology. Psychologists are the ones who test and analyze the child, write reports on his or her progress, meet with parents to discuss the child's development or academic problems, examine the student for vocational suitability, and provide preliminary diagnoses of any learning problems. Assisting in these efforts to determine children's success in their transition from "primitives" to "moderns" are scores of psychologically based tests and assessments. The results of these tests determine the student's future educational and vocational trajectory. Those who score high are tracked for college-preparatory classes and professional careers. Those who score low are relegated to special education classes or vocational training.

These tests are designed to reveal not only such attributes as intelligence, motivation level and career aspirations but also the sources of dysfunction. Children who score outside of the norm (either high or low) are labeled "exceptional," and their test results are seen as holding the secret of their peculiarities. For psychologists, it is a student's unique underlying psychological makeup that is responsible for his or her extraordinariness. For instance, children who are inattentive are concealing hyperactive disorders, and children who lack inspiration are hiding motivation disorders. As Stratton (1903: 184) put it a century ago, "A child who cannot learn to spell, should be regarded as a rare and inviting individual who may not be dismissed until he has yielded up the secret of his defective memory." Arguably, however, students are neither extraordinary nor secretive until the test makes them so. In its quest to find and fix the developmentally abnormal, psychology serves not as just another form of social control, as is often claimed by cultural critics, but as an arbiter of what the social norm will be.

The movement of psychological concepts into the lives of children was not limited to activities occurring in twentieth-century school systems, however. These psychological concepts and practices also greatly shaped other "extracurricular" groups concerned with training children and promoting social change. Organizations such as the Boy Scouts, the Playground Movement, the YMCA, and the 4-H often imported the ideas of Hall and other leading educational and developmental psychologists into their programs. For example, John Alexander, a founder of 4-H and author of the *Boy Scout Manual*, was an avid follower of G. Stanley Hall. His model for the programs of 4-H was largely based on Hall's understanding of child development. Likewise, Henry Curtis and Joseph Lee, central figures in the movement to build playgrounds throughout urban areas, were disciples of Hall's brand of child and developmental psychology (see Kett, 1977: 224–225).

The activities of psychologists and teachers, coupled with the work of various "moral entrepreneurs" (Becker, 1963), such 4-H and the Boy Scouts, helped "regularize" childhood (Cohen, 1985: 292). Under the influence of psychology and other disciplines and movements, childhood became an object of expert regulation and dependence upon adults. The child was to undergo a type of teacher and parent-supervised "quarantine" before being "allowed to join the adult world" (Aries, 1962: 412). He or she needed a "carefully structured and special education" before being considered "properly prepared for adulthood" (Empey, 1978: 51). Psychology contributed to this regularization of childhood by identifying, defining, measuring, and solidifying such traits as instincts, motivation, intelligence, attitudes, imagination and attention span. Assessments and measurements of these "essential psychological traits" could then be used to predict the child's mental health and eventual success, as well as mobilize action on such child-related issues as education and social welfare.

By the 1950s the psychologization of contemporary childhood education was largely complete (see Kett, 1977: 245). New classifications and definitions of childhood and youth had been forged, distinct stages of psychological development had been accepted as standard knowledge, intelligence testing had become an ordinary practice and modern and psychologically based teaching methods had been formed and implemented. Psychology, in conjunction with other groups and organizations, had recast both children and schools. In this process, psychologists had made their knowledge indispensable for education. Educating a child without psychological expertise became as unthinkable as self-diagnosing a disease or cooking without a cookbook. Psychologists had acquired this authority within pedagogy without a direct conquest of education; rather, they had succeeded at planting their particular epistemological vision and conceptual tools into the field. Education simply provided one of the key arenas wherein psychologists rewrote and redefined both education and children. As a result of this alliance with education, psychology took an important step toward becoming an integral part of the social landscape. Schools and school children had become one of the principal arenas where society was being made psychological.

CONCLUSION: WHY THE ALLIANCE BETWEEN PSYCHOLOGY AND EDUCATION?

Historians and sociologists of science have pointed out that if any knowledge is to become successful, it must make itself indispensable to others by establishing itself as an "obligatory point of passage" (Latour, 1987). Without the ability to insinuate itself into the activities of other knowledge-producing groups via these points of passage, new knowledge always risks isolation and disintegration (see Shapin and Schaffer, 1985). Psychology proved itself to be particularly skillful in the endeavor to become indispensable. By the early twenty-first century it had been able to become "an obligatory crossing point" not only for education but "for anyone interested in the advancement of culture, everyday life, philosophy and the sciences" (Kusch, 1995: 151). Education, however, was where this ability to insinuate itself into other groups' activities was initially forged. Over the course of a few decades psychology became the primary supplier of educational concepts and a means through which education could channel its problems or anomalies. With regard to the latter role, psychology became a central means for sorting students and for implementing "educational crisis management." It provided education with the conceptual tools and scientific legitimation to handle classroom instruction, disruptive students, intrusive parents and a host of other problems facing schools.

As James and most early psychologists recognized, knowledge that wants to become successful and all-encompassing must also recruit allies outside of its point of production or face isolation and extinction. Knowledge that remains embedded in the restricted local networks in which it is produced will always have limited impact and appeal. In this sense, "no instruments can be developed, no discipline can become autonomous, no new institution can be founded" without the development of alliances that enable a knowledge form to grow (Latour, 1999: 103). In other words, knowledge without attachments always remains local knowledge. This local knowledge may coordinate action within its limited territory; however, it will never be able to establish itself as a universalistic way of knowing or become truth. Usually only powerful and well-established knowledge producers have either the ability or luxury to insulate themselves from outsiders. In addition, the legitimacy of a new knowledge form is often dependent upon how useful it proves to be to the aims and objectives of those outside of the domain where it is produced. In this case, it is always up to others to demonstrate the effectiveness of adopting or adapting the new field's concepts, methods and theories (see Latour, 1987).

Potential sites for the movement of a new knowledge form often include other, less prestigious or more loosely organized disciplines, emerging professions, industries or corporations, governmental agencies and the general public (see Brown, 1992). For a number of political and practical reasons, these groups are seldom in the position of producing their own "hard" or "official" knowledge. Often they must rely on the established knowledge products of those already "in the know." In this regard, the professionalization of teachers could not have taken place without "a well-developed body of knowledge on teaching that [could] guide teaching practices" (Labaree, 1997: 140). For early psychology, the field of education proved to be a prime site for the exportation of its knowledge—education needed a body of scientific knowledge in order to achieve its own goals of professionalization and modernization.

Soon after the turn of the twentieth century, the association between education and psychology became quite well established: the *Journal of Educational Psychology* had been founded, a number of child-research laboratories had been launched and the separate subdisciplines of development and educational psychology had emerged (Danziger, 1990: 104). Such a close relationship between the two areas prompted G. Stanley Hall (in Birnbaum, 1955: 25–26) to proclaim, "America believes, as does no other country, that education must be based on the study of psychology." The interdependence of psychology and education had proven beneficial to both parties. Education received many of the conceptual tools and testing instruments necessary to transform itself from a relatively weak occupation with little public respect to a somewhat more powerful profession. Psychology also provided education the capacity to show a skeptical public that its pedagogical and administrative practices were based on the methods of science and were not simply ad hoc control strategies. On the other hand, psychology, although initially skeptical about becoming too closely linked with teachers (Lagemann, 2000: 21), found in them a reliable conduit for the flow of its knowledge and in education a place of employment for its applied practitioners. It had also found an opportunity to prove its own scientific status and practicality to other fields that were still suspicious of psychology's merits as a discipline and a profession.

Today, the practical outcomes of the alliance between education and psychology are unmistakable. Most schools have psychologists on their payroll; teachers in most states are required to receive training in child development and adolescent psychology; and teacher workshops are often conducted on psychological topics, such as self-esteem, motivation and child development. Schools generally do not rely on social workers, theologians, philosophers, sociologists, anthropologists or other related experts, as could have been the case, but instead call upon psychologists—to administer intelligence tests, provide training workshops for teachers and conduct vocational and emotional counseling for students. In addition, the conceptual language of psychology has largely been subsumed in the language of education. Teachers have borrowed some of the key concepts of psychology—such as self-esteem, attention span, motivation, development and aptitude—as means to organize and think about pedagogy, students and their classrooms. Also, students themselves are seen as exhibiting the "inherent" psychological conditions of "maladaptive behavior," "learning disabilities," "attention deficit disorder," "conformity," "intelligence" and "peer conformance."

As with psychology's efforts at making connection to the natural sciences and medicine described in the last chapter, the association with education should not be seen the result of a natural affinity between these two endeavors. There existed other disciplines—such as social work, philosophy, medicine, sociology, and even anthropology—with which education could have forged as strong connections as it did psychology. Under other conditions, in fact, education might have been able to strike out alone, with its own, unique knowledge-making institutions and procedures.[10] An example of other fields with the potential to contribute to the methods and language of education is sociology. Despite great fanfare in the early decades of the twentieth century about the importance of sociology for education, by midcentury courses in the sociology of education decreased in number after reaching their peak in the 1920s; the National Society for the Study of Educational Sociology, established in 1923, failed as an organization; and membership in the American Sociological Association's educational section declined significantly from earlier decades (Brookover, 1949: 407). It appeared by midcentury, according to one educational sociologist, that "in the past few years relatively few sociologists have been interested in sociology, and apparently there has been no increase in interest in departments of education" (Brookover, 1949: 407).

Psychology's alliance with education reveals the vicissitudes of the struggles to expand the knowledge of the discipline. In one sense, psychology simply arrived on the scene first, with the largest number of advocates. Once there, these advocates were particularly adept at linking themselves with a loyal and needy ally. Also, psychology succeeded because its conceptual innovations were less likely to cause dramatic disruptions in the field of education than were those of other disciplines. For instance, sociological concepts derived from Chicago School sociology or philosophical concepts from Dewey's philosophy of education often called for thorough reorganization of the education system. In contrast, most psychological concepts, such as intelligence and motivation, were adaptable to the prevailing system. They also placed the imperative to change squarely on the student rather than the entire educational system. These features of psychological concepts kept the cost of innovation low. In such a case, the lower the cost of innovation, "the more likely its adoption" (Katz, 1999: 150).

The relationship of psychology and education illustrates that the path that a new knowledge form follows as it moves from the obscurity of the margins to the prominence of the center is determined by a complex political dialectic between advocates and potential allies. It is rarely a case of one field completely conquering and colonizing another, as is clearly the case with psychology's relationship with education, but rather a situation where a "trading zone" between cooperating fields and groups is established (Galison, 1997). Like the gift exchange in the Trobriand Island described by Marcel Mauss, this knowledge-based trading zone allows a place for discrete and often hierarchically dissimilar groups to exchange concepts, methods and perspectives (see Galison, 1997). This allows a field to adopt some of the ideas and materials of another while maintaining some degree of autonomy. So, while education was undoubtedly scientifically and professionally weaker than psychology, it managed to alter the direction of psychology perhaps as much as psychology changed the course of twentieth-century education. The discipline of psychology was led or in some ways forced to become a more applied knowledge form in order to expand, find employment for its students and legitimate its claims to be a science.

NOTES

1. As Danziger (1997: 182) has pointed out, this involved a careful balance between "the ideal of a universalistic and uninvolved science and accommodation to the requirements of local sectoral interests." Psychology needed scientific authority for its truth claims, while it needed the applied domains for employment and other forms of support.

2. At the time of these lectures James was married to Boston schoolteacher Alice Gibbens. In the preface to the published version of these lectures, James (1962 [1899]: v) apologized to his academic colleagues for producing knowledge that was "practical and popular to the extreme." Such defensiveness provides some indication of the reluctance some psychologist felt at becoming involved in education, as well as of the perceived status gap between psychology and education that existed during the late nineteenth century (see Lagemann, 2000).

3. Hall was known as a prolific lecturer. He later estimated that he had delivered as many as 2,500 lectures outside of his position at Clark University between 1889 and 1923 (see Adams, 1931: 80).

4. The original idea of recording children's development dated back as early as the late eighteenth century (see Claparede, 1911).

5. Thorndike is also known for developing a list of the most commonly used words in American society. The "Thorndike List" was used by a host of editors seeking to make works readable to the American public (see Stille, 1998: 18).

6. In the same year, James Sully opened a psychological laboratory for the study of "difficult children" in Great Britain (Reisman, 1991: 43).

7. By the late 1920s the number of school psychologists who were APA members had grown to eighty-seven (Hildreth, 1930: 23).

8. Terman's advocacy of the usefulness of intelligence testing corresponded with the efforts of psychologists in Missouri and Illinois to enact legislation requiring the administration of measures of intelligence before a child could be sent to a school for the mentally defective (Reisman, 1991: 115).

9. Of course, there were also many critics of intelligence testing.

10. This is somewhat the case today for the field of education. However, much of its indigenous knowledge is still highly psychological in nature.

4

Molding Morals and Minds: Psychology and the Modernization of Parenting

A KNOWLEDGE FORM'S CONCEPTS AND IDEAS OFTEN OPERATE like consumer products in the marketplace. Concepts and ideas, like consumer products, must be marketed and advertised, demand must be fabricated, follow-up services must be offered and finally the product must be sold to the enthusiastic and receptive consumer. A common strategy in such a merchandizing campaign is the development of the so-called spin-off product. Here, demand is created for a new product by linking it with a successful old one. Such a marketing tactic often has the paradoxical effect of increasing the sales of both the original and the spin-off.[1]

Although it would be misleading to claim that the psychological knowledge has operated in some great "marketplace of ideas," a marketing analogy is, nevertheless, applicable to another of psychology's great twentieth-century affiliations, parenting and parenting advice. The relationship psychology established with education in the late nineteenth and early twentieth centuries showed itself useful in reorganizing the educational experiences of teachers, school administrators and children. The relationship made teachers more professional and modern and school administrators more efficient "human resource managers"; children became redefined as immature adults in need of the guiding hand of a developmentally sensitive pedagogy. Psychologists too reaped important benefits from the alliance. First and foremost, they found an arena where they could show skeptics of the discipline, as well as the educated public, that their new science had practical applications far beyond the experimental confines of their early academic laboratories.

If the knowledge produced by scientific psychology was so central to teachers' and school administrators' efforts to reorganize and "modernize" education, it obviously would be of great assistance to parents raising children. It seemed that early-twentieth-century parents were as backward and ill informed as nineteenth-century teachers as to the proper, scientifically tested methods for transforming undisciplined children into responsible adults. Like the nineteenth-century teachers described by John Dewey (1978 [1899]: 66), the direct exposure of turn-of-the-century parents to the "unanalyzed personality" of their children was no indication that they knew very much about what was really going on with them.

In the late nineteenth and early twentieth centuries, psychologists undertook an effort to expose not only teachers but also parents to the newly crafted concepts and principles of psychology. Educational psychologists such as Gertrude Hildreth (1930: 211) argued that 90 percent of student problems could be solved "by better understanding on the part of parents of newer movements in education and need for acquiring objective attitudes toward child behavior." To accomplish this modernization of parenting, psychologists and allied organizations used not only traditional avenues of dissemination, such as popular books, public lectures and seminars, but also established connections with a number of emerging social movements and organizations concerned with parenting, motherhood and children. In these efforts psychologists often teamed up with such groups as the National Congress of Mothers, the Young Men's Christian Association (YMCA), the Boy Scouts, the Children's Foundation, the National Council on Parent Education, and the 4-H to provide instruction to parents on a host of general psychological principles regarding the proper, modern way to carry out their responsibilities.

In this chapter I explore a few of the ways psychology began to redirect the way children are raised and the way parents and children relate to one another over the course of the last century. Specifically, I examine psychology's contribution to the formation of entirely new notions of childhood and adolescence. In the opening section, I investigate how early psychology was mobilized to aid social reformers' efforts to control child and adolescent sexuality. Here, I inspect how psychology was able to use a late-nineteenth-century panic over adolescent sexuality to establish itself as an important purveyor of parenting advice. The second section explores the discipline's influence on the development and growth of parenting manuals and advice. In this section, I survey some of the suggestions that psychologists gave to parents on child rearing throughout the twentieth century. I also investigate how these suggestions slowly became benchmarks for defining the meaning of modern parenthood and for setting the boundaries of competent parenting. In the third section, I discuss how the concept of self-esteem began to redirect discussions of the psychodynamics of childhood and to redefine parental responsibility in the late twentieth century. Finally, in the concluding section, I explore how psychology set up particular notions of normal child and adult relationships and how this construction contributed to both the emergence of a child-centered family life and a growing dependency on psychological advice for bringing up children the "right way."

FORBIDDEN JOY: PSYCHOLOGY AND THE CONTROL OF ADOLESCENT SEXUALITY

In the late nineteenth century a "moral panic" involving the perils of unchecked child and adolescent sexuality began to sweep America and Europe (see Hall, 1992; Neubauer, 1992: 152; Hunt, 1998). For many commentators, the apparent lack of sexual control by children and adolescents represented the inherent danger posed by the lure of the "primitive." For some, adolescent sexuality, with its appeal of immediate fulfillment and spontaneity, threatened to unravel the carefully woven fabric of modern civilization. Physicians were the first to respond to this dire sexual situation. Building on a two-century-old concern over childhood sexuality, physicians began dispensing advice to parents, headmasters of boarding schools and other concerned parties on ways to spot and control aberrant sexual behavior (see Hunt, 1998). Soon, however, psychologists also began to use the panic as a means to promote their new science. In doing so they often conceptualized these "bad sexual habits" as forms of "moral insanity" (Ellis, 1890: 211). As a response to this "moral insanity," many early psychologists began to provide parents, teachers, clergy and other authority figures with advice on understanding and redirecting a variety of children's "maladaptive sexual behaviors."

Central to this late-nineteenth-century teenage sex panic was concern over the effects of adolescent masturbation. This rediscovered fear had its origins in earlier linkages of masturbation and mental deficiencies. Physicians in England had proposed a link between masturbation and insanity as early as 1700, with the publication of the moral tract *Onania; or the Heinous Sin of Self-Pollution* (see Gilman, 1988: 70). Such a view found a more scientific and popular audience in Europe with the publication of Samuel Tissot's *L'Onanisme* in 1758. Tissot connected masturbation with a number of mental ailments, including insanity, a general lack of drive, idleness and self-absorption. In light of a late-nineteenth-century emphasis on educational reform measures to mold children into responsible citizens, adolescent masturbation seemed a serious threat to the carefully planned transition of both child and society from barbarism to civilization.

As the nineteenth-century moral panic over sexuality grew, psychologists focused their research attention on diagnosis and treatment. Parents were given advice on issues ranging from how to spot early evidence of autoeroticism in infants to teaching self-control to young children (see Hardyment, 1983). The leading child psychologist of the day and the first president of the American Psychological Association, G. Stanley Hall , devoted a substantial portion of his influential 1904 book series *Adolescence* to the psychological analysis of the dangers associated with unchecked adolescent sexual development.[2] Although described by fellow psychologist Edward Thorndike (in Joncich, 1968: 244) as "chock full of errors, masturbation and Jesus," *Adolescence* was one of the first academic treatments of the subject of adolescence. In the ensuing decades the book series would sell over twenty-five thousand copies and greatly influence the attitudes of professionals and parents about the importance of controlling and redirecting child and adolescent sexuality (Karier, 1986: 161). Hall argued (1969 [1904]: xv) that "sex asserts its mastery in field after field, and works its havoc in the form of secret vice, debauch, disease, and enfeebled heredity." Particularly insidious for Hall was the "dangerous malady" of masturbation, which was "most liable to occur in individuals who lack stamina" (Hall, 1969 [1904]: 434). It was "the very saddest of all the aspects of human weakness" (Hall, 1969 [1904]: 432). Hall (1969 [1904]: 434) argued that masturbation's "octopus-grasp" was most likely to occur in institutions that housed the "defective classes." This, he reasoned, was the result of both the underdeveloped mental state of the "defective classes" and a reflection of their link with civilization's past barbarism. For Hall (1969 [1904]: 452), the adolescent masturbator's goal of immediate sense pleasure was always "bought at the cost of the higher life." Masturbation corrupted the mind and moral constitution of the growing adolescent making him or her throw away the "potency of good heredity" for the "acme of selfishness" (Hall, 1969 [1904]: 452). In the end, it made "life blasé" and created "a burnt-out cinder," where "admiration, enthusiasm, and high ambitions are weakened or gone, and the soul is tainted with indifference or discouragement" (Hall, 1969 [1904]: 322).

Echoing previous medical diagnoses, Hall linked adolescent masturbation to a host of physical and mental disorders, such as weakness, depression, convulsion, neurasthenia, cerebrasthenia, spinal neurasthenia, psychic impotence, light sensations, optical cramps, sluggishness of heart action and dry cough, to name but a few. However, in Hall's view some of the most dangerous effects of masturbation came from its influence on the adolescent's moral character. In his words, "The power of pity and sympathy is often almost extinguished. Self-control and will-power, purposive self-direction, resolute ability to grapple with difficulties mental or physical, to carry work that is begun through to its completion, are certain to decline" (Hall, 1969 [1904]: 443). The adolescent who had "tasted these forbidden joys" loses interest in the intellect and "lapses to a *nil admirari* indifference" (Hall, 1969 [1904]: 443).

Hall (1969 [1904]: 459) suggested that the only means for adverting adolescents from traveling down "the gloomy pathway to Avernus" was to rely on the moral guidance of "father, pastor, mentor, or mature friend." These figures should serve to instill self-control in the adolescent and save them from the plague of "masturbatory insanity" (see Griffin, 1997: 19). Hall (1969 [1904]: xv), however, maintained that "neither parents, teachers, preachers or physicians know how to deal with its problems." A full understanding had to come from psychologists and other experts on childhood who had carefully studied and analyzed the problem. Correcting these problems required an intimate knowledge of the psychological processes of child development and training and the workings of the adolescent mind.

The leaders of the Boston-based religious and psychotherapy group known as the Emmanuel Movement also warned of the role of masturbation in producing "nervous debility" in the young (Worcester, McComb and Coriat, 1908: 143; see also chapter 8 of present work). Lead by Elwood Worcester, who had obtained a Ph.D. in psychology and had trained with Wundt in Germany, the Emmanuel group argued that "no one can deny that serious moral and nervous affections follow the habitual practice of masturbation, and these are more serious in early life, and when, as is often the case, the victim is temporarily nervous and delicate. The physical symptoms are weakness, pallor and backache and general debility. The effects on the brain and nervous system are more serious" (Worcester et al., 1908: 144). Worcester, McComb and Coriat (1908: 144) also associated masturbation with "listlessness, apathy, moroseness and morbid irritability, in short a general perversion of character." It was, they contended, up to the parents to provide the "delicate truth" of the effects of masturbation on their bodies and minds.

Other psychologists of the time recommended a response similar to Hall's and that of the Emmanuel Movement. Christabel Meredith (1916) argued that the raw energy of teenage sexuality should be channeled into positive and constructive directions. For Meredith (1916: 129) adolescent sexual energy should be redirected into activities such as "poetry, painting and all forms of art." In Meredith's view, transforming the child's primitive callings to constructive social pursuits preserved the child's social and cognitive development and kept society from sliding into barbarism. Other psychologists moved their analysis away from the act of masturbation itself to the guilt that accompanied it. Havelock Ellis's *Studies in the Psychology of Sex* (1910) attacked what he considered to be the exaggerated warnings of prior unscientific treatments of sexuality. Ellis believed that these past treatments were responsible for creating much of the sexual anxiety of adolescents. Instead, he recommended that concerned parties "desexualize" masturbation so that the adolescents would learn better to control it.

For some psychologists and psychoanalysts, female masturbation posed a more serious threat to an adolescent's well-being. Ernest Jones (1920) insisted that female masturbation, with its emphasis on clitoral stimulation, disrupted a women's psychological transition to womanhood. Jones contended that while male masturbation was often a passing phase that had inconsequential effects on a child's cognitive and moral development, continued clitoral stimulation made women unable to appreciate the "more mature form" of male/female sexual intercourse. It was, therefore, responsible for a host of neuroses afflicting adult women. Some experts advised dietary restrictions on adolescent girls, including the avoidance of caffeine and spicy food. Such food aversions, coupled with cold water and Spartan bed furnishings, would help curtail female sexual excitement (see Neubauer, 1992: 159). Others, such as K. Menzies (1921) believed that the only way of treating masturbation was through employing prolonged psychoanalysis. In his words, "the better method of *festina lente* may be proposed, and effort directed toward gradually decreasing the extent of the indulgence. Where the habit is deeply rooted, victory is not immediately to be expected, but may be worked for in proportion as self-confidence and self-respect are gradually restored" (Menzies, 1921: 92). In this psychoanalytic approach, masturbation was to be stripped of its moral underpinnings. The chronic masturbator was to be "encouraged to analyze freely and aloud in the presence of his confidant the feelings of distress and remorse" (Menzies, 1921: 90).

In many instances, early psychology's assessment of adolescent sexuality was linked to the child's inherent barbarism and even criminality. As such it threatened, not only the moral development of the child, but civilization itself. For Ellis (1890: 212), the child was "by his organisation, nearer to the animal, the savage, to the criminal, than the adult." Joseph Jastrow (1928: 148) saw undirected adolescent sexuality as responsible for such behaviors as stealing and truancy— activities that eroded the bases of civilized societies. In his view, "stealing is a sort of substitute excitement, and sometimes is a substitute for sex excitement" (Jastrow, 1928: 148). G. Stanley Hall considered adolescent masturbation as also violating "the preservation of the race." It was a deficiency "handed down" from generation to generation. Masturbation was "the sins of the parents that are visited on their children, devitalizing, arresting their full development, and finally exterminating them" (Hall, 1969 [1904]: 438–439).

As not-yet-civilized humans, pre-adolescents were, William Hall (1924) argued, particularly prone to such "primitive vulgarities."

Vulgarity seems to be part of our heritage from barbarism. The barbarian boy seems inherently vulgar; or if not precisely that, we all must admit that if ever a boy may easily drift into, or be easily led into, vulgarity in thought, language and habits, those are the crucial years. It is because of this mental attitude more than anything else that the pre-adolescent child, perhaps especially the boy, is so extremely likely to acquire the habit of self-abuse (W. Hall, 1924: 312).

Accordingly, adolescent sexuality was not just a problem for the child's psychological development but a larger social problem that required the immediate attention of parents and teachers. As Jastrow (1928: 100) cautioned, "Civilization can exist only if we do not let one another run wild."

The "saving of civilization" required the diligent and coordinated efforts of the school and home (W. Hall, 1924: 313). William Hall believed that young men and women needed to be taught the sacredness of life, the body, family life and parenthood. Fathers needed to instruct their boys that semen should not be wasted (W. Hall, 1924: 315). Meanwhile, mothers should teach their girls that the ovaries produce the venerable "elixir of life" that flows through their blood (W. Hall, 1924: 316). If parents performed these tasks, both young girls and boys would learn to respect the sacredness of life and abandon the self-destructive practice of masturbation.

However powerful the role psychology played in instigating and sustaining the turn-of-the-century moral panic over adolescent sexuality, it had an equally important role in its ending. By the 1940s psychologist and psychiatrists had begun arguing that adolescent sexuality was not so threatening after all, at least if properly controlled and directed. Post-1940s psychological advice began to recognize masturbation as a means for diffusing other, more serious and risky, forms of adolescent sexuality. Masturbation was now considered a normal part of the sexual exploration of childhood. It was no longer a threat to a child's psychological well-being or to the evolution of the social order but a stage in a child's emotional and sexual development. However, concern over adolescent sexuality again flared in the 1960s, when teen pregnancy became an important focus of psychological expertise.

What is perhaps most important about psychologists' late-nineteenth and early-twentieth-century venture into the issue of adolescent in sexuality was not so much their specific revelations about childhood and adolescent behavior or the treatment strategies they recommended but their ability to use the sex panic to establish an opening with respect to parenting concerns and child-care issues. As with the area of education, psychology had begun to establish itself as an obligatory touchstone for parents in search of answers about their children's behavior, wishing to learn whether or not it was normal. Adolescent sexuality was, consequently, among the first vehicles by which psychology was able to establish its presence in the much broader area of advice to parents. Psychology's turn of the twentieth century discussion of children's sexuality had shown that it could provide useful advice to parents on correcting their children's actions. It also illustrated that psychology could play an important role in helping authorities and parents to pinpoint pathological and "psychologically unhealthy" behavior in their children.

HOW TO RAISE A WELL-ADJUSTED CHILD: PSYCHOLOGY AND THE ADVENT OF CHILD-CARE MANUALS

As we saw in the last chapter, psychologists sought to show teachers and school administrators that established pedagogues and practices were insufficient for the demands of the modern world. Teaching that used older, nonscientific methods was not only ineffective but actually threatened the psychological development of children and the larger preservation of the social order. The outmoded educational system produced children who were unable to endure life in a modern, industrial society. Early psychologists used a similar strategy in their efforts to promote the necessity of scientifically based parenting advice. Parents too, they argued, needed new models and techniques, advice based on the sound foundations of experimental and clinical psychology, to raise their children. Without these scientific strategies, parents, like the outmoded educator, were putting both the future success and mental health of their children in jeopardy.

One of the earliest instances of the new psychology's linkage with parenting concerns occurred in 1897, when G. Stanley Hall was invited to speak to the first gathering of the newly formed National Congress of Mothers (NCM) (see Kett, 1977: 229). Hall shared the congress's conviction that the only proper avenue for saving the child, and modern society in general, was the exportation of new scientific conceptualizations of childhood to mothers and fathers. Alarmed by increases in the number of women working outside of the home, the NCM sought to establish motherhood and home life as the solution to a series of pressing social problems. For the group's members, Hall's analysis of child development provided further verification of the importance of involved parents, particularly mothers, for the success of both children and industrial society. For Hall, the meeting furnished an opportunity to show how the new science of psychology could provide useful advice for parents and groups seeking to effect social change.

The connection initiated by Hall with parenting organizations was strengthened by Michael V. O'Shea in the early twentieth century. O'Shea, a Cornell-trained psychologist and educator, spent most of his career as a professor of education at the University of Wisconsin (Malone, 1934: 82–83). He also served as chairman of the Department of Education of the National Congress of Mothers and as educational director for the congress's primary publication, *Mother's*

Magazine and Home Life (O'Shea, 1920a: 7). O'Shea (1929: 29) believed that "the home is lagging behind the school" in incorporating new methods of teaching children. He described his influential Childhood and Youth series (in Fisher, 1916: 245) as "the first systematic attempt to give to parents, teachers, social workers, and all others interested in the care and training of the young, the best modern knowledge about children in a manner easily understood and thoroughly interesting." To accomplish this task, O'Shea assembled a variety of contributors, primarily from psychology and education. Each title in the series provided advice to parents and educators on specific childhood issues and problems, such as learning problems (Swift, 1914), dealing with the high school years (King, 1914), the physical maturation of the child (Crampton, 1908), and how to instill honesty and a capacity for hard work (Healy, 1915).

O'Shea also wrote several influential volumes on parenting as part of the Parent's Library series, published by Frederick J. Drake of Chicago, including *First Steps in Child Training* (1920a), *The Trend of the Teens* (1920b), *The Faults of Childhood and Youth* (1920c) and *Everyday Problems in Child Training* (1920d). He also authored several elementary school textbooks and served as an advisor to the YMCA (Malone, 1934: 83). Like many other early parenting experts, O'Shea (1929: 321) recommended that parents make their homes "school[s] of practice," in order to coordinate more closely the efforts of parents and teachers. Parents should construct a child's home activities to reinforce the more formal lessons being taught in the schools. To accomplish this goal, O'Shea (1929: 415–419) provided parents with three central "resolutions" in training and dealing with children: (1) to maintain poise; (2) to be firm, decisive, and consistent; and (3) to be positive and constructive rather than negative and prohibitive. In O'Shea's scheme, children were to be given more freedom to make choices. However, the limits of these choices were to be set by parents and teachers acting in concert. Proper parenting skills on the parts of the mother and father would produce respectful and self-reliant children and would mirror the efforts of the now reorganized education system.

O'Shea's efforts at providing parents with psychologically sound advice on child rearing was found in a number of similar works of the era, such as the publications of H. Addington Bruce (1910; 1911; 1915), the Children's Foundation, and the Infant Care series published by the Federal Children's Bureau.

Bruce, perhaps psychology's most prolific early popularizer (see chapter 6), published a number of articles between 1907 and 1916 on children and parenting advice in such publications as *American Magazine* and *Good Housekeeping* (see Bruce, 1910; 1911; 1915). The Children's Foundation was organized in 1921 in Valparaiso, Indiana, to provide parents and others with the "present-day knowledge relating to the nature, well-being, and education of children" (Myers, 1924: v). Under the editorship of O'Shea, the foundation published its first collection, *The Child: His Nature and His Needs*, in 1924. Of the sixteen contributors, ten were professors of psychology or educational psychologists. The first collection contained essays on topics ranging from children's instincts to preventing delinquency to moral development to caring for an "intellectually inferior" child (see O'Shea, 1924).

Other works, such as Dorothy C. Fisher's (1916) *Self-Reliance*, part of O'Shea's Childhood and Youth series, sought to aid parents in cultivating responsible and self-reliant children. For Fisher the individualistic demands of modern society required parents to move away from traditional and authoritarian modes of child rearing. Modern children needed to "learn for themselves that lasting satisfaction comes from a wise employment of their own energies and capacities, and not from a passive ownership of things" (Fisher, 1916: 10). To accomplish this transformation, parents needed to "find new formulas and devices" (Fisher, 1916: 4). Parents were encouraged to loosen their control by giving children allowances, providing them with tools to stimulate creativity, allowing them to develop their own lists of chores and providing them opportunities to take active roles in planning family trips. This new parenting strategy would result in a child who fully understood the "energy and purposefulness of his own life" (Fisher, 1916: 38).[3]

The early efforts of psychologists and members of allied groups to provide popular advice to parents reached an important milestone in 1926 with the first appearance of the magazine *Children, a Magazine for Parents* (later changed to *Parents Magazine*). Subsidized by the Laura Spelman Rockefeller Fund, the magazine contained a wide range of practical advice for parents, written by a hodgepodge of psychologists, educators and lay commentators. By the end of its first decade of publication, the magazine's circulation had reached over three hundred thousand. By the end of its third decade, circulation had climbed to more than one and a half million, making it the most popular parenting periodical in the world (Costner, 1980: 119). Today the magazine has a circulation of over twelve million.

Psychological advice to parents took a somewhat unusual turn in 1928 with the publication of J.B. Watson's behaviorist manual *Psychological Care of Infant and Child*. Watson (1928) dedicated the book to the "first mother who brings up a happy child." He (1928: 7) contended that the failure to bring up a happy and well-adjusted child "falls upon the parents' shoulders." For Watson, even the vocational choice of the child ultimately rested on the methods of child rearing employed by parents (see Watson, 1928: 39). Because the happiness and economic livelihood of the child were at stake, Watson believed it was imperative that the science of psychology and the doctrines of behaviorism be brought into service. As psychologists had charged with regard to education, parenthood was too serious of a business to be left to haphazard instincts or myths handed down through the centuries. Too many children had been ruined by the absence of a scientific approach to parenthood. In Watson's (1928: 44) words, "Mothers just do not know, when they kiss their children and pick them up and rock them, caress them and jiggle them on their knee, that they are slowly building up a human being totally unable to cope with the world it must later live in." A type of "tough love" was needed, to ensure that coddling parents did not forever spoil their children. Watson (1928: 12–13) concluded that "parenthood, instead of being an instinctive art, is a science, the details of which must be worked out by patient laboratory methods." Luckily for the parent there existed a large repository of knowledge already collected by the laboratories of behaviorists. Earlier Watson called for the establishment of "infant laboratories" where mothers "could be guided and warned about the way the children were tending to develop" and receive "expert guidance and intelligent help" (Watson, 1917: 82). Watson further popularized his views on child rearing in articles written for *Parents Magazine, Cosmopolitan, Collier's* and *Harper's*. Although his framework for raising children never really caught on with the public, several of his concepts were incorporated into the leading child-care manuals of the late 1920s and 1930s (Weiss, 1977: 530). These included the popular U.S. Department of Labor booklet *Infant and Child Care*, which reached an audience larger than any other government publication of its time (Birnbaum, 1955: 29).[4]

By the 1930s, psychologists and other individuals trained in psychology had become collectively a dominant force in the dispensing of parenting and child-rearing advice. Psychologists had managed slowly to edge out the many "amateurs" who had dominated the parenting marketplace earlier in the century (see Costner, 1980: 122–

123) and to challenge directly other professions that were also handing out advice to parents. During this time, regular feature articles on parenting written by psychologists began appearing in magazines such as *Ladies' Home Journal* and the *New York Times Magazine* (Costner, 1980: 123). By the 1940s opinion polls indicated that the public saw psychologists as the people to see for guidance about their children (see Guest, 1948).

However, unlike in the field of education, where psychologists held a virtual monopoly over the dispensation of expert advice, in the area of parenting advice psychologists were in competition with other professional groups. Medical doctors, psychiatrists, social scientists, religious leaders and government bureaucrats also produced works on parenting and child care. Some authors, particularly medical doctors, found psychological ideas "so muddled" that they advised parents to avoid them (Weiss, 1977: 531). However, many of the works produced by these nonpsychological professional groups had the effect of spreading psychological ideas and concepts on child development to new audiences.

Two of the most important in this regard were Margaret Mead's (1942) influential *And Keep Your Powder Dry* and Benjamin Spock's (1946) *The Common Sense Book of Baby and Child Care*. Although written by an anthropologist and a physician, respectively, these works disseminated many of the basic ideas of early psychology and psychoanalysis to parents (Matthews, 1988: 345, 352; also see Weiss, 1977: 531). For example, Spock's baby-care book advanced early psychology's idea that self-formation is "uniquely individual and universally patterned" (Schnog, 1997: 6), as well as the importance of an active role of parents in the proper development of the child. These works also marked an important shift from the more restrictive parenting style advocated by Watson and other early, leading parenting authorities toward a looser, less restrained type of parenting. The first generation of parenting experts had argued for the importance of fixed schedules and rigid parental regulations. The post-1940 psychological works began to proclaim a more relaxed outlook and flexible approach to child rearing.

By 1975, *Books in Print* listed over two hundred books on child care (Clarke-Stewart, 1978: 360). During this time and for the next two decades, the change in tone that had begun in the 1940s reached its apex. Gone were the rigid parenting guidelines and strong emphases on moral and social development proposed earlier in the century (see Costner, 1980). Parents were still at the center of the child's activities;

however, they no longer need to develop and enforce strict moral or mental regimens for their children (see Shiff, 1987). Parents now needed to focus on developing "congenial parent child relations" (Costner, 1980: 208). One now needed only to be "a good enough parent" (Bettelheim, 1988). Parents were to focus on making the child "well-adjusted," by exercising "unconditional love" and practicing the "art of sensitive parenting" (see Kersey, 1983). This was to be accomplished by allowing the child "to do what comes naturally" (Costner, 1980: 235). In this new version of parenting the well-adjusted child "may not necessarily become a success in the eyes of the world, but ... will on reflection be well pleased with the way he was raised" (Bettelheim, 1988: 3).

Now, in the early twenty-first century, the infiltration of expert advice on child rearing is so complete and widespread that "the modern mother takes for granted that she will have the advice of experts and will not have to rely on the advice of her mother" (Jolly, 1986: 1). Today the number of books on child care in print is well over 1,300.[5] These books have spawned book clubs, reading groups and their own sections in most bookstores. In addition, most parenting magazines and children's television programs now have psychologists on their editorial boards or as contributors and consultants. When people become parents today, they often first seek assistance in the bookstore rather than from parents or grandparents.[6] In doing so, they unwittingly partake of the historical legacy of psychological knowledge.

SELF-ESTEEM, THE GREATEST GIFT

Among the many psychological ideas introduced to parents through parenting manuals and magazines, few have been more influential than the concept of *self-esteem*. Since it first entered the vocabulary of psychology in the late nineteenth century, self-esteem has become one of the most important and fruitful concepts in psychological research, psychotherapy, parenting advice and popular discussions of the self and self-help. While the concept was first limited to educational attainment and self-improvement, it slowly began to influence parenting advice more broadly throughout the latter half of the twentieth century. Today, the development of high levels of self-esteem in children is said to lead to a host of positive attributes, such as good academic performance (Dukes and Lorch, 1989), good psychological adjustment (Buri, Kirchner and Walsh, 1987), happy relationships (Thornstam, 1992), and healthy adult sex lives (Hally and Pollack, 1993). In contrast, low levels of self-esteem have been linked to such widely varying childhood and adult problems as unwanted pregnancy (Crockenberg and Soby, 1989), suicide (Choquet, Kovess, and Poutignat, 1993), fire starting (Stewart, 1993), and homicide (see Lowenstein, 1989).

The first reference to the concept of self-esteem in American psychology can be found in William James's *Principles of Psychology* (1952 [1890]). James borrowed the idea, at least to some extent, from groups such as New Thought and its concern with character development, self-potential and growth (see chapter 8). While self-esteem was not a central concern of James, he viewed "self-complacency" and "self-dissatisfaction" as "direct and elementary endowments of our nature" (James, 1952 [1890]: 306). James (1952 [1890]: 310) argued that self-esteem "is determined by the ratio of our actualities to our supposed potentialities." As people improve this basic human ratio, they feel a sense of self-satisfaction that builds their self-appreciation. Although James argued that self-esteem derives from a basic need for self-manifestation, he also maintained that "self-feeling is in our power" to control (James 1952 [1890]: 311). This led him to argue that a well-adjusted person was one who could successfully balance actuality with potentiality.

After its initial introduction by James, the concept largely lay dormant until the 1940s and '50s, when self-psychology, which had been overshadowed by experimental psychology and behaviorism, began to make a comeback in the field. It was during this time that the first comprehensive psychological clinical and experimental studies of self-esteem began to appear. Among the first clinical studies were Abraham Maslow's (1942) examination of self-esteem (dominance feeling) and of women's sexuality, and V.C. Raimy's (1949) analysis of self-reference in counseling sessions (see Rosenberg, 1965: 271; Hamachek, 1992: 3). Using "semi-psychiatric" interviews, Maslow connected self-esteem with a variety of sexual problems and issues, including "homosexual behavior," sexual position, and frequency and type of orgasm. Maslow also connected self-esteem with marital happiness and success. One of his conclusions was that "the best marriages in our society . . . seem to be those in which the husband and wife are at the same level of dominance-feeling or in which the husband is somewhat higher in dominance-feeling than the wife" (Maslow, 1942: 278). Raimy's (1949: 154) clinical study argued that an "individual's perception of himself is of ultimate psychological significance in organized behavior." In reviewing the outcome of counseling sessions, Raimy (1949: 161) concluded that "successful cases showed a vast predominance of self-approval: the unsuccessful cases showed a predominance of self-disapproval and ambivalence."

Maslow and Raimy's clinical studies spawned a series of other clinical studies on the relationship between self-esteem and such issues as schizophrenia (Rogers, 1958), Rorschach characteristics (Bills, 1953), marital happiness (Eastman, 1958), the attitudes of psychiatric patients (Tolor, 1957; Zuckerman, Baer, and Monashkin, 1956) and psychopathology (Zuckerman and Monashkin, 1957). During this period, self-esteem also became associated with other positions in counseling and clinical psychology, particularly the "client-centered therapy" of Carl Rogers (see Rogers, 1951; Rogers and Dymond, 1954). (In Rogers's more "humanistic approach," the central goal of counseling was the development of the client's sense of self-worth and potential.) These clinical studies, along with a growing interest in self-esteem in already established forms of therapy, helped link the concept of self-esteem to success in therapy. This move expanded the concept's usefulness beyond theoretical understandings of human behavior, making it one of the diagnostic tools of practitioners. During this time the concept began to have practical significance for professionals seeking to study or alter behavior and those interested in unleashing human potential.

From the 1940s to the early 1970s, self-esteem not only became attached to "humanistic" psychology and the "human potential" movement but emerged as a central concept in experimental and survey studies in psychology and social psychology (Wylie, 1961: 2). Articles in leading psychology and human-science journals began to relate self-concept and self-esteem to such issues as ethnocentrism (Pearl, 1954), social class (Klausner, 1953), stress (Levanway, 1955; Sharma, 1956), performance (Benjamins, 1950), ingroup/outgroup preference (Brodbeck and Perlmutter, 1954), aspiration and motivation (Cohen, 1954; Mussen and Jones, 1957), level of social interaction (Manis, 1955), delinquency (Reckless, Dinitz, and Kay, 1957) and "private and public failure" (Stotland and Zander, 1958). In this new use, self-esteem, once a concept used to ground new innovations in personality theory and to treat patients, became a standard feature of basic psychological research.

During the 1960s empirical work on self-esteem began to multiply at a rapid pace (Wells and Marwell, 1976). During the decade two important books were published that helped to establish self-esteem further as an indispensable concept for both psychological research and parenting. The first of these was Morris Rosenberg's *Society and the Adolescent Self-Image* (1965). Rosenberg was among the first to use large-scale survey research techniques to explore the factors that influence self-esteem. Rosenberg identified a number of elements that affect the self-esteem level of adolescents, such as family structure, social class, ethnicity and religion. He also tied self-esteem to a series of personality and social problems, such as anxiety, low occupational motivation, leadership potential and social isolation. Rosenberg concluded that parenting and educational tactics were two of the most important factors influencing the development of self-esteem in children and adolescents.

A second influential book of the sixties was Stanley Coopersmith's *The Antecedents of Self-Esteem* (1967). Coopersmith (1967: 236) held that "parents of children with high self-esteem are concerned and attentive toward their children, that they structure the worlds of their children along lines they believe to be proper and appropriate, and that they permit great freedom within the structures they establish." Coopersmith's work helped establish a link between parenting style and self-esteem in children and adolescents. This connection, in turn, was said to be an important determinant of the ability of an individual to lead a successful and productive life.[7]

Two factors emerging during the period from the 1940s through the early 1970s were crucial for the expansion of the concept of self-esteem. First, self-esteem began to become part of the normal knowledge of clinical and experimental psychology. In this process it was translated and directed into the daily practice of clinical and experimental psychology. This move allowed promoters of the concept to recruit and expand into the vocabulary and practices of a new set of users. Second, the stage was set for the importation of self-esteem into areas outside of the direct professional domain of psychology. This is particularly true with regard to the work of Rosenberg and Coopersmith. Rosenberg was able to introduce self-esteem into the concerns of policy makers (interested in using the concept to solve social problems) and educators (who wished to increase academic performance and discipline). Coopersmith, on the other hand, was able to link self-esteem with parenting roles and obligations. Both of these works would later prove essential in the expansion of self-esteem into self-help literature, parenting manuals, public policy, educational pedagogy and the discourse of TV talk shows.

By the early 1970s psychologists had amassed hundreds of studies of the antecedents of self-esteem and the effects of self-esteem on an array of personal and social issues (Wells and Marwell, 1976: 5). Yet during this period of peak production of work on self-esteem, people outside of psychology and related fields remained largely "uneducated" about the concept and its meaning for their lives. This began to change in the late 1960s and early 1970s as the concept of self-esteem began to move beyond psychology. In these years the concept was linked to a number of social movements and popular issues, such as educational pedagogy, social policy, business success, women's issues and, most importantly, parenting advice.

Another important attachment during this period was the one established with the growing self-help movement—a connection spawned in part by humanist psychology. In the United States, self-help literature can be traced to the Puritan goal of obtaining "Christian goodness" (Simonds, 1992: 140). However, beginning in the 1950s, particularly with the publication of Norman Vincent Peale's *The Power of Positive Thinking* (1952), the idea that "material attainment and personal well-being are the results of properly focused desire" was generally revitalized (Simonds, 1992: 144). This view was given a psychological basis in the humanistic psychology associated with Carl Rogers and Abraham Maslow. One of the first important works to link personal success and fulfillment with self-esteem was Nathaniel Branden's *The Psychology of Self-Esteem* (1969, see Baumeister, 1993: vii). Branden (1969: 103) maintained that self-esteem "is the single most significant key to behavior." Echoing previous constructions of self-esteem, Branden (1969: 103–104) argued that self-esteem is "an urgent imperative[,] . . . a basic need" that is "inherent in his nature." Branden (1969: 182–203) linked self-esteem with success in marriage, sexuality and "romantic love." One of his key arguments was that "healthy masculinity requires a self-confidence that permits the man to be free, uninhibited and benevolently self-assertive in the role of romantic initiator and aggressor" (Branden, 1969: 193). In a later writing, Branden (1984: 12) maintained that he could not "think of a single psychological problem— from anxiety and depression, to fear of intimacy or of success, to spouse battery or child molestation—that is not traceable to the problem of poor self-esteem."

After Branden's early work, most self-esteem literature reflected his contention that if an individual is to overcome adversity in life, he or she must first come to appreciate and respect his or her self. As Deborah Hazelton (1991: 1) put it, "If you expect to truly love others, you need to start by first learning to love yourself." According to these books, the first step in this process is to realize that the only person responsible for how one feels is oneself. Other writers, like Gloria Steinem, saw self-esteem in broader, more political terms, linking it with the empowerment of women and other oppressed groups.[8] Steinem wrote,

No matter who we are, the journey toward recovering the self-esteem that should have been our birthright follows similar steps: a first experience of seeing through our own eyes instead of through the eyes of others . . . ; achieving empowerment and self-government[;] . . . and finally, achieving a balance of independence and interdependence, and taking one's place in a circle of true selves. (Steinem 1992: 44–45)

Aside from the attachments made with the self-help movement during this period, self-esteem also became one of the central ideas in the related area of parenting advice. Among the first manuals to associate parenting style directly with self-esteem was Dorothy C. Briggs's *Your Child's Self-Esteem: A Key to His Life* (1970). Borrowing from "mounting research" and "accumulated evidence," Briggs (1970: xiv) declared that her book would show, "step by step[,] . . . how to build a solid sense of self-worth in your child." In her view, "if your child has high self-esteem, he has it made" (Briggs, 1970: 2–3). She argued that the key factor determining a child's development and level of self-esteem is "the child's feelings about being loved or unloved" (Briggs, 1970: 4). A youngster who was the beneficiary of her advice was "slated for personal happiness in all areas of his life" (Briggs, 1970: xiv).

Most manuals advised parents that if they wanted to raise responsible children they needed to be attentive to their self-esteem at a very early age. Even for children as young as fifteen months, parents were told that "expecting more than your toddler can deliver may be daunting, discouraging, and damaging to his or her self-esteem" (Eisenberg, Murkoff and Hathaway, 1994: 82). In lieu of criticizing a child for his or her performance, parents were encouraged to use phrases like, "I was pleased to be there and be your parent," "I can see you have made lots of progress since your last effort," and "I am glad you played and participated" (Dinkmeyer and McKay, 1973: 97). Other manuals declared, "Self-esteem is the greatest gift you can give your child—and yourself. . . . [I]t is the cornerstone of mental health, learning, and happiness" (Hart, 1987: 5). One popular children's book, *The Loveable in the Kingdom of Self-Esteem*, brought the concept to young readers, introducing such characters as Daniel Dolphin, "who loves others as they are," and Greta Goat, whose "very own best friend is me [that is, herself]" (Loomans, 1991).

Some manuals went so far as to warn parents that if they did not build their child's self-esteem, the child—particularly if a young girl—was at risk of becoming an "insecure, unhappy teenager" (Eagle and Coleman, 1993: 14). Girls with low self-esteem were said to be in danger of developing depression, becoming victims of crime, involving themselves in destructive relationships, practicing unsafe sex and being unable to compete in the high-tech job market (Eagle and Coleman, 1993: 14–15). Other works, particularly Mary Pipher's (1994) best-selling book *Reviving Ophelia,* took self-esteem even farther. Pipher linked low self-esteem with the development of eating disorders in young girls. Self-esteem was now regarded as a matter of life or death.

Perhaps one of the most important and unusual linkages in the history of the concept arose from the establishment in 1987 of the California Task Force to Promote Self-Esteem and Personal and Social Responsibility. Formed to investigate the influence of self-esteem on an array of social problems, the task force concluded in its final report that "the lack of self-esteem is central to most personal and social ills plaguing our state and nation" (1990: 4). John Vasconcellos, the California lawmaker responsible for the establishment of the task force, compared the new emphasis on self-esteem to unlocking the secrets of the atom and the mysteries of space (Vasconcellos, 1989: xi). He went so far as to connect self-esteem with governmental budget deficits, arguing that "people with self-esteem produce income and pay taxes[;] . . . those without tend to be users of taxes" (quoted in Baumeister, 1993: viii). In the task force's report, persons with low levels of self-esteem were described as victims, traumatized and deprived of self-potential. By 1994, in response to this report and the efforts of the National Council for Self-Esteem (established in 1986), thirty states had enacted over 170 statutes seeking to promote the self-esteem of their citizens, mostly by school-based programs (Nolan, 1999: 117). States such as Utah, Georgia, Florida and Wisconsin began requiring schools to offer self-esteem enhancement as part of their curricula. The state of Ohio even held hearings on self-esteem and its occurrence in disadvantaged groups (Moskowitz, 2001: 4).

What had begun as a fragile statement by William James in 1890 had, over the course of the twentieth century, expanded to become an essential tool for explaining and directing the self. With the development of an attachment between self-esteem, self-help and parenting, the concept moved into new areas and developed a larger, more encompassing, network of support. Self-esteem thus became a vital concept for understanding and approaching groups as widely varied as teenagers, the poor, fire starters, marriage partners, drug addicts and educational underachievers. It also became an essential tool for policy makers and parents seeking to understand and control particular situations. In the process, self-esteem became not just part of the specialized jargon of psychologists but a basic psychological truth of human existence and a tool for conducting everyday life.

CONCLUSION: PSYCHOLOGY AND THE CHILD-CENTERED FAMILY

Hidden within the scientifically based parenting advice of twentieth-century psychologists were a number of subtle moral imperatives for raising the right kind of child, as well as norms for evaluating parenting practices. The right kind of child was responsible, honest, internally motivated and had a high self-concept as well as a sense of control—perhaps ironically, a child who was simultaneously independent-minded and directed by parental authority. The modern, psychologically informed parent was also a complex figure: open and honest; firm yet flexible; understanding but demanding; and above all, ever vigilant with regard to his or her child's psychological development. Psychologists were successful in establishing today's taken-for-granted assumption, unlike views espoused in previous centuries, that children do not correctly develop on their own. The supposedly ad hoc techniques of previous centuries' parents—like the preprofessionalized, intuitive approaches of turn-of-the-century teachers—simply would not meet the multifaceted demands of the modern world. The modern child's proper development required the preoccupation and watchfulness of a psychologically informed parent. This modern parent, who needed to be well versed on the latest theories and concepts of the new psychology, would manage the course of his or her child's development across the early lifecourse in much the same way that an architect oversees the construction of a building.

The child psychologist Michael O'Shea (1929: 5) had predicted in the late 1920s that the twentieth century would be "an era when the welfare of the child will be the chief concern of the home, the community, and the nation." O'Shea foretold one of the vital requirements of twentieth-century parenting—that modern family life would be centered around the moral and cognitive development of children (see Strickland and Ambrose, 1985: 538). For O'Shea and most other twentieth-century psychologists, the proper development of the child required a "child-centered" family, one that placed child development and training at the very heart of its activities. In fact, in the view of some experts, this was the primary reason for the institution of the family in the first place. In the words of Dr. Miriam Stoppard's *Baby Care Book*, "The basic family unit as we know it today has been found in every race or tribe since people first inhabited the earth. The family has been, and still is, the cornerstone of society and its main function is to create a secure environment in which children can be raised" (Stoppard, 1983: 9). Such heightened parental attention to children would, it was believed, pay very high dividends. The child would develop normally, acquire high self-esteem, and become well adjusted, highly motivated, dedicated to his or her studies, and eventually a responsible, competent and moral adult. Parental failure to take the development of their children seriously, or without the benefit of expert advice, would inevitably lead to a host of personal problems for the child, such as unemployment, criminality, psychological maladjustment, disruptive behavior, low self-esteem, poverty and even, should anorexia or bulimia develop, death. The burden of the mental and financial well-being of the child now rested on the actions of parents. Proper attention in the home could make or break a child's future.

Psychology's reform of parenthood also entailed a new, emotion-centered model of the family. This new, modern family was conceived as a "field of dynamic interchanges" between various family members (Rose, 1985: 176). This interconnected "family system" involved the active relationships between mother and father, sister and brother, and mother and father and children. This new psychological system was seen as being fueled by inherent psychological traits, such as emotions, feelings, guilt, self-esteem, jealously and fantasy (Rose, 1985: 176). Its viability rested upon the proper interplay and balance of the elements within the system. Breakdowns would create "dys-functionality" within the family and, as a consequence, problem behavior in the child.

Taken as a whole, the examination of the influence of psychology on parenting in the twentieth century reveals three central themes. First, psychologists and other allied professionals were able to mold and establish particular notions of normal child behavior and parent-child relations. In the course of the twentieth century, psychologists constructed the child in two different ways, at different times. The pre-1940s child was, in Joseph Jastrow's (1928: 99) words, "a selfish, cruel tyrant" in need of the strict moral guidance of psychologically informed parents. The post-1940s child was a creative, enterprising being who needed parents to serve as role models and as "cognitive stimulators" of his or her imagination. In both cases, however, parents were viewed as needing the expert intervention of psychologists to maximize their chances of success. The pre-1940s parent required the help of psychologists to develop schedules, exercise proper discipline and set ground rules of behavior. The post-1940s parent needed their advice on self-esteem and stimulating toys, and their help to relieve them of parental anxieties and assist in fashioning their child's individuality and cognitive development. In each case, psychology would be able to assess whether the child had received the proper parental training and if the family system was working effectively.

Second, once established as a important conveyor of parental advice, psychology was able to offer its services as both an evaluator of adherence to proper developmental norms and as a rehabilitating force to correct unacceptable variations. The modern parent was responsible for providing a structured and caring environment for the cognitive, moral and biological nourishment of the child. The child, if psychologically normal, would respond to these conditions in "developmentally determinable" ways. If he or she failed to adhere to these developmental standards, either the family system was in peril or the child might harbor some psychological abnormality—which could be identified, tested, assessed and perhaps corrected. Psychology helped establish and promote the developmental standards of normality and then provided means of assessing adherence to those standards.

A third trend can be identified in the movement of psychological advice away from an emphasis on the moral development of children toward a concern for children's cognitive or brain development. This trend paralleled the movement of the discipline of psychology itself from concern with moral developmental in the early part of the twentieth century toward the brain and cognitive science of the latter half of the century (see Bruer, 1999). In popular education movements— such as Rob Reiner's "I Am Your Child" campaign, George H. W. Bush's "Decade of the Brain" and the 1997 White House Conference on Early Childhood Development and Learning—parents were advised to be active catalysts of the cognitive development of their children, particularly in the first three years of development (Tavris,

1999: 14). Concern for a child's "wiring" in the first few years, when synapses are being formed, would pay off in rapid cognitive development and future educational and occupational success. As had the panics over adolescent sexuality and low self-esteem, this new moral imperative required psychological intervention in order to avoid potentially serious psychological harm.

The linkage of psychology with parenting concerns, child-care issues and "progressivist social movements" proved to be one of the most fruitful and consequential in the discipline's history. Having often been shut out of, or marginalized in, the mental health field by psychiatrists, psychologists were forced to move into areas, such as parenting and education, that offered less resistance. Within the discipline, the alliance with parenting stimulated the rapid growth of the subdisciplines of child, clinical, counseling and developmental psychology. This in turn greatly expanded the employment opportunities for the discipline's students, and it generated generous research funding from the state and organizations seeking to promote social change. Outside of the discipline, the alliance served as a precursor of what is today called "popular psychology" (see chapter 6). This popularization would transform psychology from a marginal academic enterprise at the turn of the twentieth century to a household word by midcentury. It would also help establish psychology as the place to which parents and other ordinary people could turn for advice on molding and managing the minds and selves of their children.

In the end, psychology's attachment to parenting concerns contributed to the construction of radically new definitions of parenthood. Parents, like their children, became "psychologized" as they grew familiar with and began utilizing psychological concepts to understand their roles as parents. Today, traditional or "embodied" knowledge about the roles of children and parenting seem rather old-fashioned. Developing the child's mind, whether at home or at school, is seen as too serious an undertaking to go unmanaged. Psychology, in conjunction with allied professions and organization, has managed so to erode older parenting strategies as to make them appear no longer viable or even possible. Traditional parenting strategies simply cannot compete with the now ubiquitous network of the new science of child rearing. As a result of psychology's influence, "both birth and death become foci of societal scrutiny, along with each step in between" (Meyer, 1988: 53).

NOTES

1. However, as is sometimes the case with consumer products, a knowledge form's concepts are always in danger of being co-opted and marketed by others. When this occurs the producer may have little control over what happens to the ideas once they have left his or her domain. However, if the product has sufficient "brand recognition" and is backed by the trademark legislation of the state, it may still flourish even when the original producer has lost control of it (see Barnes, 1995: 134).

2. *Adolescence* was among early psychology's most widely distributed works, with over twenty-five thousand copies sold in the first few years after publication (Karier, 1986: 161).

3. Psychological advice on parenting was often directly marketed among women. In 1914, *Good Housekeeping* published an article entitled "Mothercraft: A New Profession for Women." The article maintained that the "amateur mother of yesterday" would soon be replaced "with the professional mother of tomorrow."

4. A. Geoffrey Steere (1968) has pointed out the child-rearing manuals of the 1920s were strangely devoid of large-scale Freudian influences. While Freudian ideas were rampant in popular psychology and film, they were only a minor presence in the child-rearing literature of the time.

5. This does not include the allied areas of child-care services or child-care workers.

6. According to psychologists, some 12 percent of children and adolescents in the United States now experience significant behavioral or emotional problems (Weisz, Weiss and Donenberg, 1992). In instances where the child-rearing efforts of parents have proven "unsuccessful," psychologists and psychiatrists have developed new diagnostic categories, such as one that the *Diagnostic and Statistical Manual of Mental Disorders*, 4th edition (1994: 93–94), has recently identified as "oppositional defiant disorder." This label is used to describe "a pattern of negativistic, hostile, and defiant behavior lasting at least six months" (DSM, 1994: 93). These behaviors range from "often loses temper" to "often deliberately annoys people," to "is often spiteful or vindictive" (DSM, 1994: 93–94).

7. The early years (1942–73) of empirical work on self-esteem also saw the production of a series of scales by which to measure the concept. Instruments such as the Twenty Statements, Sherwood's Self-Concept Inventory, the Tennessee Self-Concept Scale, the Self-Esteem Scale, Social Self-Esteem Scale, and the Inferred Self-Concept Scale were used in numerous studies of the causes and effects of self-esteem. This period also spawned debates as to which of these measures were most effective or had the greatest degree of internal and external validity (Wells and Marwell, 1976: 148–149; Wylie, 1961).

8. Ellen Herman (1995) and others have pointed out that psychology, particularly its humanistic branch, was influential in the growth of feminism in the United States after the 1960s. In addition, it is important to note that Betty Freidan had extensive training in psychology and was the first woman to be offered a fellowship in psychology at the University of California (Street, 1994: 350).

5

Minds, Measures and Machines: The Materialization of Psychological Ideas

IN A *POPULAR SCIENCE MONTHLY* ARTICLE PUBLISHED IN 1893, James McKeen Cattell (1893b: 784) predicted that "the measurements and statistics of psychology . . . may in the end become the most important factor in the progress of society." Thirty-four years later, the controversial British psychologist Cyril Burt (1927) confidently proclaimed that psychology "aims at almost mathematical precision, and proposes nothing less that the measurement of mental power." For Cattell, Burt and many other early psychologists, the success of psychology as both an experimental science and form of applied knowledge was predicated upon its ability to replicate the mathematical precision and predictive validity found in the natural sciences. Psychologists maintained that if the emerging discipline was to become a respected experimental science, it needed to forecast human behavior and mental activity just as chemists calculated the outcome of chemical reactions or astronomers predicted the movement of planets. To do this, psychologists, like their counterparts in other scientific fields, needed their own laboratories, machines and measures.[1]

Something unusual happened to the measures of psychology, however. Unlike those utilized in the natural sciences, many in psychology managed to escape the laboratory. For instance, while measures of neutrons or alkalinity only occasionally roam beyond the corridors of a physics or chemistry laboratory, many of the measures of psychology move freely about in the corridors of everyday life. Today people are exposed to a host of psychological tests, inventories and measures in a variety of settings and throughout their lives (see Hanson, 1993). In early life, teachers and school psychologists measure such psychologically identified attributes as intelligence, motivation, aptitude and vocational interest. In adulthood, employers, bureaucratic agencies and consumer research companies measure such characteristics as personality, trustworthiness and moral reasoning.[2] Often little attention is given to how these measures were devised or to their role in reproducing psychologically derived notions of the mind and self, either within the discipline of psychology or in everyday life. Psychological tests and measures seem to constitute a necessary and ordinary means of proper evaluation and decision making. As such, they have become natural and institutionalized features of everyday life, much like school psychologists and childcare manuals. However, the activities of these "nonhuman actants" (Latour, 1987) are arguably as important as those of the legions of counselors, psychotherapists and school, sports and industrial psychologists in creating and sustaining the normalcy and naturalness of psychological knowledge. These tests and measures have had the effect of concealing the concepts and assumptions of the discipline of psychology in the material, nonhuman environments of machines and testing instruments. As with the algorithms of a computer program, it became no longer necessary to ask how they got there or what assumptions they concealed, but only how and where the instruments could be used.

Up to this point I have followed human actors as they went about the work of assembling components of the elaborate network supporting psychological knowledge. If, however, we were to see psychology's practical success over the last century only as an outcome of professional discourse, persuasive rhetoric, clever political maneuvering or human activity, we would miss some of the more important material aspects of its achievements—that is, the fact that building knowledge, particularly building knowledge into something as pervasive and heterogeneous as contemporary psychology, involved much more than the human actions of rhetorical and political strategizing. While the maneuvering found in textbooks, parenting manuals and APA presidential speeches were undoubtedly crucial for establishing and promoting the discipline, alone they would never have been enough either to organize psychology into the self-perpetuating knowledge form we know today or to establish its facticity and omnipresence in everyday life. It is important, therefore, to look at the actions of the nonhuman actants of psychology, such as its laboratories, machines and measures, and examine their role in establishing and solidifying the discipline and in expanding and congealing the vast network of contemporary psychological knowledge.[3] These nonhumans are simultaneously symbolic and material; they are both representations of the ideals and values held by the network of knowledge producers, and vital and independent components of the built and enduring environments that constitute and support a system of knowing (Bowker and Star, 1999: 39).

In this chapter, I examine part of the material culture of psychology and its role in the proliferating psychological knowledge. In the first section I discuss the founding of university and hospital psychology laboratories in the United States and their role in promoting and organizing psychological knowledge. In the second section I examine some of the machines housed in these laboratories and how their operation led to the dominance of certain psychological concepts and methods over others. Next, I consider psychology's attempt to construct and measure the elusive concepts of "self" and "personality," and how, once constructed, these measures were integrated into the decision-making processes of courts, correctional facilities, corporations, clinics and social service agencies. I conclude the chapter with an examination of what these laboratories, measures and machines meant for the discipline of psychology, the proliferation of its knowledge form and the overall stabilization of psychological content. Principally I argue that psychological measures provided a compact and economic means for spreading psychological concepts into new areas even when no psychologists were present.

A PLACE OF THEIR OWN: PSYCHOLOGISTS AND THEIR LABORATORIES

As early as the 1860s, Gustav Fechner (1966 [1860]: xxix) argued that it was time for psychology to have "its own laboratory, its own apparatus, its own methods." Fechner's call was finally realized in late 1878 when Wilhelm Wundt established the first psychology laboratory in Leipzig, Germany. Wundt's lab was small by later standards, with only two rooms; however, by 1894 it had grown into an institute comprising some eighteen rooms and had gained a worldwide reputation for its work on perception and sensations (Harper, 1950: 161). When Wundt's American students returned home from their doc-

toral studies in Germany, they used his laboratory as the basic pro-
totype for a number of laboratories they later founded in the United
States.

The first of these American laboratories was the one established by
G. Stanley Hall at Johns Hopkins University in 1883 (see Hilgard,
1987: 32–33). Hall, along with James Cattell and Joseph Jastrow, put
together the laboratory in a small room in a structure next to the
main university buildings (Ross, 1972: 154). In early 1884 the laboratory was moved to a larger room in the new biology building.
Within ten years of the establishment of the first laboratory, other
laboratories had been founded—at the University of Wisconsin, Indiana University, Harvard University, Cornell University, the Uni-
versity of Iowa, the University of Michigan, Yale University,
Wellesley College, the University of Pennsylvania and a number of
other elite colleges and universities throughout the country (Littman,
1979: 50).

These early psychology laboratories sought to reproduce the design
and often the instruments found in the physiology labs that were also
being opened in the late nineteenth century (see Borell, 1993). This
emulation helped direct the way American psychology laboratories
were utilized. Unlike the German laboratories, which almost exclusively emphasized research, the typical psychological laboratory in the
United States in the late nineteenth and early twentieth centuries was
often designed for the threefold purposes of demonstration, "drill"
and research (Popplestone and McPherson, 1984: 198). Areas of the
laboratories were designed to demonstrate to students, and in a few
cases the general public, the experimental prowess of the emerging
field of psychology. Some areas of the laboratories were set aside for
students of psychology participating in "drill work," while other sections were left for psychologists doing their own experiments. Most
of these early laboratories were also divided into a number of rooms
serving distinct experimental functions. There was a dark room, a
silent room, an optics room, rooms for observing subjects, and rooms
housing machines like the heliostat and Hipp Chronoscope, to test
perception and reflex (see Sanford, 1893; Krohn, 1891; Titchener,
1898).

Two of the largest and most elaborate early laboratories were at
Harvard, opened by William James and directed by Hugo Muensterberg; and at Cornell, opened by Frank Angell and directed by E.B.
Titchener.[4] Muensterberg (in Lundy, 1992: 789) provided the following description of his laboratory at Harvard:

Our Harvard laboratory has not less than forty rooms. The electric wires bring different currents to every wall. Large instrument cases recall the apparatus of a physical laboratory. A big workshop with its lathe for metal work in which a mechanic is busy from morning to night provides students with the newest equipment for special researches. Eight rooms are entirely black so that no light may be reflected from their surface; one room is soundproof. In some, very subtle instruments are installed to measure the shortest time intervals with the exactness of a thousandth of a second; in others very complicated arrangements allow the worker to take a record of the smallest changes in pulse or breathing, in muscle contractions or in the flowing of the blood to the arm. In short, everything suggests interest in bodily material processes, and nothing betrays the predominant activity of this scientific institute, the study of the mind.

Titchener's Cornell laboratory, opened in 1891, with only twelve rooms, was considerably smaller than Harvard's. Like most of the early laboratories, however, it set aside rooms for optics, acoustics, haptics (studies related to touch), reaction-time experiments and for studying what he referred to as "affective consciousness," consisting of "pulse, respiration, volume and muscular tone" (Titchener, 1898: 315). Titchener also developed elaborate plans for what he referred to as the "ideal laboratory." He envisioned this laboratory as a three-story building with a basement for experimental work on larger animals and an attic for work on smaller animals (Titchener, 1900: 253). The building would also would contain a floor for a drill laboratory (for student experiments) and a floor reserved for a research laboratory. Titchener (1900: 254) maintained that "experimental psychology is advancing so steadily along the beaten paths, is developing so many new branches, and, above all, is holding out so bravely against pedagogical and philosophical attack, that the realization of a laboratory on the scale indicated can but be a matter of time."[5]

By the early twentieth century, laboratories were not only becoming a staple of most elite psychology programs in the United States but being introduced into a number of hospitals and schools for "feebleminded" children.[6] The first hospital laboratories fulfilled a vision held by some of the early founders that "degenerations which escape the common observation and even the practiced eye of the physician, can be detected and measured by scientific methods" (Cattell, 1893b: 779). In these settings psychologists introduced a new type of "experimental psychopathology" that applied empirical research on perception and learning to mapping and diagnosing "mental deficiency." Advocates of experimental psychopathology held that mental hospitals provided the ideal environment in which to study disruptions in sensation and perception. Among the first of these clinical laboratories was one established by August Hoch and later directed by Shepherd Ivory Franz at McLean Hospital in Belmont, Massachusetts. Franz, a student of Cattell at Columbia, later established a psychology laboratory at the Government Hospital for the Insane in Washington, D.C. (Maher and Maher, 1979: 575). Frederick Wells, another student of Cattell, replaced Franz at McLean Hospital. William Krohn, who had received his Ph.D. at Yale, established a similar psychology laboratory at the Illinois Eastern Hospital for the Insane in 1897 (Popplestone and McPherson, 1984: 212). From the late 1890s until 1910, other important laboratories were established at Worcester State Hospital in Massachusetts, the New York State Psychiatric Institute, the Minnesota School for Idiots and Imbeciles, the New York Infirmary for Women and Children and the New Jersey Training School for Feeble-Minded Boys and Girls at Vineland. Experiments at these hospital and "training school" laboratories usually resembled those taking place at most university laboratories. Subjects participated in a series of perception and sensation experiments, such as reaction times given various stimuli, color perception, word association, electrical resistance of the skin and maze negotiation. Such experiments were meant to identify and diagnosis various types of psychopathologies and to determine the range and possibilities of human intelligence and thought (see Scripture, 1916). By the 1920s, however, the hope of establishing a large-scale experimental psychopathology had been eroded by the onslaught of psychotherapy and the success of the mental-testing movement.

As a result of the efforts of American experimentalists, by the early 1900s twenty-five of the forty-seven laboratories in existence throughout the world were located in the United States (Harper, 1950: 161). By this time, most major private and public universities with psychology programs had opened some type of laboratory (Littman, 1979: 50). Accompanying this "Americanization" of experimental psychology was the advent of a "laboratory genre" in psychology publications. From the 1880s to around 1920, psychologists wrote almost incessantly about their laboratories, including detailed analyses of budgets, types of plumbing, electricity needs and the proper ways for students to store instruments (see, for example, Titchener, 1898). Such "obsession" over the creation and running of laboratory space reflected both a material and symbolic concern among early experimental psychologists. In the first place, the laboratory and its objects committed students and other practitioners to psychology as an experimental science; it was material testimony that psychology had entered the age of science and was an important player in the overall advancement of scientific knowledge. In this sense the early psychology laboratories did much more than simply provide sites for research; they also concentrated resources, people, equipment and objects into centralized locations. This concentration influenced the activities of people outside the laboratories and professionals within them. The concentration of people and resources allowed outsiders to observer that there was much more than mental philosophy, psychic research or philosophical speculation going on within the laboratories' walls. The existence of laboratories served notice to other disciplines and the public that unlike the "old psychology," the new scientific psychology involved much more than pen and paper to function. As E.W. Scripture (1895: 295) put it in 1895,

mere observation and speculation will not serve to build a locomotive, paint a picture, run a gas factory, or teach psychology. Long, long years of special training and laborious experimenting must first be spent in the workshop, the studio, the chemical laboratory, or the psychological laboratory. To do any of these things a man must be a specialist. As long as psychology was an arm-chair science, anybody could teach it; to-day no one but a carefully trained man do so.

Scripture (1895: 24) further argued that "for several thousand years psychologists have been waiting and watching; it never occurred to them to labor also." The psychological laboratory provided a place for this labor to happen. The new psychology required adequate space, specialized equipment and a technical expertise that would, in the view of the experimentalists, allow for a "dissection of consciousness, an analysis of a piece of the mental mechanism" (Titchener, 1971 [1902]: xi).

Laboratories symbolized that psychology should be recognized as a serious science with its own dedicated space and specialized instruments. They were icons of the "transcendent power of scientific knowledge" (Capshew, 1992: 132). Psychological experimentation required discipline, adherence to experimental methodology, mathematical precision, and the assistance of machines to produce its knowledge, just as in the natural sciences. The days of mental philosophers contemplating the relationship between mind and matter or utilizing exclusively introspective methodologies were over. Such speculative accounts were to be replaced, or at least supplemented by, an experimental science that would provide a final settlement of competing truth claims.

PSYCHOLOGICAL IDEAS IN BRASS AND STEEL

Early psychologists were not only concerned with finding a space within the university, or occasionally the hospital, to set up shop but were also keen on equipping these spaces with the latest in experiment hardware. In this quest psychologists began adapting machines from industry, physiology and the natural sciences, as well as manufacturing and designing their own equipment, to be used as testing equipment. Following up experiments conducted by Wundt in his Leipzig laboratory, most of these machines were used to measure object perception and sensations. Also following Wundt, American experimentalists sought to use laboratory apparatuses to break perception into the basic elements of sensation in order to dissect its fundamental building blocks (see Boring, 1942; Hochberg, 1979).

Of the early advocates of the instrumentation of psychology, few were more vocal or active than E.B. Titchener and James Cattell.[7] Like their mentor, Wilhelm Wundt, Titchener and Cattell were determined to make psychology a respected experiment science. To accomplish this, they, like any scientist, needed the right instruments for precise measurement and certainty. Titchener argued (1898: 320), "It is of little use to have ideas, if you have no means of realizing them in brass and steel." Like Wundt, Titchener believed that psychology could distinguish itself from philosophy only through detailed, timed studies of mental activities. To do this psychologists needed to acquire the "technical knowledge" necessary to use machines that were highly accurate, well calibrated and reliable (Titchener, 1898: 311). A detailed list of the equipment at his Cornell laboratory compiled in the late 1890s contained 368 items used to test auditory and visual sensations, "haptics and organic sensation," taste and smell, "affective processes," action and attention (Titchener, 1900). Likewise, Hugo Muensterberg's (1893) inventory of the equipment at Harvard listed three hundred items used in his laboratory to test these attributes.[8]

As the leading American laboratories competed with one another for standing within the field, a consensus soon developed on the types of machines that all psychology laboratories should have and the types of experiments that they were to perform. Reflecting Wundt's laboratory's strong emphasis on sensation and perception experiments, most of this research measured sensations in vision, hearing, taste and touch; the duration of mental processes; "the time senses" and attention; memory and the association of ideas (Cattell, 1888 [1947]; Boring, 1950: 340). Describing the function of the visual and acoustical instruments Titchener wrote:

The optics apparatus, e.g., includes instruments for the investigation of visual sensation, visual space perception, visual memory, visual recognition, visual attention, imagination, etc, and for the giving of visual stimuli, simple and compound, in reaction work; the acoustical apparatus includes the instruments necessary for the investigation of tonal fusion, of clang analysis, of auditory rhythm, of auditory memory, attention and recognition, of the localization of sounds, etc. and for the giving of auditory stimuli in reaction work (Titchener, 1898: 315–316).

At Yale's laboratory, similar experiments were performed to test the reaction time to acoustical tones, the rapidity of "movements of the arm and hand carrying a pen," electrical stimulation and sensation and "the monocular accommodation" (Krohn, 1891: 1150). At Clark University, early experiments were performed on "sensations of contact," "muscle sense," sensations of taste and smell and sensations of pressure (Krohn, 1891: 1141). Experiments at the University of Pennsylvania were directed at measuring reaction time to sound, time required to name colors, rate of movement and "number of letters remembered at one hearing" (Cattell, 1890: 373). In addition to these laboratory experiments, students in undergraduate psychology courses throughout the country were given manual-based drill work in such areas as reaction times, cutaneous and thermal sensations, visual sensations, muscular and mental fatigue, optical illusions and fluctuations of attention (see Sanford, 1898; Myers and Bartlett, 1911).

In early psychology several machines became necessities for psychologists in their quest to describe mental process in "quantitative terms" (Cattell, 1904: 184). Since most of the early psychology experiments were centered on measuring reactions to various bodily sensations—or "mental chronometry," as it came to be called—some of the new instruments were designed to provide precise measurements of time. Of these timing instruments few were more widely used or highly touted than the Hipp Chronoscope. The chronoscope was originally developed in 1840 by Charles Wheatstone to measure the velocity of artillery shells. Two years later the device was redesigned by a Swiss watchmaker, Mathias Hipp (Perera and Haupt, 2001). In the 1870s Wundt began using the Hipp Chronoscope as part of his early psychology experiments. Later it became an important piece of hardware in his psychology laboratory at Leipzig. As Wundt's American students returned home, they saw the chronoscope as indispensable for doing scientific psychology and began stocking their new psychology laboratories with the device. The chronoscope utilized a heavy weight to rotate a clockwork mechanism. It could be stopped and started using a clutch that engaged or disengaged the clock. If properly calibrated, the device allowed psychologists to perform time measurements in thousandths of a second. Other reaction-time devices—such as the vertical drum kymograph, the Fall Chronometer, the Stanford swinging reaction-time apparatus and the dual-pendulum Vernier chronoscope—soon followed the Hipp Chronoscope as instruments for timing reactions in various sensory experiments.

Other experimental instruments, such as the pythescope and the aesthesiometric compass, were used in various tactile experiments. The pythescope measured reaction to various stimuli. A subject's hand and forearm were immersed in a container of warm water; increases in the water level corresponded to various physiological changes as the result of various external stimuli being introduced (Hilgard, 1987). The aesthesiometric compass was used to test a subject's ability to discern the number of pressure points placed on the skin (see Baldwin, 1902: 611–612). The device allowed detailed studies to be conducted to determine which parts of the body were the most sensitive to tactile stimulation. Both apparatuses allowed experimentalists to provide detailed graphs and charts of the physiological effects of various stimuli.

Such devices as the tachistoscope, the hand and Wheatstone stereoscopes and the Phi Phenomenon Apparatus were used to measure visual sensations and perception. The tachistoscope used the quick exposure of some visual stimulus to measure a respondent's speed of recognition or comprehension. The hand and Wheatstone stereoscopes used two mirrors reflecting drawings to create a stereoscopic effect, enabling psychologists to conduct experiments on depth perception. The Phi Phenomenon Apparatus allowed psychologists to examine the perception of apparent movement of light by flashing two stationary lights successively. Acoustical equipment ranged from simple tuning forks to such more complex equipment as Helmholtz Resonators and the Stern Variator. These devices were used to examine reactions to variations in tonality and pitch.

Another relatively simple fixture of some early laboratories, partic ularly those interested in comparative psychology and mental testing, was the maze. Using books from William James's library at Harvard, Edward Thorndike built a small labyrinth in 1895 to study the learning process of chickens (Sokal, Davis and Merzbach, 1976: 63). The maze functioned as a crude forerunner of the puzzle boxes that Thorndike would later develop to study animal behavior. It also served as an impetus for devising tests of intelligence. In this role, the maze was used to test learning-skill acquisition, intelligence and dexterity. By World War I a later version of these early mazes, the Stenquish Construction Series, was being used to test the mechanical abilities of new army recruits (Sokal et al., 1976: 63). Later, the Stylus maze and the Hampton maze, and others, were used to study the acquisition of skill by recording the time required to move through the maze and the number of errors. Also, devices such as the memory drum, in which material to be memorized rotated around a drum, were used to test for intelligence and memory.

The rapid instrumentalization of psychology is reflected in the increasing expenditures on laboratory equipment from 1890 until the 1920s. When the APA was founded in 1893, the estimated total value of psychological materials in the United States was around thirty thousand dollars. Ten years later the total amount was estimated to be around a hundred thousand dollars (Miner, 1904: 303). Yale's laboratory alone had equipment valued at nearly ten thousand dollars. By the mid-1920s the Chicago Laboratory Supply and Scale Company, the largest American manufacturer and supplier of psychological apparatus, had sales of about five hundred thousand dollars (over five million in current U.S. dollars) (Ruckmick, 1926: 583).

In the early 1890s Cattell (1893a: 320) had argued that "the advance of science will demand a more exact definition of the subject matter" of psychology. In this sense one of the most important outcomes initiated by the instrumentalization of psychology was the reconfiguring and discarding of the discipline's early central concepts. Gone, or at least greatly transformed, were methods and concepts derived from mental philosophy and psychical research. Instrumentation enabled psychologists to redirect the older modes of psychological decision making and redefine psychological terms to fit the aims and objectives of an experimentally based psychology (Hornstein, 1988).

In the first instance, advocates of experimental psychology needed to illustrate that the use of such methods as logical coherence, plausibility, introspection and other strategies of inquiry that had been borrowed from the older mental philosophy were ill suited for the new experimental research. The redefining of concepts also required that experimentalists eliminate terms that were not readily amenable to quantification and instrumentalization (see Danziger, 1997). As a result, such concepts as "consciousness," "spirit," "character" and "will" were discarded as useless. Unless definitions of concepts could be "settled in the laboratory" (Kao, 1924: 427), they were deemed unworthy of further service. As a consequence, the method of psychological introspection was presented as "cramped and unnatural" and as placing psychology at "a striking disadvantage compared with the natural sciences" (Stratton, 1903: 2). It had either to be discarded as too unreliable for an experimental science or enhanced by machines to make it more precise and standardized (see Dunlap, 1912). There was little room for introspection in a discipline that had spent so much time showing, with its laboratory equipment, the limitations of human sensation and perception. In the place of the discarded concepts came more empirically measurable terms, such as "perception," "intelligence," "personality" and "learning"—concepts that were to become standard psychological truths in the twentieth century (Hornstein, 1988: 2). In the place of introspection arose the rigid procedures of experimentation and measurement construction.

The early instruments of the psychological laboratory were also responsible for transforming the amorphous and theoretical philosophies of the mind into tangible and concrete empirical entities. For instance, the Hipp Chronoscope, with its exact time measurements, helped establish "mental chronometry" as the centerpiece of experimental psychology during its early years. In the process humans, now redefined as "subjects," came to be seen as possessing measurable "attributes," such as perception, intelligence and, by the late 1910s, personality. In turn, timings of subjects identifying letters, answering math questions, responding to sounds or filling out inventories became both representations of these attributes and verifications of their existence. Detailed, timed studies allowed people to be rated along a continuum based on how long it took them to perform certain tasks or respond to particular stimuli. The data could then be aggregated to find statistical norms and standard deviations. This created a means for economizing on the other steps of investigation by determining how groups should be compared and what scores could be used (Hornstein, 1988: 23).

The statistical normalization provided by testing instruments paved the way for the expansion of standardized tests to measure such attributes as perception and mental ability—tests that were to become the hallmark of the discipline in the early twentieth century. Until the development of such instruments, statements about the psyche or mind were left to the isolated commentator or observer. In a discipline that sought to model itself after the natural sciences, such speculative approaches simply would not do. With the incorporation of machines, the speculation of mental philosophers could be transformed into something solid, measurable and quantifiable. One need no longer look to the pronouncements of the philosophically oriented early psychologists but could simply observe, count, and report the findings as they were recorded on the objectifying machines. In the long run this permitted psychological knowledge to become solidified, or "black boxed." In this instance, the actions of individual psychologists disappeared into the objectifying technical apparatuses. It was no longer a matter of "subjective" psychologists looking inward in order to represent consciousness but of "objective" machines providing "readings" about the workings of the mind. Opinion and interpretation became homogenized as observers stood witness to the findings of experimentalists (see Shapin and Shaffer, 1985).

The instrumentalization of psychology also set the discipline on a path that would influence the direction of the field until the dramatic growth of clinical psychology tipped the balance of power in the 1950s. Psychologists' attachment to such work objects as white mice, Hipp Chronoscopes, Ludwig kymographies and plethysmographies, and later memory drums, pursuit rotors, conditioning apparatuses and puzzle boxes dictated that their object of study would be the mind and that their method would be measurement and experimentation. The mind was thought of as a machine that could be mapped by other machines. Any subfields that wished to develop would have to adhere to these constructs and standards if they were to exist under the flag of psychology. In this sense, as Bachelard (1984 [1934]: 13) put it, "Instruments are nothing but theories materialized." They are particular moral visions of the ways things are and how they should be put in durable form (see Latour, 1991).

SELFHOOD RECONFIGURED: MEASURING PERSONALITY

In 1879 the father of mental testing, Francis Galton (1879: 147), declared that "until the phenomena of any branch of knowledge have been submitted to measurement and number, it cannot assume the status and dignity of a science." Echoing this view, Cattell (1893a: 316) argued that "the history of science is the history of measurement." Responding to these imperatives, many early psychologists not only set about the task of creating and furnishing their laboratories but also began to construct a host of scales, inventories and indexes to measure various aspects of their newly reconstituted and "dephilosophized" concept of the mind. Given this emphasis on visual and auditory acuity, the nature of the laboratory instruments used in the late nineteenth century dictated that most of the efforts of psychologists would be directed at constructing measures of perception, sensations, mental abilities and human and animal intelligence. Indeed, psychology's early practical success can in large part be attributed to its creation and promotion of intelligence testing (see chapter 3). However, a number of changes in the early twentieth century would force a reformulization of these foci and a reexamination of the dominant experimental notion within the discipline.

First among these changes was the rise of the applied wings of psychology in hospital laboratories and public schools. Here psychologists began to see complex experimental hardware as unnecessary for their immediate tasks of analyzing patients or students. What they needed were simpler modes of assessment that were capable of being transported from placed to place.[9] The second was growing criticism over the limited focus on sensations found in most of the discipline's experimental work. Some critics charged that "modern psychology is a psychology without even consciousness" (Ward, 1893: 55). For these critics, psychology's exclusive focus on sensation and perception had obliterated other important aspects of the mind and self (see Tweney and Budzynski, 2000). Another important change that began to reshape psychology was the general turn toward psychotherapy evident in psychiatry and medicine in the early part of the twentieth century. This change led psychologists to focus attention on measuring personality, psychopathology and selfhood. As psychiatry gained control over psychotherapy, psychologists were often relegated to the role of measurers of personality rather than its caretaker, until the situation changed dramatically after World War II (see chapter 8).

"Consciousness" and the "self" had been left behind by the experimental emphasis on perception and the measurement of sensations and intelligence in the late nineteenth and early twentieth centuries. For instance, the *Psychological Index* lists only a handful of works using the heading of "self" written from 1894 to 1935 (Viney, 1969: 349).

With the exception of William James and a few of his students, most psychologists deemed consciousness and selfhood, with idiosyncratic and amorphous meanings firmly embedded in mental philosophy, unworthy of experimental investigation. Kuo (1924: 427), for example, argued that "the so-called consciousness, if it exists at all, must be reducible to physical terms and capable of objective and quantitative treatment[;] . . . otherwise there is no justification for the existence of any such controversies or problems in the science." However, beginning in the early 1900s the concepts of self and consciousness began to undergo an empirical and experimental makeover. Consciousness now began to be listed under "cognition" in the *Psychological Index* (Viney, 1969: 349), and empirical studies began measuring the "traits" that compose the self (see Titchener, 1911). The effort to reintroduce and measure experimentally the concept of self was led primarily by Mary Calkins, a student of James's (see Calkins, 1915). Much of her work sought to show that the self could be adapted to modern psychology by examining it under controlled experimental conditions.

Calkins's efforts to revitalize the concept of the self began to fuse with the techniques of the mental-testing movement that was already well under way in the discipline, with the older notion of "character" and with Cattell's (1903) earlier efforts to construct a statistical profile of well-known scientists to form the concept of "personality." Essentially, personality was the self in new empirical garb. However, unlike the existing conceptualizations of the self, personality was something that could be broken down into traits and then observed and counted. Personality became, in the words of Morton Prince (1929: 171), the founder of the *Journal of Abnormal Psychology*, "the sum-total of traits, and that differences of personality depend upon differences in traits, on the one hand, and on the varying conditions of them, on the other." This new empirical self was now the reservoir of phobias, impulsions, aversions, neuroses, confidence and a host of other observable and measurable entities (see Prince, 1929: 174).

Although Francis Galton had used word-association tests in his mental testing and Muensterberg (1908) had used association tests to detect lying in legal cases, it was not until the work of Carl Jung and his visit to the United States that attempts to measure personality using word association began in earnest. Jung (1910) maintained that the projective technique of word association could be used to reveal "complex indicators" of personality. Grace Kent, a psychologist, and Aaron Rosanoff, a psychiatrist, began using Jung's word-association test as part of their clinical work at King's Park State Hospital in

New York (Kent and Rosanoff, 1910). Kent and Rosanoff constructed a table of frequencies based on the responses of a thousand "normal subjects" to various words. The frequencies were then compared with the responses of those at the hospital. Differences between the populations reflected areas indicative of the existence of a mental pathology.

In the 1910s the assessment of personality moved in two general directions. The first path, following Jung, used what were later called "projective techniques" to access personality. This approach compared answers to word associations or reactions to drawings, handwriting or inkblots of normal and pathological populations. Such an approach would come to its culmination with the development of Hermann Rorschach's (1942 [1921]) inkblot test in the early 1920s and Morgan and Murray's (1935) Thematic Apperception Test, published in the mid-1930s. The other path employed a more "subjective approach," using paper and pen instruments to ask respondents questions regarding behaviors and attitudes. In some cases the results of these questions were compared with those of a "pathological population," while in other instances they were simply rational or "face value" indicators of personality traits or personality disorders. With their growing control of psychotherapy and treatment, psychiatrists often utilized the "projective techniques," while psychologists, who were often on the sidelines of treatment, tended to develop the more "subjective" assessments of personality.

The first pen-and-paper personality assessment, the Woodworth Personal Data Sheet, was developed in 1917 by Robert S. Woodworth (1917) to screen American recruits for service in World War I. At the time of its development Woodworth had been experimenting with different instruments for assessing personality for almost a decade and was serving as chairman of the Committee on Problems on Emotional Characteristics, Self-Control, Etc., in Their Relations to Military Demands (Hilgard, 1987: 512). Gen. John J. Pershing, the commander of American Expeditionary Force in France, was concerned with the large number of psychiatric casualties and turned to Woodworth to develop a screening device for new recruits. Woodworth's final data sheet was entitled the "Scale of Psychoneurotic Tendencies"; it contained 116 questions using simple "yes," "no" and "don't know" answers to ascertain mood, morale, anxiety, fears, complaints and a host of other "neurotic personality characteristics." The test was developed by comparing the results of tests of "well-adjusted" college students with those of diagnosed neurotics (Dahlstrom, 1985:

85). Respondents were asked to answer such questions as "Do you feel tired most of the time?" "Has any of your family been a drunkard?" and "Does it make you uneasy to cross a wide street or open square?" (see Ferguson, 1952: 147–149). After the war the sheet was modified and widely used in businesses, schools and clinics (Dahlstrom, 1985).

The success of Woodworth's personal data sheet prompted the production of a number of other similar personality tests in the 1920s and '30s. In the early 1920s Floyd, Allport and Gordon Allport (1921) began work on classifying and measuring personality using a multidimensional approach. This approach broke the concept of personality into four dimensions—intelligence, temperament, self-expression and sociality. Self-expression was further broken down into the areas of extroversion-introversion, ascendance-submission, expansion-reclusion, compensation-insight and self-evaluation. Each of these dimensions was then measured using a "Personality Rating Scale" in combination with intelligence tests. Nearly a decade later the Personality Rating Scale began to evolve into a much more elaborate "Test for Personal Values" (Vernon and Allport, 1931).

In the late 1920s, L.L. Thurstone and Thelma Thurstone (1930) of the Psychological Laboratory at the University of Chicago developed a 223-question personality schedule to measure "neurotic tendencies." The schedule used questions obtained from a number of existing sources, including the scales constructed by Woodworth and the Allports. It was initially used on first-year students entering the University of Chicago in 1928. The schedule contained such questions to indicate neurosis as "Do you find it difficult to get rid of strangers?" "Would you rather work indoors than outdoors?" and "Can you stand disgusting smells?" A high score on the schedule indicated "an emotionally unstable person which has many of the specific traits described by various writers as neurotic personality" (Thurstone and Thurstone, 1930: 13–14). Thurstone and Thurstone concluded that "the fundamental characteristic of the neurotic personality is an imagination that fails to express itself effectively on external social reality" (Thurstone and Thurstone, 1930: 27).

Of the tests devised in the 1920s and '30s, one of the most prolific was the Bernreuter Personality Inventory, developed by Robert Bernreuter at Pennsylvania State College on the basis of his dissertation at Stanford. Bernreuter (in Ferguson, 1952: 174) maintained that "behavior of an individual in a single situation may be symptomatic of several traits." In order to capture what he referred to as the "total integrated personality" (Bernreuter, 1933: 387), Bernreuter used 125 questions combining existing measures of neurotic tendency, self-sufficiency, ascendance-submission and extroversion-introversion into one scale, known as the "P-I Test." Bernreuter (1933: 402) concluded that a person who scores high on the neurotic scale "often feels miserable, is sensitive to blame, is troubled by useless thoughts, by shyness, and by feelings of inferiority." A person who scores low on the self-sufficiency scale "is dependent on others for his enjoyments." A person who scores high on the introversion-extroversion scale "shows signs of a neurotic condition." Finally, a person who scores low on the ascendance-submission scale "lacks self-confidence, keeps in the background at social functions, and rarely takes the initiative in directing people or activities" (Bernreuter, 1933: 403).

Throughout the 1930s a number of other personality measures were added to the Thurstone and Thurstone scale and the Bernreuter inventory (see Goldberg, 1971). Measures such as Bell's (1935) Adjustment Inventory, which produced scores on home, health, social and emotional adjustment; the California Test of Personality, which tested the personality of children; and Humm and Wadsworth's (1935) Temperament Schedule, used to test for psychopathology—all supplemented and expanded the work on personality measures conducted in the 1920s. However, the widespread use of these and previous scales was hampered by what critics considered to be their unreliability due to lying and misrepresentation. Such skepticism began to wane somewhat in the early 1940s, when Minnesota psychologist Starke Hathaway and neuropsychiatrist J.C. McKinley presented an inventory to measure personality pathology in psychiatric faculties (Hathaway and McKinley, 1943). The Minnesota Multiphasic Personality Inventory (or MMPI) would, over the next few decades, become the most widely used personality inventory in the United States (Reynolds and Sundberg, 1976). It helped establish personality tests as a standard part of assessment not only in clinics and hospitals but also in schools, correctional facilities, courtrooms and corporations.

Work on the MMPI began in the late 1930s and was funded in part by a grant from the Works Progress Administration (Buchanan, 1994). Hathaway and McKenley's goal was to construct a multidimensional test of personality based on established and empirically verifiable criteria of psychopathology and to devise an instrument that would meet the criticism that personality inventories were untrustworthy. To accomplish these goals, Hathaway and McKenley used an empirical approach to inventory construction pioneered by E.K.

Strong in the development of his Vocational Interest Bank in the late 1920s. The original personality inventory Hathaway and McKenley (1940) developed contained 504 statements, in four control scales and ten clinical scales. Later the number of questions was expanded to 550, of which only three hundred items were scored. Respondents were asked to respond to a series of statements by answering "true," "false" and "does not apply." The control scales were composed of the *?* or "Cannot Say" scale, the L scale, the F scale and the K scale. High scores on the *?* scale indicated a subject who is "evasive, defensive and/or indecisive" (Edward, 1970: 54). The L (or "Lie") scale was devised to identify those who were likely to lie or misrepresent themselves. The F scale was used to identify those who are were not paying attention to the questions or who wished to call attention to themselves by giving outlandish answers. The final control device, the K scale, was used to capture defensiveness that may have altered respondents' answers on the clinical scales.

The clinical scales contained in the inventory were used to measure hypochondriasis, depression, hysteria, psychopathic deviate, paranoia, psychasthenia, schizophrenia, hypomania and later masculinity-femininity and social introversion.[10] High scores on the scales were indicators of the likelihood of the existence of a personality pathology: low scores were indicative of its absence. The construction of these clinical scales was made by comparing a group of "Minnesota normals," which consisted of 724 relatives and visitors of patients at the University of Minnesota Hospitals, 265 WPA workers, 265 recent high school graduates and 243 medical patients without psychiatric diagnoses, with a group of diagnosed psychiatric patients at the University of Minnesota Hospitals (Hathaway and McKinley, 1940). The typical "Minnesota normal" was white, thirty-five, married, lived in a small town, had an average of eight years of education and worked in a skilled or semiskilled job. Only those questions that differentiated the two populations were included in the final clinical scales.

Although clinicians and counselors often criticized the MMPI and the various other personality tests over the ensuing decades for their theoretical simplicity and reduction of personality to a few crude traits (see Peterson, 1968), the tests continued to enjoy widespread use. From the time of initial use of the MMPI, the number of scales in it rapidly expanded. Psychologists began to see the test "had many implications for general personality measurement beyond the clinical syndromes on which they were constructed" (Dahlstrom and Dahlstrom, 1980: 5). Psychologists began using existing questions to construct new markers of personality. By the mid-1950s there were already some hundred additional scales devised for the instrument (Welsh and Dahlstrom, 1956: 178). By the time of the production of the MMPI-2 in the late 1980s, the inventory had expanded to include eight validity scales, ten clinical scales, fifteen content scales, twenty-seven content-component scales, twenty supplementary scales, thirty-one clinical subscales and five superlative self-presentation scales (Butcher and Megargee, 1989).[11] The inventory was now used to measure not only the original personality traits but also such characteristics as cynicism, low self-esteem, family problems, amorality, denial of social anxiety and naiveté. In addition, ironically, in the MMPI-2 the opposite of neurotic—imperturbability—became a diagnosable personality characteristic.

The practical success of the MMPI led to the development of a number of other multidimensional empirical and logical tests of personality in the 1950s. Tests such as the California Personality Inventory (which borrowed a number of items from the MMPI), the Myers-Briggs Type Indicator, the Sixteen Personality Factor Questionnaire, the Guilford-Zimmerman Temperament Survey and the Edwards Personal Preference Schedule all expanded on the conceptualization of personality articulated in previous scales and inventories. These newer scales were based upon much more elaborated notions of self and personality. Personality was seen not only as containing such traits as dominance, subordinance, anxiety or neurotic tendencies, as in the older inventories but as the harbinger of such "attributes" as achievement, aggression, original thinking, cautiousness, vigor, adequate outlook and goals, reflectiveness, leadership potential and "personal frankness." In addition, in subsequent tests many of the characteristics identified in early inventories were further segmented into subcategories. For example, by the late 1960s the concept of dominance had been broken down into thirty to forty facets (Butt and Fiske, 1968), and the concept of anxiety became fractionalized into such types as test anxiety, math anxiety, reading anxiety, generalized anxiety and specific anxiety. Also, many of these inventories borrowed items from each other, thus creating an implicit, widespread consensus on what constituted personality (see Goldberg, 1971: 335).

The personality measurements constructed throughout the twentieth century allowed psychologists to increase their influence well beyond what had been possible using only the experimental hardware of the turn-of-the-century university and hospital laboratories. The bulkiness of laboratory instruments tied them to laboratory settings; however, pen-and-paper measures were capable of easily and quickly moving to a variety of places. In producing these personality inventories and scales psychologists not only expanded and reformulated some of their own central disciplinary concepts and reshaped their own political organization but created instruments that were capable of moving far beyond the walls of the discipline and its laboratories. By the 1940s, personality tests, like intelligence tests, were becoming a standard fixture of many organizations and institutions. During World War II, personality tests were used to identify "submissive personalities" and "potential troublemakers" for the army (Baritz, 1960: 159). Later, in the 1950s, personality tests were employed in corporations to assess managers and other employees. For example, during this period, Sears and Roebuck became one of the first companies to administer tests of intelligence, vocational interest and personality as part of their efforts to place and promote employees (Hanson, 1993: 243). By the late 1990s, 28 percent of American companies were using personality tests to assess employees and managers (Lavelle, 1998). Recently one company has gone so far as to include color-coded name badges revealing how managers scored on the Myers-Briggs Type Indicator, in order to ease interactions and facilitate communication between people of different personality types (*Fortune*, 1998: 80). Psychologists often lauded these tests as "a good, accurate, not-discriminatory means for choosing employees" (Arnold in Lavelle, 1998: B01).

Perhaps the most versatile, portable and widely used of the tests developed over the last century was the MMPI. Soon after its first use, the inventory began to migrate from clinical settings to colleges and universities, where it was used to help students select careers, and to corporations, where it was used to assess the suitability for employment in certain high-risk occupations. However, its most influential arena outside of clinics has been courtrooms. Here, it is often used to evaluate pain and suffering in personal injury cases, the ability of a defendant to stand trial, sentencing appropriateness and parental fitness in custody cases (see Peyrot, 1995: 575; Maynard, 1982). The inventory's popularity in law has resulted from its ability to speed or economize the decision-making process of courts and move cases toward closure. The MMPI is often seen as an objective, professional "witness" that allows for a neutral assessment and disposition of a situation. For example, in the spring of 2001 a jury in a personal injury case awarded a Philadelphia woman 1.5 million in a settlement after the MMPI helped establish that she suffered from depression and anxiety resulting from a posttraumatic stress disorder caused by an accident in a store (Song, 2001).

Psychology's personality tests can be seen as serving as what Star and Griesemer (1989) have referred to as "boundary objects." Such objects have the malleability and versatility needed to move from setting to setting without becoming diluted. They are also pliable enough to fulfill the eclectic needs of the various groups utilizing them. Such pliability partially explains the widespread diffusion of personality tests. By 1970, 513 tests of personality had been developed. Of these, 379, or 75 percent, were still in print (Buros, 1970: xxi). Of the tests in print, almost 80 percent were of the nonprojective types favored by most psychologists. Almost thirty years later, in 1998, tests of personality continued to be the most widely referenced tests in psychology, and they still made up the largest percentage of new or revised tests (Impare and Plake, 1998: xi). Today there are some 2,500 publishers of personality tests (*Psychology Today*, 2000: 14). In this sense, the true value of the MMPI and other personality measures comes not so much from the ability to accurately assess personality, but rather, as in the case of intelligence tests in schools, from the capacity to move decision makers toward a particular version of events and form of action. In doing so, these measures allow psychological knowledge to be in places and influence decisions even if psychologists themselves are not on hand.

CONCLUSION: LABORATORIES, MACHINES, MEASURES AND THE STABILIZATION OF PSYCHOLOGICAL CONTENT

In order to be successful, knowledge makers need somehow to write themselves into standardized procedures and practices. In other words, they must find ways to make their ideas material. Psychology did this, at least in part, though its various measures and machines. Historically, the use of such measures and laboratory machines in the production of knowledge has itself often been psychologized, however. In this more philosophical version of psychologization, devices and techniques are seen as serving to unleash, hone, magnify or graphically or mathematically reproduce phenomena that are beyond human perception or intuitive calculation. In such an account, machines and measures are value-neutral instruments that merely represent or amplify what is already there for the discernment of the detached experimenter. Yet treating machines and measures as merely "perception-enhancing devices" minimizes their role as active and independent knowledge actors in the overall construction and maintenance of a knowledge form. Measures and instruments do not just amplify what is already there but embody "strategies of demonstration, work relationships in the laboratory, and material and symbolic connections to the outside cultures in which these machines have roots" (Galison, 1997: 2). In this context, measures and machines train the senses and mind in "well defined patterns of perception and reasoning" (Borell, 1993: 245). In doing so they shape what will count as observable and scientific and what will not. This structuring of perception, then, ensures that particular styles of research will persevere in a field over an extended period of time.

Measures and machines also economize procedures within a discipline, establish interaction protocols between members and provide links to those outside. In addition, machines provide a means for configuring and delimiting a discipline's object of inquiry by first narrowing inquiry exclusively to the things that can be observed or counted by the machines and then by using the results of machine or measurement work as vindication of the reality of these things. Machines and measures, consequently, move a field of knowledge into particular directions by establishing and stabilizing its work object. In this sense, statistics, machines and measures can be thought of more as "truth techniques" (Rose, 1996b: 57) than as passive purveyors of truth. Experimental devices do not represent an unmediated reality but instead secure and stabilize its meaning—or, as Ian Hacking (1983: 230) has put it, "to experiment is to create, produce, refine and stabilize phenomena."[12]

In this light, psychology's laboratories, machines and measures can be seen as playing a number of important roles in establishing and promoting psychological knowledge. Initially the laboratory provided a place for the (re)enactment of "fact-finding rituals" (Wynne, 1982). It was a space where "thoughts, acts and manufactures" merged (Hacking, 1992: 30). As such, the laboratory provided a set of prescriptions for what it meant to be a psychologist—at least, a modern scientific, experimental psychologist (see O'Donnell, 1985: 122–123). Laboratories were, in the words of the Yale psychologist E.W. Scripture (1895: 295), "the outward signs of internal forces at work in developing psychology." With its calibrated equipment and standardized procedures, the laboratory was "designed to impress upon the student the facts, the methods, and the spirit of his science" (Nichols,

1893: 406). It provided a place for the alignment of cognitive styles and modes of action for those who could rightly be called psychologists.

The measures and machines of psychology also provided what may be described as "front-stage props" and ceremonial forms for the discipline. In this role, they served to convince others outside of the discipline, in particular other scientists and professionals, of the competence and trustworthiness of the knowledge form and its practitioners. This, in turn, enabled psychologists to conduct the "boundary work" necessary to form and reproduce a collective identity (see Gieryn, 1983). Measures and machines provided some of the symbols necessary for others to separate psychological knowledge from other forms of knowledge and to distinguish psychologists who possessed the technical skill necessary to use the measures and machines from the amateurs or outsiders who did not.

In addition, machines and measures provided pedagogical and professional continuity for practitioners. In this role they were used to acculturate succeeding generations of psychological knowledge makers. Since their use often required the special and local knowledge of the original creator, a series of student/mentor ties was established that, over time, became a network of interconnected and like-minded practitioners. In this role the machines and measures of psychology provided a type of technical continuity for the field (see Galison, 1997: 21–22). They supplied technical expertise and standardized truth rituals around which new recruits could be properly socialized, and myths in which existing members could reexperience and become recommitted to the discipline and its objectives. "Just as jealousy, anger, altruism and love are myths that interpret and explain the actions of individuals, the myths of doctors, of accountants, or of the assembly line explain organizational activities" (Meyer and Rowan, 1977: 349).

The use of laboratories, experimental apparatuses and measures was also responsible for the introduction of specific codes and mechanisms for the reproduction of the discipline. These objects and machines provided the model of what it meant to do scientific psychology. They therefore served to establish certain standards of the profession. In order to develop, scientific knowledge needs means of transmitting itself to the next generation of practitioners (Ben-David and Collins, 1966: 459). The measures and machines provided these means of transmission by economizing and smoothing communications and interactions between psychologists (see Friedman,

1967). Additionally, they provided the rationale for the reduction of the world to psychological principles and the material for the assessment of the validity of psychological knowledge. These work objects allowed psychology to become further organized, complete with fact-finding rituals, journals, graduate programs, research hardware, special certifications and intellectual exemplars. Without some means of reducing the world to its concepts and some degree of shared commitment to what it meant to be a psychologist, the discipline would not have developed in the manner that it did, nor would have psychological knowledge have managed to migrate into so many corridors of everyday life. In a way reminiscent of Durkheim's (1965) description of the centrality of rituals in the maintenance of a group's collective representations, the standardization of mechanical and measurement procedures created a totem of identify and exclusion. Much like the phenomenology of the Balinese cockfight in Clifford Geertz's (1973) classic description where cockfighting is emblematic of a complex and carefully ordered cultural world, as members of a profession encounter their machines and measures that too are enveloped in an elaborate symbolic environment of a discipline. In such situations members do not need to declare repeatedly their allegiance to the discipline; they are continuously reminded of, and reintroduced to, its rules and knowledge as they undertake their work.

Also, and perhaps most importantly for the discussion here, measures and machines reproduced the knowledge form's ideas into a material and highly transportable form by creating a demonstrative or epistemic continuity and stability (Galison, 1997). While the most hard-line positivist would admit that even the most valid experimental results or measures are at best approximations of the phenomenon being studied, something important happens when a machine, measure or statistical procedure is used over and over again. The measure, originally recognized as unstable and provisional, begins to solidify, reify and take on an existence of its own. No longer is it just an approximate, incomplete representation of a phenomenon but a definition of it. Thus, for example, intelligence is no longer a slippery and amorphous phenomena, as was acknowledged by Simon and Binet in 1905, but, as the experimentalist Edwin Boring (1923: 36) put it in 1923, "what the test tests."[13]

In this role the measures and machines "recast objects of investigation by inserting them into new temporal and territorial regimes" (Knorr-Cetina, 1999: 43). The meaning of other central psychological phenomena and issues, such as motivation, social attitudes, neurotic personality, extroversion-introversion, attention span, self-esteem and alienation become stabilized and defined as the measure. Over time they become composed by the measure and, like the modern fact described by Mary Poovey (1998: 5), take on "connotations of transparency and impartiality." In the laboratory environment and scale construction, new phenomena were created that became mainstays of subsequent psychological theory (see Hacking, 1983: 220). Here, certain concepts became truisms of both the discipline of psychology and human psychology in general. Indeed, the laboratory and its instruments and measures helped erase differences between the two. Human psychology was now what psychologists said it was. Psychologists were not just producing context-dependent disciplinary knowledge but were representing a basic, universal human condition. In this process the content of psychology was further tamed as the remnants of existing psychology became transformed into disciplinary psychology. Personality tests had a similar effect. Humans became endowed with particular traits that the measures were said to capture and help reproduce. Such qualities or traits as extroversion-introversion, neurotic tendencies or hypochondria became characteristics of individuals and not the test.[14] For both the measurer and the measured, these instruments took what is arguably fleeting and contextual and transformed it into something concrete and enduring.

As measures move from place to place, they carry with them the knowledge form's understanding of the ultimate order of things. In this capacity they reinforce the field's own conceptual definitions and strengthen its professional legitimacy. An example of this can be found in the statements used in the MMPI. Many of the MMPI's scales garnered a respondent's openness to therapeutic intervention. High scorers on the clinical scales included those who both resisted therapy and who answered positively to other questions seeking to assess the pathology. For example, a subject who is "critical of therapist" and "tends to terminate therapy when therapist is perceived as not giving enough attention and support" tends to score high on the Hypochondriasis Scale (Graham, 1987: 40). Likewise, high scorers on the Psychasthenia Scale indicated a person who is "resistant to interpretations in psychotherapy" and "expresses hostility toward therapist" (Graham, 1987: 61). In this sense, the scale became, in part, self-vindicating: confirmation of its truthfulness and legitimacy was built into the structure of the test. As is the case with charges of religious heresy, where almost any response is considered heretical, rejection of the device or the test giver was a further reflection of one's own pathology.

In their various capacities, the measures and machines of psychology became moral actors in the production, maintenance and dissemination of psychological knowledge. In contrast with the account given in traditional epistemological, where instruments and measures are seen as neutral appliances for the discovery of knowledge, in the field of psychology they are fully active and productive players. Machines and measures transformed the initial "fuzzy logic" of psychologists into the predictable outcome of machine procedure and precision and measurement reliability. So, while instruments and measures of psychology undoubtedly honed perception, they did so within the confines of the already predetermined conceptual constructions of the discipline's way of knowing. Furthermore, psychological concepts were limited and defined by what the machine or measure was capable of presenting. Likewise, as the discipline changed and its measures and machines "evolved," so did the membership of the discipline and the people being tested. New machines and measures brought with them new modes of practices, and they reconstituted and redefined the discipline and the people exposed to its knowledge. In turn these machines and measures were themselves shaped by the organization mythology of various groups as they projected their own organizational images into their construction. Consequently, experimentation and measurements are never neutral representations of the way things are. Instead, "we represent in order to intervene, and we intervene in the light of representations" (Hacking, 1983: 31).

NOTES

1. Cattell (1947 [1888]: 7), for instance, maintained that the issues revealed by psychology experiments "are not less interesting or important that such as can be solved in chemical, physical or physiological laboratories."

2. For example, every football player entering the National Football League's spring draft is given a version of the Wonderlic Personnel Test to gauge basic intelligence and personality (T. Smith, 1997: 11).

3. The material culture of psychology is not only present in its machines, scales and laboratories; it can also be found in its writing style. Like machines and scales, writing style also enforces particular notions of what it means to be a psychologist and to do psychological research (see Madigan, Johnson and Linton, 1995).

4. William James is credited with first developing a rudimentary laboratory at Harvard, as early as 1875; however, it was not until the arrival of Hugo Muensterberg in 1892 that a laboratory was officially opened.

5. In 1905 E.B. Titchener advocated the formation of an "experimental club" for psychologists. The club would have "no officers, the men moving about and handling [apparatus], they visited lab to do the work, no women, smoking allowed, plenty of frank criticism and discussions, the whole atmosphere experimental" (Titchener in Furumoto, 1988: 94; see also Boring, 1967).

6. In order to emphasize their experimental status as a science, early psychologists also set up a psychology laboratory as part of the psychology exhibit at the Chicago World's Fair (Jastrow, 1893). The exhibit contained two rooms, one that reproduced a psychology laboratory and one that held the testing apparatus. The laboratory was used to conduct various tests on fair-goers.

7. Describing his invention of the gravity ghronometer at Wundt's laboratory, Cattell wrote in his journal that this was "probably the best thing I have done in psychology so far was inventing the gravity apparatuses which enables me to see letters, words, etc., for a short and measurable time" (Cattell in Sokal et al., 1976: 61).

8. Included in this elaborate inventory were a portrait of Darwin and a bust of Aristotle.

9. Another factor that influenced this change was disenchantment by some within psychology with excessive reliance on instruments. Lewis Terman (1932: 311n) wrote, "My dislike of apparatus doubtless had something to do later in turning me to test and measurements of the kind that make no demand upon mechanical skill."

10. Lewis Drake (1946) independently developed the Social Introversion Scale at the University of Wisconsin. It was later added to the MMPI's clinical scales.

11. The MMPI-2, a restandardized version of the MMPI, used a nationwide sample of 1,138 males and 1,462 females between the ages of eighteen and eighty.

12. As Nickolas Rose (1996b: 57) has put it, "Statistical techniques began a condensation of the empirical and were then reshaped in such a way that they became a materialization of the theoretical."

13. Even Binet and Simon were quite reluctant to claim that their test was actually measuring intelligence (see Binet and Simon, 1916: 253).

14. In *Organization Man*, William H. Whyte (1957: 196) condemned personality tests for creating conformity among employees. Whyte argued that the tests rewarded such qualities such as extroversion, lack of interest in the arts and acceptance of the status quo at the expense other, more individualistic characteristics.

6

A Séance or a Science? Psychology and Its Publics

B
Y 1900 THERE WERE ALREADY MORE PSYCHOLOGY LABORA-
tories in the United States than there were chairs of psychology
in Germany (Adler, 1994: 115; see also Capshew, 1999: 16). The
experimental science that had originated in Germany with Wundt was
showing signs of become thoroughly Americanized. Despite this important disciplinary accomplishment, American psychologists still
faced serious obstacles to the large-scale acceptance of their emerging
science. Regardless of psychologists' continual insistence that their
newly established field was an experimental science on a par with
physics or biology and despite their well-equipped laboratories, most
average folk in the early part of the twentieth century held what psychologists considered to be rather wrongheaded notions of what the
discipline was all about. In 1908 Joseph Jastrow (1908: 38) openly
worried that most people saw psychologists as "spook hunters" rather
than as scientists, and psychological laboratories as places for "mental
healing, telepathic mysteries, or spiritualistic performances" rather
than as places of serious scientific inquiry. At the time of Jastrow's
comments most Americans, outside of a few academics and professionals, saw psychologists as investigators of spirits and other so-
called paranormal phenomena, if indeed they knew about them at all.

As a result of the public's misguided view of what the new discipline
of psychology was all about, early advocates began utilizing a number

of strategies to promote their scientific approach to the mind and self to a variety of lay and professional audiences. Somehow they needed to illustrate to those outside of academia that psychology was a science and not a séance. In order to accomplish this goal, psychologists had to appeal to a number of different audiences with often vastly divergent objectives. "Businessmen needed to hear a somewhat different story with different leading roles than those told to mothers, policy makers, store clerks, or Sunday school teachers" (Morawski, 1986: 120). Like the artists in the art worlds described by Harrison White (1993: 143), psychologists actively sought to recruit and establish distinct "publics of recognition." They needed people to appreciate and patronize their new science. Perhaps like no other knowledge form, this desire for a multifaceted patronage led psychologists to undertake a concentrated and unparalleled public relations campaign.[1] This campaign directed much of its early effort at recruiting and converting professional groups and followers of various existing mind-cure therapies, or "folk psychologies," to the new science of psychology.[2]

In this chapter I explore the efforts of psychologists to make their discipline better known to the public. Although the term "popularization" is used throughout this chapter, it is, as we shall see, a somewhat inappropriate and misleading word for describing psychology's wide-scale acceptance and adoption. "Popularization" assumes a clear boundary between the professional knowledge produced on the inside and the public knowledge consumed somewhere "out there" (see Cooter and Pumfrey, 1994). However, such a rigid demarcation between the inside and the outside does not quite apply in the case of twentieth-century psychology. The relations between psychology and its publics involved a complex interchange between the knowledge of the discipline and the concerns and interests of its publics. This interchanged affected the internal politics and the content of the knowledge being produced within the discipline of psychology, as well as these publics' reception, acceptance and incorporation of psychological knowledge.

In the first section of this chapter, I provide an overview of some of psychology's early efforts to become a popular science, beginning with its founding in the late nineteenth century until the so-called decline of psychology in the early 1930s. Here, I focus on the development of a division between "purists" and "populists" in the early history of the profession and how the dynamics of this division set the stage for the course of dissemination in the reminder of the twentieth century. In the second section, I provide a brief survey of the relationship between psychology and the media over the last seventy years or so. Next, I consider the more recent movement of psychological knowledge from print media to television. Finally, in the concluding section, I explore the effects of popularization on both the dynamics of the discipline and the reception of psychological knowledge by psychology's various publics.

PURISTS AND POPULISTS: THE TWO PATHS TO POPULARIZATION IN EARLY PSYCHOLOGY

Attempts to place the insights of the new psychology into the popular press are as old as the discipline itself. The acknowledged founder of the new psychology, Wilhelm Wundt, contributed a number of articles to popular family magazines in Germany in the late nineteenth century (see Viney, Michaels and Ganong, 1981: 270). In the United States, John Dewey wrote on the emergence of the new psychology in the *Andover Review* as early as 1884. Likewise, another one of the American founders of the new psychology, William James, wrote several articles on the emergence of this new psychology for a number of popular magazines in the United States, including *The Nation* and *The Atlantic Monthly*. Also, excerpts from his seminal work *Principles of Psychology* appeared before its publication in *Scribner's* and *Popular Science Monthly* (see Burnham, 1987: 91).

The first organized effort to popularize the new psychology came in 1892 at a preliminary meeting of the APA in G. Stanley Hall's home in Worcester, Massachusetts. At the meeting Joseph Jastrow "asked the cooperation of all members for the Section of Psychology" at the upcoming World's Columbian Exposition in Chicago (American Psychological Association, 1892a: 2). At the exposition, Jastrow, along with the anthropologist Franz Boas and Frederic Ward Putnam of the Peabody Museum, set up a display of fifteen tests as part of the Department of Ethnology to examine attendees' mental powers and sense capacities (Napoli, 1981: 15; Sokal, 1987: 31). The results of these tests were used to compile a large database on a variety of psychophysical responses. He also developed a special section on the emerging field of developmental psychology that contained illustrations of the mental development in children, based in part on "statistical research in the school-room" (APA, 1892b: 5; also see Blumenthal, 1994: 81). Jastrow, who was perhaps the founder most deeply concerned with the public image of psychology, saw the exposition as a means to "excite interest in and show the methods of experimental psychology" (APA, 1892b: 5). It was a unique opportunity to demonstrate the explanatory power and practical uses of the new science of psychology to a public that was much more familiar with mind cures than the new scientific psychology (see Jastrow, 1901).

In 1904 an even larger exhibit was prepared for the Louisiana Purchase Exposition at the St. Louis World's Fair. This exhibit, like the Chicago one that preceded it, contained a booth for the mental testing of the public as well as numerous displays of the early testing instruments of the discipline. The St. Louis exhibit, organized by Harvard psychologist Hugo Muensterberg, drew even larger crowds than the Chicago exhibit, as well as the participation of some of the leading psychologists of the day, including G. Stanley Hall, J.B. Watson, E.B. Titchener, and Adolph Meyer (see Perloff and Perloff, 1977).

The use of experiments, mental tests and demonstrations at the St. Louis exposition exposed a division that had been developing since the APA's founding between those who wanted to expand psychology into applied settings and those who wanted to keep it a university-centered science. For some, the public displays at the two fairs mirrored too closely the sideshow demonstrations used by people promoting mind cures, spiritualism and Mesmerism. The more "purist" members of the APA, particularly E.B. Titchener, wanted psychology to become more accepted by the public; however, they were suspicious of anything that resembled the carnival-like demonstrations of Mesmerism or mind cures. In their view, the proper place for displays of the explanatory power of psychology was the laboratory, and the proper audience was professional groups like teachers, social workers and politicians. The purists generally believed that psychology's involvement with public exhibits and the popular press denigrated and defamed the discipline and its scientific goals. In their view attractions at the expositions and other highly public events merely highlighted the already existing perception that psychology was a mystical sideshow and hence indistinguishable from the stunts of psychical researchers in Britain and the United States. Echoing this view, William James allegedly referred to the 1893 Chicago exhibit as "Muensterberg's Circus," in reference to Hugo Muensterberg, one of the central participants (Benjamin, 1986: 942). Populists such as Hugo Muensterberg, Joseph Jastrow, H. Addington Bruce and later Muensterberg's student William M. Marston, however, wanted to spread the message of psychology through a variety of channels, including the popular media and public demonstrations. For these advocates, popular presentations provided opportunities to direct attention away from spiritualistic movements and toward the new psychology. Populists maintained that these exhibits provided a means to show people that psychology was indeed a serious, experimental science unconnected to earlier psychological mysticism. Popular presentations were necessary, they contended, for the ultimate advancement of the science.

The public acceptance of the new psychology was initially overshadowed by the existing popularity of various mind-cure therapies. In fact, in the late nineteenth century when people used the word "psychology" or "psychological," they usually meant some form of mind cure and not the new, scientific psychology being promoted by APA members. In the late nineteenth century, "anyone who read a daily newspaper or subscribed to a popular magazine or belonged to one the major Protestant denominations" (Parker, 1973: 152) would have been aware of the various mind-cure therapies in circulation. Public demonstrations of mind-cure therapies, such as Mesmerism, New Thought or Christian Science, were common in many large Eastern cities and had by the 1880s reached "almost epidemic proportions" (see E. Taylor, 1999: 159). Lecture bureaus, newspapers and local mind-cure groups arose to manage and publicize the growing interest.

The pivotal figure in both the networks of the new psychology and the mind-cure therapies was William James. In addition to being a founder of the new psychology and well-respected philosopher, James was a founding member of the American Society for Psychical Research (ASPR) and a well-known investigator of mind-cure therapies in Boston (see Parker, 1973). As part of his research into the efficacy of mind-cure therapies, he made several trips to mental healers in order to experience their various techniques. In the 1880s, as head of ASPR's Committees on Hypnotism and Mediumistic Phenomena, James hypnotized a number of people, including Leonora Piper, the wife of a Boston area tailor, and Governeur Charnochan, a Harvard student, in order to demonstrate empirically the existence of an altered state of consciousness distinct from sleep and wakefulness (Taylor, 1999: 157–158; 165).

James's involvement in the mind-cure movements helped introduce some of the ideas of the new psychology into public discussions of the mind and self. However, early psychologists not only faced competition from mind-cure movements in the area of public displays and lectures but were in direct competition with these groups for the acceptance of their published works and advice. Books such as Henry Wood's *Ideal Suggestion through Mental Photography* (1893); Thomas Jay Hudson's *The Law of Psychic Phenomena* (1893), which sold more than one hundred thousand copies; Ralph Waldo Trine's *In Tune with the Infinite* (1897), which sold a million and a half copies and became a favorite of Henry Ford; and Elizabeth Towne's *Practical Methods for Self-Development* (1904), which sold 100,000 copies—occupied much of the popular publication space that the new psychologists hoped to fill (see Caplan, 1998; Parker, 1973). Mind-cure authors also held prominent places in a number of serial publications, such as *Mind*, *Mental Health Monthly*, *Journal of Practical Metaphysics*, *Banner of Light* and an advice column in *Good Housekeeping* (Moskowitz, 1995: 66). By 1910 there were already about a hundred magazines and papers on mind cures (Starker, 1989: 34), garnering a readership that was estimated to be in the hundreds of thousands (Parker, 1973: 8). Psychologists began to realize that public displays and lectures alone would not be enough to circulate the ideas of their science. The battle for recognition would also have to be fought in the areas of popular books and advice.

Among the first works in the new psychology to challenge mind-cure therapies' control of popular publication was E.W. Scripture's 1895 *Thinking, Feeling, Doing*. Scripture, a founding member of the APA and an experimental psychologist at Yale, used the book as a means to popularize the ideas of Wilhelm Wundt and the experimentalism of the new psychology. He declared the book to be "written expressly for the people ... as evidence of the attitude of the science in its desire to serve humanity" (Scripture, 1895: iii). The book contained chapters explaining the latest experimental findings on such topics as attention, hearing, feeling, memory and time reaction—topics with some appeal to followers of other therapeutical movements of the time. Within five years of its publication the book had become American psychology's first "best-seller," at over twenty thousand copies (Burnham, 1987: 89). However, this number still paled in comparison to those being sold by psychology's spiritualistic rivals.

Of the early founders of the new psychology, it was Joseph Jastrow who sought to challenge directly the domination of mind-cure therapies in the popular media. As early as 1886, Jastrow argued that those who wanted to find their way onto the curriculum had to "acquaint the cultured and powerful public with the general problems and broad outlines of your science" (Jastrow, 1886: 106). In his efforts to expose more people outside of academia to psychology, Jastrow began publishing articles in a number of popular magazines, including *Popular Science Monthly* and *Harper's Monthly Magazine*. In a series of essays in these magazines he addressed the public's conflation of psychology and psychical research (Jastrow, 1900). In 1900 Jastrow published his most widely read book, *Fact and Fable in Psychology*, where he sought to debunk a host of existing folk psychologies. Jastrow was convinced that until the public both understood and appreciated how different the unsound logic of spiritualism was from the rigorous experimental science of psychology, the discipline would forever remain in the shadow of mysticism.

In the 1920s Jastrow began writing a newspaper column entitled *Keeping Mentally Fit*, to spread the ideas of the new psychology and challenge the domination of spiritualism in the popular press. In the column he often reinterpreted the concerns and topics of mind-cure advocates as related to the findings of the discipline of psychology. The column became popular enough to be syndicated in over 150 newspapers by the late 1920s (Benjamin, 1986: 943). Jastrow argued that the new psychology now spoke with "the authority of an emancipated science—no longer a dependency of philosophy nor a protectorate of physiology—and speaks also in intelligible terms with an appeal to the common interests of common men" (Jastrow, 1928: vii). Jastrow's (1928) newspaper columns explored such topics as "The Art of Being Happy," "Are You Too Bright for Your Job?" and "Subconscious Habits"—topics that had once been the prime preserve of the spiritualists and mind-cure advocates. By the 1930s, Jastrow's books were directed almost exclusively toward popular audiences (Blumenthal, 1994: 82).

Of the early popularizers of the new psychology, few were more prolific than William James's student H. Addington Bruce. Part psychologist and part journalist, Bruce published sixty-three articles and seven books on an assortment of psychological matters between 1903 and 1917 (Dennis, 1991: 756). Of the early popularizers' writings, Bruce's came the closest to mirroring directly the interest of followers of the various mind-cure movements. Bruce provided popular psychological advice on issues ranging from mental telepathy to dream analysis, to parenting strategies. Among his more provocative proposals was the construction of "psychological institutes" in town and cities. Modeled to some degree after the Emmanuel Movement's healing centers (see chapter 8), these psychological institutes would train citizens in the "utilization of the energy hidden in the resources of the subconscious" (Bruce, 1908: 79).[3] In the eyes of those who wanted psychology to be a respected science, Bruce's efforts did more harm than good. In their view, his prolific writings on telepathy, dream analysis, and the subconscious further confused the public's already blurry distinction between the science of psychology and mysticism.

Another of psychology's early popularizers, Hugo Muensterberg of Harvard University, also sought to push the insights of the new psychology into the limelight. Muensterberg wrote a series of articles for magazines such as *The Atlantic Monthly*, *Harper's* and *Mother's Companion* in the early part of the twentieth century (M. Hale, 1980: 4). He also appeared in the *New York Times* an "average of once a month with a pro-psychology opinion" (Landy, 1992: 794). Muensterberg asserted that the time was right for the psychological expert to move into the public arena and provide much-needed advice on how to conduct modern life. He maintained that "experimental psychology has reached a stage at which it seems natural and sound to give attention to its possible service for the practical needs of life" (Muensterberg, 1908: 8). So valuable was this psychological input that Muensterberg claimed that the individual "who closes his ears to their advice will never dig the finest potatoes from his acre" (quoted in Hale, 1980: 106).

By the early part of the century, Muensterberg had become one of the most visible and often-maligned psychologists in the United States. In 1907 he gained national attention by administering a lie-detector test to Harry Orchard, a government witness in the much-celebrated trial of the labor leader "Big Bill" Hayward for conspiracy to murder the governor of Idaho (Spillman and Spillman, 1993: 329). In 1908 Muensterberg created a controversy when he argued for the beneficial effects of moderate alcohol consumption in an article in *McLure's Magazine*. By the early 1910s Muensterberg's articles in popular magazines had earned his writing the label "yellow psychology." E.B. Titchener accused him of debasing psychology at Harvard in his unrelenting appeal to popular concerns (Hale, 1980: 6). Likewise, Lightner Whitmer, the founder of the psychology clinic at the University of Pennsylvania, condemned Muensterberg for the "jaunty way in which the professor of psychology at Cambridge goes around the country, claiming to have treated in his psychological laboratory hundred and hundreds of cases of this or that form of nervous disease" (Whitmer in Hale, 1980: 110).

However, such criticisms did not keep Muensterberg from carving out new areas of influence and from continuing to promote psychology widely in the media and at public lectures. In the mid-1910s he became interested in film and film theory, publishing *The Photoplay: A Psychological Study* (Muensterberg, 1916). On a visit to Hollywood, Muensterberg visited the studios of Paramount, Pathé, Vitagraph and Universal (Hale, 1980: 144). There he developed friendships with several studio executives and helped developed a short film to be shown before features, entitled *Testing the Mind*, for Paramount. The film contained several segments, such as "Are You Fitted for Your Job?" "Does Your Mind Work Quickly?" and "Can You Judge Well What Is Beautiful and Ugly?" (Hale, 1980: 221). During its run the film was seen by almost two million people.

Early psychology's efforts at popularization saw the emergence of a particular type of public psychologist—a group that would continue to shape the reputation and reception of psychological knowledge throughout the century. These psychologists essentially combined the "advisory function of the old-time pastor and the country doctor" (Bunn, 1997: 96). Much like the mind-cure psychologists, these "folksy" psychologists, such as Jastrow, Muensterberg and Bruce, allocated advice on everything from the disciplining of children to mental telepathy, to enhancing one's popularity. In so doing they sought to supplant the treatment of popular topics by mind-cure advocates with the experimental insights of the new psychology. Also, they, like their psychic competitors, sought to give advice in a manner and in language that were amenable to various publics. They often accomplished this by using the same forums, like public demonstrations, lectures and popular periodicals, as the various folk psychologies they sought to replace.

By the 1920s the discipline of psychology had undoubtedly become better known. However, the success of its early popularization efforts was not without costs to the internal politics of the discipline. Early psychologists soon become divided over the direction the discipline was taking. In the early decades of the twentieth century, this division frequently took the form of a conflict between experimentalists and clinicians (see Adams, 1928). Experimentalists typically viewed themselves as protectors of the original and true Wundtian science of psychology. In their view, clinical psychology and other, more applied wings of the field had gone too far and promised too much. Their tactics and popular messages were much too similar to psychology's psychic competitors and, as such, diluted the radical experimental message of the new psychology. The experimentalists' attack on their more populist cousins' efforts at broad popularization usually took the form of ridicule; however, on one occasion it went so far as an attempt to get one of the first populists, E.W. Scripture, removed from the APA.[4]

PSYCHOLOGY TODAY: PSYCHOLOGISTS AND THE POPULAR PRESS

The populist and purist pathways established by the earlier founders of the discipline continued to affect psychology's relationships with its publics throughout the remainder of the twentieth century. For populists it was imperative to "give psychology away" (Miller, 1969). People needed psychology in order to know "why they feel they way they do, act like they do, how to rear children, how to get more fun out of their jobs, how to solve many of their problems, how to live more up to their capabilities" (Blakeslee, 1952: 91). Populist publicizers took various opportunities to increase the public awareness of the discipline including, moving the insights of psychology into radio, television and by late in the twentieth century, the Internet. On the other hand, purists continued to maintain that psychology, while undoubtedly useful, should be cautious and reserved in its pronouncements until its results were a bit more solid. In their view, public advice should be dispensed only after long and careful empirical study in the laboratory.

By the late 1910s psychology was still far from a household word or an important component of everyday life of the kind early populist advocates wanted. This situation began to change in the 1920s, when Science Service, a federally sponsored wing of the National Research Council and an agency under the direction of the National Academy of Science and the American Association for the Advancement of Science, began to release news reports on psychology's findings to newspapers, and later radio stations (Burnham, 1987: 95; see also Whalen, 1981; Morawski, 1986). Science Service's stated goal was "to make the greatest possible use of the Press in the way of disseminating" scientific findings (Scripps in Morawski, 1986: 116). Psychological articles were distributed alongside those of astronomers', physicists' and other natural scientists'. Within a short time psychology articles became the most popular items released by the service (Rhees, 1979).

Bolstered by its success testing the IQs of students and soldiers in the 1910s and by the reports released by Science Service, psychology began to become a more widely recognized field in the 1920s. By this time psychology was, according to James McKeen Cattell (1922: 5), "on the map and on the front page." In 1921 psychologists at Columbia received front-page coverage in the *New York Times* when they released the results of a series of psychological experiments performed on Babe Ruth to determine the reason for his batting success. Under the heading "Babe Ruth's Home Run Secrets Solved by Science," the psychological experiments revealed that Ruth's "eyes, ears, his brain, and his nerves all function more rapidly than do those of the average person" (Fullerton in A. Fuchs, 1998:160). In 1923 two new psychology magazines were launched, Henry Miller's *Psychology: Health, Happiness, Success* and Orlando Miller's *The Psychological Review of Reviews*. The former sold some 30,000 copies soon after its inaugural run (Benjamin and Bryant, 1997: 587). Like previous popular works these magazines contained advice on such topics as curing depression, doing well at work and child rearing.

By the mid-1920s, psychologists were publishing almost 15 percent of all science articles appearing in mass-circulations magazines (LaFollette, 1990: 54). Newspaper writers began to laud the virtues of psychology in such popular publications as *The American Magazine, Good Housekeeping* and *Collier's Weekly*. Writers like Albert E. Wiggam (1928) began espousing how much the public needed psychological assistance in their daily lives:

Men and women never needed psychology so much as they need it today. Young men and women need it in order to measure their own mental traits and capacities. ... [A]dults need it in order to make the mental health adjustments necessary for meeting the stress and strain and keeping the swift pace of modern life; business men need it to help them select employees; parents and educators need it as an aid in rearing and educating children; all need it in order to secure the highest effectiveness and happiness (Wiggam, 1928: 13).

For Wiggam, it was impossible to be happy and successful without "the new knowledge of . . . mind and personality that the psychologists have given us" (Wiggam, 1928: 13). The practical popularity of psychology began to spawn a series of books on the "psychology of everything," such as *The Psychology of Murder* (Bjerre, 1927), *Psychology of Group Insurance, Psychology of Buying* and *Psychology and the Day's Work* (Swift, 1930).

The production of so many books and articles so quickly, coupled with the unbridled enthusiasm of populist advocates, soon spawned a backlash against psychology's popularization both outside and within the discipline. In 1924 the journalist Stephen Leacock (1924) lampooned the "outbreak of psychology" in *Harper's*. Leacock (1924: 471) proclaimed that the growing popularity of psychology had enabled "college professors of psychology [to wear] overcoats lined with fur, and [ride] around in little coupe cars like doctors." Later, critics such as James Thurber echoed this criticism in a series of articles in the *New Yorker*. Here he castigated the growing preoccupation of American society with psychological issues and elaborate psychological strategies to "fix the mind" (see Thurber, 1937).

For the more purist critics within the discipline, psychological advice to the public had proliferated much too quickly and as a result had weakened psychology's status. Echoing the earlier sentiments of her mentor, E.B. Titchener, Grace Adams, writing in *The Atlantic Monthly*, argued that the discipline's rapid popular assent had destroyed its standing as an experimental science. As evidence of the discipline's demise she cited the overall decline in references to psychology in the *Reader's Guide to Periodic Literature* in the late 1920s (Adams, 1934: 91, see also LaFollette, 1990: 54). For Adams, psychology had failed to deliver on its earlier promise of providing practical advice on the "essential nature of man"—"The public which had asked for facts realized that it was being stuffed with words" (Adams, 1934: 92). In her view, psychology "has renamed our emotions 'complexes' and our habits 'conditioned reflexes,' but it has neither changed our habits nor rid us of our emotions. We are the same blundering folk that we were twelve years ago and far less secure of ourselves" (Adams, 1934: 92). For Adams, the "happiest solution" for preserving the integrity of psychology as a discipline would be "a merger with sociology or anthropology" (Adams, 1934: 92).

By the late 1930s the number of psychology articles appearing in popular science magazines had declined significantly from the previous decade (LaFollette, 1990: 54). The scorn leveled at psychology in the 1920s and '30s seemed to have taken a toll on the popularity of the discipline. The decline also appeared to spell the end of the discipline's early success at displacing the mind-cure movement in disseminating popular advice on the conduct of life and pursuit of mental health. In response, psychologists often attributed the decline in their popular article output to the pirating of their findings by journalists, who began to push increasingly sensationalistic stories. However, this downturn concealed the fact that psychology had by this time managed to gain control over many of the popular press discussions of the mind and the self. By the 1930s publications of spiritualists, New Thought advocates, Mesmerists and other folk psychologists prevalent in the last century had gone out of vogue and been largely replaced by those of psychologists and psychiatrists (see Moskowitz, 1995: 79). This downturn also concealed the fact that psychology itself had changed, moving away from a university-centered experimentalism toward populist topics and concerns.

Yet even during the 1930s, when psychology was supposedly losing its appeal, some psychologists did manage to garner wide publicity for psychology. In 1930 the industrial psychologist Walter Bingham launched a long-running radio show called *Psychology Today* on CBS (Landy, 1993: 103). The show, which ran for 20 years, presented a range of topics on applied psychology and included presentations by some of the leading psychologists of the day, such as J.B. Watson, Floyd Allport, E.L. Thorndike, Carl Seashore and Elton Mayo (Landy, 1993: 103). However, few were more active during this period than William Moulton Marston. In the late 1920s Marston, a student of Muensterberg at Harvard and the self-proclaimed inventor of the lie detector, film consultant and future author of *Wonder Women*, performed a series of lie-detector tests on blonde, brunette and redheaded "chorus girls" at the Embassy Theatre in New York in order to measure their emotional responses to a series of personality statements (Bunn, 1997: 97). A *New York Times* article reported that Marston's experiments showed that "brunettes react far more violently to amatory stimuli than blonds" and "that brunettes enjoyed the thrill of pursuit, while blondes preferred the more passive enjoyment of being kissed" (in Bunn, 1997: 98). During the 1920s and '30s, Marston also wrote a number of popular psychology books, including *Emotions of Normal People* (1928), *You Can Be Popular* (1936) and *March On! Facing Life with Courage* (1939). In the late 1930s Marston became the resident psychologist for the widely circulated *Family Circle* magazine (Bunn, 1997: 93). In this position he, like the other populist psychologists before him, dispensed advice on topics ranging from developing a healthy mental life to disciplining children. In 1938 he published an article in *Look* magazine claiming to solve marital problems with a lie detector. In the article he illustrated how the lie detector could be used as a means to uncover the true, inner feelings of one's marital partner.

Despite the much-heralded demise of psychology in the late 1920s and early 1930s, its popularity began to soar again in the 1940s, particularly after the end of World War II. Part of this resurgence was fueled by the publication of *Psychology for the Fighting Man* (National Research Council, 1943) and the 1945 sequel *Psychology for the Armed Forces*. *Psychology for the Fighting Man* relayed psychological advice to soldiers on the waging of war. Adopting a "popular form without sacrifice of its scientific accuracy," the book contained advice on a range of topics, such as dealing with racial prejudice, sexual desire and hearing as a tool in warfare (National Research Council, 1943: xi). By the end of the war the book had sold a surprising 400,000 copies, due to its wide circulation within the armed forces (Capshew, 1999: 97). Responding in part to the interest sparked by the book, in 1949 the APA decided to hire its first public relations consultant in to order to improve psychology's public image and promote psychological findings to the media (Burnham, 1987: 104).

Psychology's popularity in the post–World War II era was also stimulated by articles in one of America's most widely read magazines, *Life*. In the 1950s *Life* hired the psychologist Clifford T. Morgan as a consultant on mental health issues. Under Morgan's direction *Life* ran a series of articles entitled "The Age of Psychology" (see Havemann, 1957). During this period *Time* magazine also became one of psychology's most important conduits of popularization. From its inception in 1923 until 1932 *Time* published over 400 items related to psychology (Gerow, 1988: 6). Later, during a ten-year period from 1937 to 1947, *Time* published 271 articles on psychology (Blake, 1948: 124). In 1969 the magazine launched a behavior department to disseminate psychological ideas further. Its articles, like those in *Life*, focused largely on functional disorders, social commentary and educational psychology (Blake, 1948: 125).[5] During the 1950s, nine of the top ten daily newspapers in the United States carried some type of psychological advice column (Havemann, 1957: 8). Columns such as "Child Behavior," "Let's Explore Your Mind," "Mirror of Your Mind" and "The Worry Clinic" appeared in newspapers with circulations in the millions (Havemann, 1957: 8). The notoriety generated by the coverage of psychology in *Life* and *Time* articles and in newspaper columns, coupled with the publication and popularity of psychologically oriented works such as *The Power of Positive Thinking*

(Peale, 1952) and *The Mature Mind* (Overstreet, 1949), began spreading psychological ideas to a vast new audience—one well beyond that of the mind cure enthusiasts of earlier in the century.

During the 1960s, psychology's popular reception continued to expand rapidly. One of the most important milestones took place in 1967, with the inaugural run of *Psychology Today*. With its first articles on topics like children's art, pain and aggression, water witching, amnesia and psychopharmacology, the magazine sought to turn the ideas of academic psychology into "lively, clear, and technically accurate" articles (Charney, 1967a: 5). The first editor, Nicholas Charney (1967b: 5), declared his faith in psychology's ability to provide "effective means for conditioning and controlling man's behavior." However, in a jibe aimed partially at the experimentalist, he stated that he wanted the new magazine to avoid "the pompous and unnecessary vocabularies generated by some psychologists in their attempts to be objective and precise" (Charney, 1967a: 5). The popular treatment of psychological issues, Charney maintained, should not come at the expense of scientific integrity. He wanted the magazine to avoid the sensationalism of past popular presentations of psychology, which had often been superficial or "just plain wrong." To accomplish this goal the magazine directed its circulation toward a readership that was, according to a 1968 advertising campaign for the magazine, "generally younger, brighter, more prosperous and classier than the readers of any other consumer magazine" (in Burnham, 1987: 125). Within a few years of its initial run, *Psychology Today* had reached a circulation of over one million readers (Burnham, 1987: 106).

During the 1970s the conflict between purists and populists began to resurface, centered around the content of *Psychology Today*. A growing number of psychologists in the APA became troubled with the magazine's portrayal of psychological concepts and ideas, as well as with its general movement away from empirically based articles. Some also were concerned that the magazine's contributors were coming more often from journalists than psychologists (see Smith and Schroeder, 1980).[6] In 1983, responding to this growing criticism, the APA purchased the magazine for 3.8 million dollars (Moran and Moran, 1990: 109). The APA hoped to "recapture control over the market for popular psychology" and therefore "upgrade its quality" (Morawski and Hornstein, 1991: 127). However, five years later mounting debt and the need for large loans to kept the magazine afloat forced the APA to sell the magazine.

During the 1970s, when the readership of *Psychology Today* was nearing its peak, it seemed that psychological knowledge was prominent in many popular magazines, particularly parenting and women's magazines. In 1974 Robert Lewis and Hugh Petersen (1974: 9) complained that "a year's subscription to a typical women's magazine is akin to an encyclopedia of applied psychology." To meet this growing demand for psychological knowledge, a number of book clubs specializing in psychological works came into existence (Burnham, Birnha 1987: 297). Also, new sections in bookstores appeared containing a hodgepodge of self-help, parenting and academic psychology texts. In response the APA developed a Public Information Office in 1974 to better handle its relationships with the media and to try in some manner to better manage the burgeoning popularity of its knowledge (Burnham, 1987: 108).[7] One of the functions of the Public Information Office was to administer the National Media Awards, given in order to "encourage outstanding media coverage that increases the public's understanding of psychology" (Zimmerman, 1983: 257).

DR. JOYCE BROTHERS AND THE PSYCHOLOGIZATION OF TELEVISION

The popularization of psychology owes much to the concentrated efforts of such people as Jastrow, Muensterberg, Bruce and Marston and to their ability to translate existing folk mediations on the mind and self into the new language of professional psychology. Its popularization is also undoubtedly due to the successful linkages forged with the media since the turn of the last century. However, the popular acceptance of psychology was also greatly shaped by forces that, at least initially, lay beyond the direct actions of its supporters.[8] The late-nineteenth and early-twentieth-century fascination with folk psychology and other "unofficial" forms of psychotherapy that provided much of the material for the growth of psychology also helped create a fervent public interest in what came to be called "psychological literature." In the late nineteenth century this psychological literature utilized the language and ideas of mind cures and other popular therapies of the time. However, after the turn of the twentieth century this literature began to borrow more and more of its terminology from the disciplines of psychology and psychiatry, particularly Freudian psychoanalysis. Plays by Eugene O'Neil and Rachel Crother began bringing the ideas of psychology and psychoanalysis to large urban audiences throughout the United States in the early part of the century (Pfister, 1997b: 173). As popular periodicals and books were reoriented by the language of the new psychology, so too were many works of fiction.

By the 1940s the themes and perspectives of psychological literature had begun to find their way into the content of motion pictures. In the 1946 film *The Dark Mirror*, a psychologist becomes the hero when he solves a crime using a variety of psychological techniques, including the Rorschach Test (see Fearing, 1947). Also during this time the term "psychological thriller" was first introduced to movie audiences, in films like Alfred Hitchcock's *Spellbound* (1945), Darryl Zanuck's *The Snake Pit* (1948) and Joseph L. Mankiewitcz's *All about Eve* (1950) (see Schnog, 1997: 5). In 1947 alone some 28 films were produced with prominent psychological themes (Gerbner, 1961: 92). By 1951 almost 20 percent of the films produced had important "psychological elements" in their content (Gerbner, 1961: 93). These films, like their literary predecessors, shared both a fascination with psychological pathologies and a notion of a deep, and often fragile, interior self. They also borrowed heavily from the language and imagery of phobias and complexes present in Freudian psychology, psychotherapy and the mental hygiene movement.

The success of psychological elements in literature and film prepared the way for the introduction of psychological knowledge into the new medium of television in the 1950s. As early as the mid-1940s, psychologists were being urged to use the emerging form of television to forge a "science of values" and achieve "culture control" (Remmers, 1944). The popularity of psychological films also set the stage for the introduction of a new persona in American culture, the TV psychologist. The birth of this new persona can be traced to the fall of 1955, when Dr. Joyce Brothers, a little-known psychologist, appeared on a quiz show, *The $64,000 Question*. By the end of the year she had become the first women to win the $64,000 question. The next year Brothers appeared on *The $64,000 Challenge* and won again. By the end of the decade she was hosting the program *Dr. Joyce Brothers* on NBC (Capshew 1999: 248). By the late 1980s as many as 20 million people were reading Brothers's newspaper column (Moran, 1989: 119). In addition, she made regular appearances on TV talk and game shows, such as *Oprah*, *The Today Show* and *Hollywood Squares*, and published such articles as "How TV Adds Spice to Your Life" (1990), "The Shows That'll Make You Feel Better" (1989a) and "Why We Need to Laugh" (1989b) in *TV Guide*. For most people Brothers became the personification of psychology. She had taken the populist role developed by some of the earlier popularizers, such as Jastrow and Muensterberg, into the realm of television.

Joyce Brothers had set the stage for the introduction of psychologists on TV talk shows and for the emergence of the psychologically inspired "therapeutic discourse of TV talk shows" (see Peck, 1995). By the late 1970s psychologists had become some of the most favored guests on radio and television talk shows (McCall and Stocking, 1982: 992). TV programs hosted by Phil Donahue, Oprah Winfrey and Sally Jessie Raphael often used psychologists as expert guests to comment on the problems of the people appearing on the shows. Also, these programs often emphasized a particular "code of the individual" (Carbaugh 1988: 39), borrowed directly from the language of psychology. Within this code, talk centers around the idea that "people are everywhere individuals" (Carbaugh 1988: 39). Often resembling therapy sessions, these programs, according to Nudelman (1997: 305), employ a "therapeutic dyad—an individual in need, speaking, and a sympathetic audience, listening." Also, as in therapy, talk shows often use a specific narrative of resolution. In this narrative, an issue is first identified as a problem; next, a guest is brought on, or a series of guests, to personify and publicly confess the problem. Then an expert, often a therapist of some type, is introduced to provide a context, give an explanation of the guest's predicament and to bring "closure." As part of this process, the audience is often expected to identify the central problem in the guests' lives, provide a moral indictment and offer solutions.

One of most successful of these therapeutically oriented talk shows is the one hosted by Oprah Winfrey. Winfrey has claimed that her show "tackles the root of all problems in the world—the lack of self-esteem" (quoted in Peck, 1995: 58). Describing a typical example from an *Oprah* episode entitled "Newlyweds at Each Other's Throat," Robin Andersen (1995) finds evidence of the presence of variety of psychological techniques in the show's production. During this particular episode John Gray, the author of the best seller *Men Are from Mars, Women Are from Venus*, is introduced to explain the root causes of the couple's problems. In his view "the underlying problem in every one of these cases is communications. Nobody's hearing the other person" (Gray in Andersen, 1995: 161). Andersen (1995: 161) contends that such programs provide a deafening "therapeutic din" that continually shuts out other, nonpsychological understandings of the couple's problems. *Oprah* now features regular visits by the clinical psychologist Phil McGraw, who is described on his Web site as "one of the world's most recognized experts in the strategy and management of life" (www.philmcgraw.com/biography). In his role as resident psychologist, McGraw dispenses advice on matters ranging from "life skills" to weight control and performs "relationship rescues" on couples in the audience.

In the 1970s and '80s, psychological themes and concepts also found their way into a variety of TV movies and programs. In the late 1970s one critic complained that TV programs like *Charlie's Angels, Family* and *Barney Miller*, and the movie *Sybil* had created "a nation of people talking like therapists" (Sklar, 1979: 63).[9] According to this critic psychology's permeation of TV programs had created a "nightmare of mulled motivations, pondered psyches, and ruminated relationships" (Sklar, 1979: 63). The decade of the 1970s also saw the first situation comedy featuring a psychologist, *The Bob Newhart Show*. Psychologists also became key players in the development of a number of popular children's programs in the 1970s, such as *Sesame Street* and *The Electric Company* (see Palmer, 1976; Lesser, 1976).[10] By the 1990s most children's television programs used developmental or child psychologists as consultants for content and modes of presentation.

Also during the 1970s and 1980s, TV shows such as *Family* and *Thirtysomething* incorporated strong psychological and therapeutic themes. *Thirtysomething*, with its emphasis on self-analysis and exploring "interpersonal relationships" became, as one writer put it, a place Americans could turn for "insights into interpersonal and psychological problems" (Pearce, 1988: 12). A 1988 *Psychology Today* article described how therapists had started using the show as part of their therapy sessions (Hersch, 1988). In addition, a survey of the same period found that people were more likely to consider using therapy after viewing the show (Faludi, 1991: 161).

Capitalizing on their success on TV in the 1970s and 1980s, psychologists began offering each other advice on how to best convey their message to the media. Zimmerman (1983: 263) advised fellow psychologists that "if you want to be taken seriously, dress appropriately. Clothing selection depends on the program, audience, and image you want to convey. Bold, bright, or deeply saturated colors reproduce poorly, can affect the camera's operation, and interfere with your communication effectiveness." Also in the 1980s the APA established a science-writer position to disseminate information about psychological research directly to the press. In 1982 a new group dedicated to the promotion of psychology in the media was formed in San Diego. First dubbed the Association for Media Psychology, the group was recognized in 1987 as an official subfield of the APA (Bouhoutsos, 1990: 54). Consisting of radio call-in hosts and other allied psychologists, the association's specific goal was to spread psychological ideas and solutions through the popular media. Talk-show psychotherapy was originally in violation of the APA's code of ethics, but the code was altered as these shows gained in popularity.

By the mid-1990s psychological knowledge had made the move to the Internet. Sites such as *Ask Dr. Tracy* (www.loveadvice.com), *Ask Dr. Victoria* (www.drvictorian.net/ehelp.html), *Ask Dr. Larry Brown* (www.askdrbarrybrown.com), the *Center for Psychological Advice* (www.psychadvisor.com) and *Conscious Choices* (www.cybertherapy.com) began dispensing advice on such psychological topics as relationships, phobias, depression, chronic pain, sexual dysfunction and getting along with teenagers. These sites provided private, fee-based counseling, and in the case of *Ask Dr. Tracy*, discounts on Tracy Cabot's books *Letting Go* and *How to Make a Man Fall in Love with You*. Other sites, such as *Self-Help & Psychology Magazine* (www.shpm.com) and *Psychological Advisor Newsletter* (www.psynews.com), were also launched during this time to bring psychological advice to people via the Web. Modeled in part on the magazines *Self* and *Psychology Today*, these "e-zines" provide psychological information, threaded discussions and self-help products such as videos and hypnosis tapes. The APA has also begun to include links for the public on its own Web site (www.apa.org/psychnet). Here people can receive brochures, look up the "latest psychological research" and obtain referrals to psychologists practicing in their area.

CONCLUSION: THE EFFECTS OF POPULARIZATION

Psychology's road to popular acceptance moved along two initially distinct, but eventually indistinguishable, paths. On one path, some psychologists sought to maintain a "respectable science" by exposing only "fellow modernizers," such as teachers, social workers and politicians, to the messages of their scientific, experimental psychology. These promoters tried to distance themselves and their new discipline from their therapeutic and mystical cousins in New Thought, Psychical Research, Metaphysical Research, and other similar movements of the late nineteenth and early twentieth centuries. On a second path, other psychologists attempted to bring the message of psychology to a wide variety of audiences. This "folksy psychology" sought to instill itself as a conveyer of everyday wisdom in the same vein as the country doctor or pastor. Along this second avenue, psychologists and their supporters sought to use an already established public fascination with various folk psychologies to enhance the recognition and acceptance of the new psychology, as well as to recruit new allies and publics to their science (see Moore, 1977: 134). Like physicians of the time, these psychologists undertook a "novel professional calculus" in order to draw the followers of spiritualism and other forms of parapsychology into the fold (Caplan, 1998a: 149).

As is clear, psychology's path to popularization, like that of most other knowledge forms, was not quite what many early advocates of psychology as an experimental science had envisioned. Psychology's early encounters with its eclectic audiences influenced the new discipline as much as the discipline wanted to shape them. Although most psychologists fought vigorously to distinguish their new science from the existing folk psychologies prevalent in America in the late nineteenth and early twentieth centuries, they would ultimately end up utilizing and sublimating the popularity of those movements to enhance the recognition and legitimacy of their own new knowledge form. This often had the effect of further blurring "boundaries between psychologists' knowledge and knowledge of psychological processes held by others" (Morawski and Hornstein, 1991: 109). Psychology's success at recruiting followers of mind-cure movements proved to be paradoxical; it sometimes stood in the way of psychology's acceptance as a serious science with the academy and created warring factions within the discipline, but the sublimation of these groups interests simultaneously allowed psychology to become one of the most influential and prolific knowledge forms of the twentieth century.[11]

Within the discipline this appeal to radically divergent audiences created and magnified already existing political divisions between experimentalists and clinicians, and forced much of the discipline onto a road that soon earned it the disparaging label "pop psychology." Throughout the twentieth century, experimentalists often presented themselves as the protectors of the original intent of the science of psychology. In their view, it was the clinicians who were guilty of spreading the science too thin, of promising too much too fast. From the clinicians' perspective, however, psychology is and always has been from its founding an applied human science. The measurements occurring in the laboratories were meaningless unless they were incorporated into daily practice. In the 1940s this political division led to a revolt by clinicians. In their view the APA represented only the interests of the experimentalists. The revolution promoted a significant reorganization of the structure of the APA. By late in the twentieth century the situation had reversed itself; the clinicians now dominated the discipline. By the 1980s most doctorates in the field were awarded in applied areas (see Reisman, 1991: 377). In 1988 the tension between the two factions became so great that a group primarily composed of experimentalists broke off from the APA to form the American Psychological Society. This new society's goal was to focus exclusively on psychology as an experimental science, although over time its structure and operation began more and more to resemble the APA's.[12]

Psychology's road to popular acceptance is undoubtedly one of the more unusual among twentieth-century sciences. Although, as other studies of science have shown, there is rarely a clear distinction between "inside" and "outside," and though no discipline can completely isolate itself from "outside influences," psychology, in contrast to physics and many of the other natural sciences, was from its inception inordinately open to a multitude of popular concerns, demands and pressures. In fact, it is this openness and the inability, or unwillingness, to create a firm insider/outsider boundary that partially explains psychology's large-scale popularity. Like religious movements, knowledge movements like psychology succeed by "remaining open networks, able to reach out and into new adjacent social networks" (Stark, 1997: 20). Remaining an open network allowed psychology to continue to nurture the "direct and intimate interpersonal attachments" necessary for a movement to spread and grow (Stark, 1997: 20). Such a process can be readily seen in the multiple networks established and utilized by such "influentials" (Katz and Lazarsfeld, 1955) as William James, H. Addington Bruce, Hugo Muensterberg and even Dr. Joyce Brothers. All used already established connections to the advantage of the various messages of psychology (James and Bruce with mind-cure enthusiasts, Muensterberg with studio executives and lawyers and Brothers with TV producers and editors). In this instance those "influential" in a network, even if the network is local, can command more authority than scores of mass-marketing campaigns (Katz and Lazarsfeld, 1955).

The history of the popularization psychology sketched here also reveals a rather new model of how knowledge is disseminated. The popularization of scientific knowledge is often treated as the struggle of enlightened souls against the ignorance and superstitions of the masses. Such diffusionist accounts divide knowledge into the special type produced in scientific and professional environments and the ordinary type found in everyday life (see Cooter and Pumfrey, 1994). The former group is said to be in possession of the truth of the matter, while the latter languishes in myth or vulgarized forms of professional knowledge. With such a separation in place between the professional and the nonprofessional, it is the task of scientists, supporters or science educators to develop strategies to teach or train those "out of the know." In these accounts the audiences of science are viewed as "large, diffuse, undifferentiated and passive" (Whitley, 1985: 4). They are acquiescent groups awaiting liberation through (or that perhaps become stubbornly resistant to) the concepts, methods and ideas of professionally produced knowledge. However, psychology's unique road to popularization reveals a much more complex relationship between a science and its publics than is conveyed in the diffusionist understandings of the movement of knowledge. While many early advocates of the new psychology wanted to preserve a purely scientific discipline, beyond the reaches of public pressures or fads, the direction psychology would take in the twentieth century owes much to its various encounters and interactions with its publics. By the end of World War I, psychologists and psychiatrists had largely managed to wrestle control of the discourse and treatment of the self away from popular folk therapeutic movements; at least, they had persuaded these movements to adopt some of their language and methods (see Moskowitz, 1995: 79). However, such an incorporation and redirection of the public also lead to the incorporation and redirection of the field of psychology. These various therapeutical movements and their specific concerns remained integral parts of the discipline throughout the century. They had, at least in part, set the agenda that psychologists would follow throughout the century. As a result psychology would not, as the purists so wanted, be able to become a completely self-contained science.

At first glance it would appear that psychology has today made little progress in its century-old pursuit of public respect. For example, most public opinion poll respondents still rank psychology near the bottom of scales of occupational prestige (see Wood, Jones and Benjamin, 1986). There is counter evidence, however, that psychology's public image has improved greatly over the century. As early as the 1960s a poll recognized psychologists as the professionals most helpful in resolving marital problems and for assessing children's intelligence (Thumin and Zebelman, 1967). This conflicting evidence reveals the complexity of psychology's relationship with its publics. On the one hand, psychological knowledge is not to be trusted, because it is sometimes seen as simply the residuals of common sense in academic garb. However, in another sense psychologists are seen as the ones to be sought out for certain types of services and treatments—services now seen as necessary for the conduct of modern life. Consequently, it would be a mistake to assume that a profession with a relatively low occupational status would not have an important influence on thought and practice. A knowledge field does not need to have high public status in order to be influential. In fact, often a type of knowledge that is concealed and diffuse, such as psychology's, can have more influence on people's ordinary activities than ones that are more open and celebrated.

If the clinicians and popularizers had not come to dominate the field as they did, it is highly unlikely that psychological knowledge would have become as all-encompassing as it is today. Psychology would perhaps more resemble fields like linguistics, philosophy, sociology or literary criticism—interesting perhaps, but relatively uncelebrated and rarely featured on TV talk shows. Over a hundred years after Jastrow's exhibit in Chicago, public displays of the explanatory power of psychology are no longer sideshow attractions at fairs and exhibits. Throughout the course of the twentieth century psychology became relatively unspectacular. This is not because people lost interest in psychology's knowledge but because it became a natural part of everyday life. Today psychology no longer needs to be "popularized," because it has become life itself.

NOTES

1. This may be related, at least to some extent, to psychologists' own early involvement with the psychology of marketing and advertising, particularly in the cases of J.B. Watson and Walter Dill Scott (see Buckley, 1982).

2. I use the phrases "folk psychologies" and "mind cures" throughout this chapter to signify an amalgamation of a number of late-nineteenth-century movements such as Mesmerism, New Thought, Christian Science, Spiritualism, Theosophy and Psychical Research. Although these movements had quite distinct philosophies, they all served as examples of the type of analyses that scientific psychology sought to replace (see chapter 8). For example, Mesmerism, associated with Franz A. Mesmer, focused on hypnosis (see Darnton, 1968). "New Thought" is a term used to group together a late-nineteenth-century movement in the United States that focused on improving the mind through scientific spiritualism (see Dresser, 1919).

3. The Emmanuel Movement was formed by two Episcopalian ministers, Elwood

Worcester and Samuel McComb, and the psychiatrist Isador Coriat in 1906 in Boston. The movement used hypnotism and autosuggestion to heal a variety of mental and physical disorders. Soon after the movement's founding, Emmanuel centers were established in such cities as New York, Newark, Buffalo, and Cleveland (Lears, 1983: 13; see also chapter 8).

4. E.B. Titchener attacked E.W. Scripture after the publication of *Thinking, Feeling, Doing* on the grounds that several large passages were virtually identical to an earlier work by Wilhelm Wundt. Titchener led an unsuccessful campaign to have Scripture expelled from the APA in the late 1890s (see Goodwin, 1985: 384).

5. During the postwar period journalists were beginning to replace psychologists and other scientists as authors of mass-circulation science pieces (Dennis, 1989: 357). Also, the venue of dissemination had moved from journals, which catered to the professional class, to magazines, and newspapers, which sought broad, mass circulation.

6. However, a content analysis of articles in *Psychology Today* failed to find evidence that the magazine's priorities changed after it was purchased by the APA (see Moran and Moran, 1990).

7. In order to gage the success of such efforts, psychologists have also conducted a number of polls on psychology's public image. Specific groups, such as teachers, children and African Americans, have been surveyed in order to get their particular impressions of psychologists (see Dollinger and Thelen, 1978; Grossack, 1954). Psychologists have also performed several analyses of how psychologists have been treated by the popular press. Other writings have sought to give psychologists practical advice on getting their insights known to the public. Some of these writings have offered pragmatic advice on how psychologists can get articles into newspapers and magazines (see Blakeslee, 1952; Carpenter, Lennon and Shoben, 1957), while others advised psychologists on the types of clothing that should and should not be worn on television.

8. For example, Gerbner's (1961) study of early trends in the treatment of psychology in the mass media found that the popularity of psychology tended to increase in good economic times and decline in times of economic stagnation.

9. Joel Pfister (1997a: 24) also maintains that much of the folk rock of the late 1960s and 1970s also contained lyrics that "helped sell the romance of white psychological individualism to many."

10. Gerald Lesser (1976: 135), a psychologist at the Laboratory of Human Development, asserts that the development psychology behind *Sesame Street* was "to help prepare 3-, 4-, and 5-year old children—especially those from inner cities—by teaching them some of the basic intellectual skills they would need in order to move rapidly and comfortably into the early grades of school."

11. Members of most knowledge fields also have ambivalent attitudes toward popularization. On the one hand, a popular field may receive generous funding, an abundance of students and jobs, and high public status. However, there is sometimes a fear that popularization may lead to the intellectual and organizational "contamination" of the field. From this view, popularization is an act of sacrilege that blurs the line between audience and practitioners. Often critics also see popularization as watering down the field's message as throngs of uncredentialed "copycats" attempt to reap for themselves the success of the field. This explains the mixed feelings some

hold toward their colleagues who are frequently quoted in the newspapers or on TV. Purists often feel that the ideas and concepts of the discipline are too complex to be reduced to the jingoism of a popular presentation.

12. Earlier in 1959 a group of purists had broken off from the APA to form the Psychonomic Society.

7

Psychological Codes of Civility and the Practice of Everyday Life

IN *THE CIVILIZING PROCESS*, NORBERT ELIAS (1978) ARGUED that modernity is best seen as the outcome of the evolution of particular codes of behavior. These modern codes, which began to emerge as early as the thirteenth century, have influenced everyday activities ranging from the blowing of one's nose to sleeping positions, to the proper way to greet a stranger. For Elias, modernity is defined by a particular cultural division drawn between the things, orientations and actions that belong to the realm of the "civilized" and those that do not. The specific content contained within and regulated by the codes is relatively unimportant; only that they are used to create and sustain group membership, exclude offending outsiders and create radical new modes of selfhood and ways of acting toward others. Over the course of several centuries, the modern codes of civility described by Elias began to shape and put into place a new definition of what it means to be a "modern individual." They did this, at least in part, by introducing what Joel Pfister (1997a: 26) has called "new thresholds of shame." These thresholds helped establish modern notions of inferiority, privacy, modes of self-presentation and protocols of interaction. As these thresholds solidified across the centuries, there came into existence a new ethical being that placed supreme importance on understanding and managing the emotions, which were seen as threatening the full manifestation of humanity's inherent rationality.

As the dominant discipline of the mind and self, psychology has become one of the means through which these modern codes of civility have spread and become recast. Indeed, one of the most striking influences of psychological knowledge has been felt through the importation of its own unique professional language and particular "codes of civility" into everyday life. These codes of civility encourage, and increasingly require people to act toward others and situations in "psychologically appropriate ways." The proliferation of these psychological codes of civility have been made possible by the movement of psychological knowledge into various domains of everyday life, particularly the areas of work and family. In these settings, psychological civility has slowly remade the way selves are conceived, discourse is enacted and affairs are conducted.

Drawn largely from the language and practices of industrial/organizational (I/O) psychology, family therapy, psychotherapy, popular psychology and more recently political and policy discourse, these psychological codes of civility have begun to shape the types of interactions people are expected to have with one another. At their core, these psychological codes are based on the possession, assessment and expression of "underlying emotional states." Individuals are viewed as possessing various inherent "psychological needs," "personality traits," "psychological issues" or levels of "emotional intelligence," which in turn shape their actions and require expression. Interaction with others requires both intimate awareness of these personality characteristics and modes of interaction that respect the inviolability of a person's psychological makeup. In the workplace and family life these characteristics can make for either a psychologically "healthy" environment, with smooth, conflict-free interactions and harmony, or an "unhealthy" setting, with conflict, hostility and antagonism.

Managing these personality traits and emotions requires a highly reflexive self that is capable of conjuring up and presenting this deep interior, as well as some type of psychological expert to aid the individual in discovering and conceptualizing his or her bottled-up emotional life. One of psychologists' goals in this revelatory process, particularly in industrial/organizational psychology and family and marriage therapy, is to assess and aid the individual in correcting the personality characteristics and interpersonal distortions that get in the way of proper emotional release, the satisfaction of individual needs and conflict-free communication and interaction.

In this chapter I look at a few more of the places where psychological knowledge has traveled in the twentieth and twenty-first centuries. Specifically, I examine how psychology has contributed to the construction of modern emotional life by reconfiguring the quality and styles of interactions people are expected to have with one another. In the first section, I use the history of industrial and organizational psychology to explore the effects of psychological knowledge on workplace relations and interactions. Here, I consider the transition of I/O psychology from the "reinforcement models" found in its early history to the therapeutical techniques of worker management found in more recent programs, such as Total Quality Management. In the second section I investigate the psychological codes of civility introduced into family life by marriage and family counselors. In this section I look at the emergence of various marriage and family communication models and how they have influenced the language and practices of intimate relationships. Finally, I conclude this chapter with a discussion of the institutionalization of psychological scripts and "feeling rules" into everyday life and the resulting "ethic of emotivism" that they spawn and support.

EMOTIONAL WORKERS AND THE RISE OF THE THERAPEUTIC CORPORATION

The growing reliance on psychological codes of civility to interpret and conduct life is evident in a number of places, including TV news programs, movies and talk shows (see White, 1992). However, one of their most influential areas has been in the world of work. Over the past hundred years or so, psychological knowledge and practices have become an integral part of the managerial strategies used by organizations to control and regulate their employees. They have also become crucial means through which corporations manage crises or control anomalous "interpersonal situations" that may disrupt the functioning of an organization. As such, psychological knowledge and techniques have increasingly become standard parts of the repertoire both managers and employees use to negotiate the organizational dynamics of the contemporary corporate world. The introduction of psychological codes of civility into the workplace can be traced to the expansion of industrial psychology in the early part of the twentieth century.

As part of his larger efforts to move psychology into applied settings, Hugo Muensterberg published the first work in industrial psychology, *Psychology and Industrial Efficiency*, in 1913.[1] Muensterberg used the book to link the findings of the new experimental psychology with the applied needs of industries and businesses. Muensterberg (1913: 243) conceptualized work as the product of the "psyche of personalities." Accordingly, the newly emerging branch of applied psychology could be used by companies to determine "what mind is best fitted for the particular kind of work, and how the mind can be led to the best output of work" (Muensterberg, 1913: 243). For Muensterberg (1913: 128), psychological assistance in personnel selection would enable employers to "secure the selection of the fit workman." Such selection would be good for both the manager and the worker. For workers, it would "insure not only greater success and gain, but above all greater joy in the work, deeper satisfaction, and more harmonious unfolding of personality" (Muensterberg, 1913: 36). To illustrate the relevance of psychology to business, Muensterberg developed a series of tests for hiring groups as diverse as ship captains, production workers, telephone operators, sales representatives and drivers and motormen (Landy, 1993: 90).

Muensterberg's vision of utilizing psychological testing techniques for personnel selection inspired the establishment of a number of consulting groups and research centers in the 1910s and 1920s. Among the first was Walter Van Dyke Bingham's Bureau of Salesmanship Research, at the Carnegie Institute of Technology in Pittsburgh. Established with the support of thirty companies that agreed to pay five hundred dollars each for the research center's services, the bureau aided companies in developing selection tests for potential employees (Lundy, 1993: 101). In 1919 Walter Dill Scott, another leading industrial psychologist and former director of the Bureau of Salesman Research under Bingham, opened the Scott Company in Philadelphia. Like the Bureau of Salesman Research, the Scott Company sold its services to companies seeking psychological advice on testing and training employees and on developing effective management strategies.

In the late 1910s, John B. Watson brought his behaviorist perspective to the emerging subfield of industrial psychology. While working for Western Union Company, Watson was recruited to study employees who "were not particularly efficient" (Buckley, 1982: 210). In 1920 he and a Baltimore physician, Edward Magruder, established the Industrial Service Corporation to provide services to companies in personnel selection. In exchange for Watson's help, Magruder agreed to set up a program to train Ph.D.s in industrial psychology (Buckley, 1982: 210). Also during this time, James McKeen Cattell launched the Psychological Corporation, providing psychologists as consultants to companies and industries. The board of directors consisted of some of the luminaries of early psychology, such as William McDougall, G. Stanley Hall, Walter Dill Scott, E.L. Thorndike and J.B. Watson (Cattell, 1923). By the late 1920s the corporation's income had risen to around $1,600. By the late 1960s, when the corporation was sold, sales had grown to almost five million dollars (Landy, 1993: 97–98). By the 1920s the demand for industrial psychologists was expanding so rapidly that there were not enough psychologists to meet the growing interest of corporations and industries (Arthur and Benjamin, 1999: 103). By this time many larger personnel departments contained psychologists as either employees or consultants (Arthur and Benjamin, 1999: 101). In these departments psychologists primarily analyzed job tasks and tested employees or potential employees for their suitability for particular jobs (Arthur and Benjamin, 1999: 101). In some instances these personnel departments became a company's own psychological laboratories, where managers could determine which employees would remain loyal to the company and what personality traits were useful in various departments (Arthur and Benjamin, 1999: 101). Elise Bregman, a student of John McKeen Cattell, established one of the first such large psychology laboratories, at Macy's department store in the 1920s. In this position she used a variety of psychological tests to examine some twenty thousand people in order to determine their suitability for sales and clerical jobs (Bregman, 1922).

Other companies began using industrial psychologists to identify people for particular jobs as well as to counsel employees and help establish "worker happiness." Echoing Muensterberg's pronouncements two decades earlier, Walter Bingham (1932b: 35) maintained that industrial psychology was not just concerned with the selection of appropriate personnel but "aims to increase the zest of accomplishment as well as to remove irritations, worries, and hindrances that breed discontent." To do this, psychologists were "measuring and studying the human factor in relation to the conditions, both material and personal, which underlie all happiness in work" (Bingham, 1932b: 271). With the advice of industrial psychologists, managers began to "recognize that it was not enough to manage jobs; efficiency and profits could be improved only if workers were managed as people with feelings and emotional attachments to their work" (Leahey, 2000: 435). As part of such efforts in 1922 Metropolitan Life started one of the first employee counseling services in order to identify psychological problems and aid in adjustments at work (Stearns and

Stearns, 1986: 116). By the early 1930s 31 percent of all large corporations in the United States had established industrial relations departments, a few of which offered counseling services to their employees (Stearns and Stearns, 1986: 116). By 1935, of large firms with over five thousand employees, some 80 percent had established personnel departments (Baritz, 1960: 120).

Attention to the "emotional needs" of workers also became an important feature of the famous four-year study conducted in the 1920s at the Western Electric Company's Hawthorne Works in Cicero, Illinois. The results of the Hawthorne study attributed increased productivity to the attention paid by management to workers' "needs," "relationships" and "team development" (see Mayo, 1933). Two researchers on the project, Fritz Roethlisberger and William Dickson (1939: 601), contended that many of the "human problems" found in the study were the result of: "(1) adjustment of the individual to industrial structure; (2) communications and control; and (3) changes in the social structure." Elton Mayo, one of the lead investigators, and his associates believed that psychological concepts and techniques were key for easing the adjustment of workers to the realities of modern industrial life. Specifically, Mayo introduced Jean Piaget's (1929) *The Child's Conception of the World* to Roethlisberger, Dickson and others involved in the study in order to illustrate both how to conduct interviews with workers and how to understand their "irrational," "emotional" and often "infantile" responses to their working conditions (Gillespie, 1993: 134). Mayo believed it was important to show workers and supervisors how their reactions to work were often rooted in the psychological clash of parent and child desires, as outlined by Piaget.

In Mayo and his associates' view, beneath most labor disputes lay individual psychological problems associated with adjustment to the new organization of work in an industrial economy. Citing a hypothetical example they wrote:

Suppose a worker, B, complains that the piece rates on his job are too low. In the interview it is also revealed that his wife is in the hospital and that he is worried about the doctor's bill he has incurred. In this case the latent content of the complaint consists of the fact that B's present earnings, due to his wife's illness, are insufficient to meet his current financial obligations (Roethlisberger and Dickson, 1939: 267).

In such situations managers were encouraged to allow workers to express themselves in order to allow for "emotional release" (Roethlisberger and Dickson, 1939: 269). It was the job of the personnel manager to "help to control and redirect the evaluation the individual makes of himself and of his situation" (Roethlisberger and Dickson, 1939: 602). If that was properly done, workers would "find in the direct collaboration with the factory all they need in the way of personal self-expression and of adequate consideration" (Whitehead, 1936: 155).The study aided management in creating well-adjusted workers by initiating a plan of "personnel counseling" to attend to workers' emotional needs. The program provided psychologically trained peer counselors to whom workers could go with their complaints and concerns. By 1954 some sixty-four peer counselors worked full-time in various Western Electric plants throughout the United States (Baritz, 1960: 106). This program remained in place long after the experiments themselves ended, and they served as models for other large firms in the 1950s (Dickson, 1950).

The Hawthorne study created an "assumption that workers act from emotions and generalized feelings, while management responds to logic" (Baritz, 1960: 1134). Many managers felt that worker complaints concealed deep-seated psychological issues rather than substantive challenges to their authority or the industrial order. Workers unhappy with managerial practices or working conditions were sometimes seen as "projecting their own maladjustments upon a conjured monster, the capitalists" (Hepner, 1938: 96). In this view, angry or dissatisfied workers mistook their own psychological issues or "adjustment anxiety" for social or organizational problems. Bottled-up and misdirected anger made the worker, in the words of one industrial psychologist, incapable of "dealing with his problems in a corrective way" (Tead, 1933: 40). The goal of the new breed of industrial psychologists created at Hawthorne was to develop programs and initiatives to aid workers in adjusting to the new realities of industrial work. Among these initiatives was the satisfaction of the "profound need" of people to live in "relationships with other persons" by creating a type of "fictional kinship" system (Mayo, 1937: 697). To accomplish this, psychologists would provide ways "to encourage employees to think constructively" (Baritz, 1960: 104), to manage their emotions, to live in cooperative work communities and to channel worker anger. Organizations using modern psychological techniques of management and personnel would, in the words of Alex Inkeles (in Baritz, 1960: 26), set "an example of rational behavior, emotional balance, open communication, and respect for the opinions, the feelings and the dignity of worker, which can be a powerful example of the principles and practices of modern living."

By the mid-1940s hundreds of large companies, as well as such government agencies as the Department of Agriculture, the Tennessee Valley Authority and the Social Security Board, had begun using psychologically trained counselors in their personnel departments (Baritz, 1960: 163). Like the Hawthorne program, these initiatives provided avenues in which workers could express their frustrations and "talk out" their problems. As one industrial counselor during this period described their role,

At least half of the grievances of the average employee can be relieved merely by giving him an opportunity to "talk them out." It may not even be necessary to take any action on them. All that they require is a patient and courteous hearing, supplemented, when necessary, by an explanation of why nothing can be done. . . . It is not always necessary to yield to the worker's requests in order to satisfy them (McMurry, 1944: 13–14).

In 1947, Standard Oil of New Jersey started one of the largest such efforts when it began offering counseling to its employees. By 1955 some six thousand interviews had been conducted with Standard Oil workers (Baritz, 1960: 164). These interviews became, in the words of one critic, "a safety valve for the angry, a stimulant for the bored, an escape for the frustrated, a refuge of the fearful" (Roessle in Baritz, 1960: 164).

By 1946 a survey of large corporations found that 30 percent had professionally trained psychologists working in their organizations and that 50 percent thought having a psychologist on staff was a good idea (Baritz, 1960: 142). Part of the importance attributed to industrial psychologists was a result of their selection testing during World War II; personnel-selection tests developed by psychologists over the previous decades had been put to wide use to support the war effort. Bingham, working as the chief psychologist of the War Department during World War II, helped develop the Army General Classification Test to match soldiers to particular jobs and assignments by analyzing their aptitudes and personalities (Katzell and Austin, 1992: 811). By the next decade psychological tests had become a standard fixture of personnel management in the United States. At that time almost 70 percent of businesses used psychological testing in some manner (Guinn, 1991: 66). Central among these tests was the Aptitude Index Battery, first developed at Bingham's Carnegie Institute research center in the 1910s. This battery, which contained a mental alertness test, was used by a number of large companies, including the Life Insurance Agency Management Association, to search for suitable employees (Katzell and Austin, 1992: 804). Other tests, such as the Bernreuter Personality Inventory, also had wide dissemination, with over a million copies sold by 1953 (Whyte, 1957: 209). Likewise, such tests as the Watson-Glaser Critical Thinking Appraisal, the Guilford-Zimmerman Temperament Survey, the California Personality Inventory and the Wesman Personnel Classification Test became integrated into the assessment of workers in a large number of organizations (see Ryan and Sackett, 1987). Also during the 1950s, many large companies, including General Electric, Prudential Insurance, Metropolitan Life, Sears-Roebuck and Standard Oil of New Jersey began to develop large, highly specialized research groups staffed with industrial psychologists and other organizational specialists (Dunnette, 1962).

As in other applied branches of psychology, until the late 1950s and 1960s two models of industrial and organization psychology competed for acceptance by corporations and businesses. One approach, that of the behaviorists, used empirical tests and the models introduced by Watson and other early I/O advocates to aid managers in controlling "employee and customer behavior to accomplish the goals of the organization" (Judd and Winder, 1995: 287). This approach used psychological concepts and measures to aid managers in selecting employees, establishing incentives and determining employee rewards and punishments. Its goal, in Watson's words (in Birnbaum, 1955: 19), was to "mold the good worker—not the griper or clock watcher." The other, psychoanalytic, approach used counseling and therapeutic techniques to adjust workers to the requirements of modern organization. However, during the 1960s, new "humanistic" modes of psychologically influenced management began to appear. Drawn in part from "third force" psychology associated with Carl Rogers and Abraham Maslow, these approaches sought to align work with the emotional needs of workers, creating "self-actualized" employees.[2] In this perspective, the "basic needs of workers" demanded the creation of "esteemable and fulfilling jobs" (*Work in America*, 1973: 12).

Among the first of these humanistic approaches were the Assessment Centers established at AT&T by Douglas Bray, Donald Grant, Richard Campbell and Ann Howard. Echoing in some respect the approach used in the Hawthorne counseling centers, these new centers examined employees "behavioral dimensions or competencies such as team building, decision making, organizing and planning" (Arthur and Benjamin, 1999: 105).[3] The centers were also used to examine the mental health of workers, including conducting a long-term study on the changing mental characteristics of managers (Bray, Campbell and Grant, 1974). Their central goal was to make work fulfill workers "basic emotional needs."

Programs such as the AT &T Assessment Centers foreshadowed the development and expansion of newer models of administration that began to emerge during the 1980s, such as Work Groups and Total Quality Management (TQM). Like humanistic psychology, TQM encouraged workers, in the words of one critic, "to become self-actualized in the workplace by identifying with their bosses' interests" (Cloud, 1998: 4). The central theoretician of TQM, W. Edward Deming (1986; 1993), borrowed extensively from the self-actualization movement and Maslow's "hierarchy of needs." He included psychology as one of the four elements of the "profound knowledge" necessary for the successful implementation of TQM. For Deming (1993: 11), psychology was a necessary prerequisite for understanding "people, interaction between people and circumstances, interaction between customer and supplier, interaction between teacher and pupil, interaction between a manager and his people and any system of management." To this end, TQM focused on fulfilling the "basic intrinsic psychological needs" of workers. Whereas many past managerial strategies had dealt only with reward and punishment, through such "extrinsic" measures as pay, promotion and merit raises, TQM sought to incorporate a worker's entire heart and head into the production process. Deming (1993: 111) maintained that "people are born with a need for relationships with other people, and a need for love and esteem by others." In turn, "good management helps us to nurture and preserve these positive innate attributes of people" (Deming, 1993: 111). As Judd and Winder, advocates of this approach describe it (1995: 289), "in place of employees merely being compensated for their work and customers simply being given a standard product in exchange for their money, their human needs for meaningful social interaction can be addressed." As this happens the employee can "engage in actualization through contributing their own core competencies to the common good that becomes their common vision" (Judd and Winder, 1995: 289).

TQM's psychological approach to management has also become instrumental in the establishment of a number of recent counseling initiatives in the workplace. Recently Digital Equipment Corporation used psychologists in implementing a round of layoffs associated with reorganization. Likewise, the U.S. Postal Service began to use psychological counselors to reduce assaults by employees after a wave of violence in its post offices in the 1990s (see Spector, 2000: 3). Such approaches can also be seen in the introduction of a number of workplace seminars developed over the last twenty years. One such seminar program, entitled "Conquering Workplace Negativity," seeks to use information from I/O psychology and management studies to uncover "negativity in your organization, negativity in your team and negativity in yourself." According to the seminars advertisement, "negativity is natural in circumstances like these. It's based on specific fears. It surfaces and then recedes as a person evaluates the situation and acts either to change it or adjust it. But some people are habitually negative" (CareerTrack, n.d.: 3). As part of the seminar, participants would learn "what makes negative people the way they are[;] . . . what, if anything, you can do to clue them in[;] . . . and how to safeguard yourself from catching their 'bug'" (CareerTrack, n.d.: 3).

The historical movement of psychological knowledge into the workplace, particularly such all-encompassing programs as the Hawthorne counseling centers, AT&T Assessment Centers and TQM, contributed to the development of what some have recently called the "therapeutic corporation" (Tucker, 1999). This "emotional transformation of the workplace" (Stearns, 1988: 124) emerged as the internal organization of corporations moved from a bureaucratic style of social organization, where authority was embedded in a rigid, top-down hierarchical structure, to a "postbureaucratic" form marked by more dispersed authority. In bureaucratic organizations, behavior is held in check by a central authority structure that channels decision making continuously upward, and by formal rules of procedure that regulate individual action within a larger system of rules and regulations. In this type of managerial arrangement, I/O psychologists are called upon to provide assistance in selecting fit employees and developing effective punishment and reward structures.

In contrast, in the postbureaucratic form of organization, decision making became much more dispersed or regionalized. This regionalization of authority requires new modes of managing employees, approaches that emphasize "institutional dialogue" based on "persuasion rather than official position" (Heckscher, 1994: 25). Such an approach seeks to utilize employees' mental and emotional states to create and sustain loyalty to the organization. Here, the organization is seen not as a elaborate system of reward and punishment to be doled out but as an "emotional landscape" that must be continuously nurtured and attended to if it is to run efficiently. In this type of management style, I/O psychologists aid employees in adjusting to the organization and provide management information on how best to satisfy workers' basic psychological needs. In the therapeutic corporation, conflict and individual deviation are not viewed as challenges to authority or violations of rules, as was often the case in the older bureaucratic model, but are reframed as internalized problems of interpersonal communication, personality conflicts or psychological pathology that can be resolved through mediation, counseling and discussion.

Of central concern among these new managerial strategies found in the postbureaucratic organization have been the need to control "interpersonal conflicts" that threaten the smooth flow of institutionalized dialogue, decision making and workplace consensus. For example, a worker's failure to get along with his or her boss or coworkers is treated as a "personnel problem" resulting from "personal characteristics or circumstances" (Tucker, 1999: 18). Accordingly, today's "uncooperative employee," much like the "belligerent worker" described by early industrial psychologists, needs adjustment—not to the new industrial order but to the complex interpersonal world of the postindustrial corporation. Unlike that of the early belligerent worker, this new adjustment is to be achieved through counseling, sensitivity training, conflict management, or communication workshops rather than punishment and reward. In this strategy managers, like therapists, are to "let people help themselves" (Tucker, 1999: 49). Managers are called upon to take on the role of counselor or therapist in order to encourage employees to talk through and mediate their problems, or create situations where things can be "worked out" between conflicting parties. With the emergence of the therapeutic corporation over the last one hundred years, managers, as Alistair MacIntyre (1981: 29) has described them, have increasingly become indistinguishable from therapists.[4]

"WHAT I HEAR YOU SAYING...": THE ESTABLISHMENT OF PSYCHOLOGICAL CODES OF CIVILITY IN FAMILY LIFE

Over the last century the psychological codes of civility found in work life have also become increasing commonplace at home. As early as the 1940s, cultural analysts were beginning to take note of the growing psychologizing of domestic and intimate relations. In "The Meaning of a Literary Idea," literary critic Lionel Trilling (1951: 285) remarked that "people will eventually be unable to say, 'They fell in love and married,' let alone understand the language of Romeo and Juliet, but will as a matter of course say, 'Their libidinal impulses being reciprocal, they activated their individual erotic drives and integrated them within the same frame of reference.'" Trilling's satirical prediction reveals the mid-twentieth-century preoccupation with psychologically inspired, specifically Freudian, vocabularies, technologies and formulas of self. While the twentieth century did not see the demise of the concept and discourse of romantic love in quite the Freudian-inspired manner Trilling predicted, psychological conceptualizations of intimate or family relationships, and the resulting codes of interpersonal civility nonetheless reframed the way marital and family relationships are played out, represented and assessed. In doing so they created new definitions of those relationships and radically redefined what it means to have a good marriage, a successful intimate relationship or a happy family life.

In the United States the passage of psychological frameworks into marriage and family relations was set into motion by the Family Life Education Movement, which began in the late nineteenth century. Groups within this movement, such as the American Home Economics Association, saw the family as the central place in which to teach the emerging scientific principles of life and home management and to aid in the modernization of family life (Broderick and Schrader, 1981). As we saw in chapter 4, part of these efforts was directed toward creating modern, psychologically informed parents. Another important feature, however, was modernizing the internal organization of marriage and family life. For these early advocates, the institutions of the family remained one of the last stubborn vestiges of traditional domestic relations within a society that was increasingly and inevitably becoming modern. The family, however, needed updating to keep pace with the demands of modernity.

One arena where this vision of modernizing family life came to fruition was the field of marriage and family counseling. Early family and marriage counselors were a rather loose amalgamation of psychiatrists, biologists, psychologists, sociologists and religious figures. The first official marriage counseling can be traced to the late 1920s and the services offered by physicians Abraham and Hannah Stone in New York. The Stones established the Marriage Advice Center to aid couples experiencing marital problems. A few months later the biologist and eugenist Paul Popenoe opened the Institute of Family Relations in Los Angeles to provide consultation on "family problems." Popenoe (1946: 487) saw his institute as a "laboratory where marriage problems were classified, studied, and solved." He is credited with first using the term "marriage counseling" and went on to write a popular monthly series entitled "Can this Marriage be Saved?" for the *Ladies Home Journal*, and to provide material for the TV program *Divorce Court* (Gladding, 1998: 68). Within a few years Popenoe claimed to have helped over five thousand people with marital problems, with none experiencing a divorce (Moskowitz, 2001: 79). Popenoe's institute also served as the site for Lewis Terman's (1938) study *Psychological Factor in Marital Happiness*, which became the first large-scale psychological study of marital happiness.

Emily Mudd's Marriage Counsel in Philadelphia soon followed Poponoe's Institute of Family Relations in 1932. Like Poponoe's institute, Mudd's Marriage Counsel sought to aid in establishing what she referred to as "marital hygiene." Its success led to the establishment of thirty-two family consultations centers throughout the United States by the mid-1930s (Foster, 1937: 764). All of these centers sought to "disseminate information designed to further adjustments in marriage and family relationships" (Foster, 1937: 764). In 1939 interest in family matters prompted the formation of the National Council on Family Relations. The council united the various factions interested in promoting family life and began disseminating their ideas in a journal entitled *Living* (later changed to the *Journal of Marriage and the Family*) (Nichols, 1992: 2). The council also began to publish articles on a host of family issues, including the importance of counseling for maintaining a stable marriage and successful family life. Such publicity provided the impetus for the formation of the American Association of Marriage Counselors (AAMC) in 1942 (Gladding, 1998: 69).

While the origins of marriage and family therapy can be traced to developments in the 1930s and 1940s, it took several decades to build it into a legitimate subfield within clinical psychology and psychiatry. Also, it was not until the 1960s and 1970s that family counseling "caught on" with the public and practitioners began to develop lists of faithful clients (Wierzbicki, 1999: 319). During the 1960s and 1970s particular schools of thought emerged, with different strategies for treating marital and family problems. Approaches such as those of the Milan group, the Mental Research Institute (MRI), strategic therapy and structuralism began to dominate the way counseling with couples and families was to occur (see Maranhao, 1986: 82).

In a movement away from the more individualistic focus of Freudian psychology, family and marriage psychology, specifically the MRI group, began to regard family and marital problems in terms of communicative acts that were "meaningful only within the communicative matrix in which they arose as responses to other acts" (Maranhao, 1986: 51). As with relationships between workers in corporations, relations within the family were seen as being based on the utilization of effective "communication styles." Effective styles were defined as those capable of conjuring up underlying emotional states and making alterations of the individual and his or her "family system" possible. In contrast, ineffective communication styles were seen as those that leave emotional states unexpressed and the individual and family system incapable of modification. These "dysfunctional communications" (Satir, 1967) eventually eroded family life, dissolved marriages and created emotional problems in children. For example, Tomm (in Gladding, 1998: 50) distinguishes between family patterns that exhibit "pathologizing interpersonal patterns," such as the failure to talk or communicate effectively, and "wellness interpersonal patterns," where communications between family members are open and honest. "Optimal family communications situations . . . include seeking and sharing patterns," involve the free exchange of feelings over a wide variety of topics, particularly frustrations, and include open discussions of family roles, expectations and obligations (Brock and Barnard, 1992: 25).

In this conception of the family, communications styles led to either a "healthy family" or a dysfunctional and distressed one (see Textor, 1989). As Gladding (1998: 35) put it, "When families are healthy, members attend to the messages from one another and pick up on subtle as well as obvious points. Within these families there is support, understanding, and empathy." In contrast, "distressed families exhibit a greater frequency of aversive communications and blaming statements than nondistressed families" (Melidonis and Bry, 1995: 451). The healthy family allows for individuation, mutuality, flexibility, stability, role reciprocity and clear perceptions of others' roles within the "family system" (Barnhill, 1979). It is also characterized by "a legitimate source of authority, a stable rule system, nurturing behavior, effective childrearing and marriage-maintenance practices, the establishment of individual and family goals and adaptability" (Becvar and Becvar, 1982: 74).

The role of the therapist in this process of "family healing" is "to help the family become family centered rather than individual centered" (Grunwald and McAbee, 1998: 91). In this process the family therapist must, in the words of Salvador Minuchin (1974: 111), a leading family therapist, "intervene so as to unbalance the system" in order to "enhance the operation of the family system" (Minuchin, 1974: 111). To accomplish this, therapists should become "coaches," who become involved in the family's communication matrix "in order to steer their negotiations from within" (Maranhao, 1986: 53). According to Minuchin, therapists are to help the family by joining "the family in a position of leadership," by unearthing and evaluating "the underlying family structure" and by creating "circumstances that will allow the transformation of the structure" (Minuchin, 1974: 111). In this endeavor therapists often employ a technique commonly referred to as "active listening." This approach, most often used in marriage counseling, encourages one partner to verbalize his or her feelings using "nonblaming I statements," while the other partner listens and repeats back their statements using the phrase "what I hear you saying." The goal of active listening is to create better communications between couples by focusing attention on the importance of the communicative process and by promoting an understanding of each other's point of view.

In order to assess the functionality of a family's or couple's "communication matrix," the therapist often uses a series of marital and family scales, such as Family Adaptability and Cohesion Evaluation, Marital Instability Scale, Waring Intimacy Questionnaire or the McMaster Family Assessment Device (see Fredman and Sherman, 1987). One such measure, Millard Bienvenu's "Marital Communication Inventory," was developed with the assumption that "if a married couple are to live together in harmony[,] . . . they must establish honest, uninhibited and workable systems of communication" (Bienvenue in Fredman and Sherman, 1987: 103). To assess a couple's success in accomplishing such a "workable system," respondents are asked to respond to a series of questions about their marriage and communication patterns. Another test, the Abbreviated Barrett-Lennard Relationship Inventory (Schumm, Bollman and Jurich, 1981), measures a couple's level of communication through responses to a series of Likert statements, such as "My husband (wife) realizes what I mean even when I have difficulty saying it," and "My husband (wife) usually understands the whole meaning of what I say to him (her)." Other scales, such as the "Caring Relationship Inventory" (Shostrom, 1975), contain an eighty-three-item inventory to measure such marital traits as "friendship," "empathy," "eros" and "deficiency love."

The psychological approach to "family healing" can also be found in the establishment of a number of professional and lay marriage and family counseling programs developed over the past four decades. Programs like the Association of Couples for Marriage Enrichment, Marriage Encounters and Conjugal Relationship Enhancement all seek to improve the communication patterns that are seen as at the heart of all marital conflict. One of the more famous programs, the Minnesota Couples Communication Program (MCCP) (now simply the Couples Communication Program), "stresses disclosure, receptivity, and the teaching of skills" that enable "more efficient ways to communicate" (L'Abate, 1981: 634–635). Based on strategies detailed in the 1975 book *Alive and Aware: Improving Communication in Relationships* (Miller, Nunnally, and Wackman, 1975), couples in the MCCP counseling sessions are first taught the definition of the "awareness wheel" that involves "acting, sensing, thinking, wanting, and feeling" (L'Abate, 1981: 635). Afterward, a number of skills sessions are used to teach people "how to exchange important communication accurately with one partner through a shared meaning framework, which consists of checking out, stating intention and asking for acknowledgment, acknowledging the sender's message, confirming and clarifying" (L'Abate, 1981: 635). Other programs, such as Communication Training, ask couples to record and code their everyday conversations to identify problems in listening and communicating (Gottman, Markman, Notarius and Gonso, 1976).

Another recent program, based in part on the best-selling book *The Seven Principles for Making Marriage Work*, written by John Gottman and Nan Silver (1999), uses extensive research from the Gottman Institute in Seattle to provide "scientific evidence" as to what makes a successful marriage. Gottman claims that his approach of videotaping couples interacting allows him to predict with 85 percent accuracy the viability of a marriage for the next six years (Nussbaum, 2000: 25). For Gottman, the way couples fight is a strong indicator of the future success of the marriage. Marriages in which criticism, defensiveness, stonewalling and contempt are common are the most likely to fail (Nussbaum, 2000: 27). He believes that soon his method of identifying the traits of successful marriages will become so commonplace that it will become "like brushing your teeth or flossing"— they will simply become common sense about how couples can maintain their marriages (Gottman in Nussbaum, 2000: 32).

Other recent programs, such as the Ohio-based Family Wellness Project, seek to extend the focus on marital communications to the entire family. One of the project's parameters involves what advocates call the "Family Wellness Checkup." Two of the central architects of the program, Talen and Warfield (1997: 315), describe the checkups as "regular oil changes and tune-ups" for the family. They argue that in families, as with cars, "costly engine repairs can be avoided if fluids are regularly monitored and changed. Likewise, regularly attending to our children's growth and development can enhance their self-esteem and social relationships while helping to avoid future problems (e.g., aggressive behaviors, low self-esteem, abuse)" (Talen and Warfield, 1997: 315). In addition to the administration of the Early Screening Profile (ESP) and the Child Behavior Checklist (CBCL), families are assessed using the Marschak Interaction Method (MIM). In the MIM, an adult and child are videotaped playing with two stuffed animals, putting lotion on each other's hands, building a structure with five blocks and feeding each other. The interactions between parent and child are observed to "support and reinforce positive parenting," provide "information about how to understand their child's needs and normal child behaviors" and to make "suggestions for enhancing their parenting skills" (Talen and Warfield, 1997: 316). After the assessment parents may opt for a follow-up session that uses "thera-play" to identify further family problems.

Of the various versions of marriage and family therapies in use, one of the most influential is based on *Men Are from Mars, Women Are from Venus*, by John Gray (1992), the self-proclaimed "best-selling relationships author of all time" (www.marsvenus.com), and a series of follow-up publications such as *Mars and Venus on a Date*, *Mars and Venus in the Bedroom*, *Mars and Venus in Love* and *Mars and Venus Together Forever*. With sales of over seven million copies, *Men Are from Mars, Women Are from Venus* has also spawned videos, TV programs, a Web site, a weekly newspaper column, counseling centers, workshops, seminars, audiotapes, a Mattel board game and recently a weekday TV talk show. Like many other marriage and family counselors, Gray (1992: 59) begins with the assumption that the secret of a successful relationship is "good communication." To encourage effective communication, partners need to know the various "worlds" (i.e., Venus and Mars) that make men and women who they are. Gray (1992: 36) argues that a woman "instinctively feels a need to talk about her feelings and all the possible problems that are associated with her feelings," while a man will retreat into "his cave" in order to think through problems. For Gray the path to overcoming such opposition is to engage in an open and honest dialogue. Couples are encouraged to write letters to each other, make their communication more direct and take time to listen in order to fix and maintain their relationships.

Another recent and highly influential program in the area of family therapy is based on the writings, videos, counseling centers and lecture series of John Bradshaw. Bradshaw, whose background includes "graduate work in psychology and religion" and experience as a counselor, theologian, management consultant and public speaker (www.creativegrowth.com/johres.htm), maintains that 96 percent of families are in some manner "emotionally impaired" (Bradshaw, 1988). This emotional impairment results from the shame and guilt introduced by "adult children raising children who will become adult children" (Bradshaw, 1988: 4). Bradshaw (1988: 31) maintains "family systems fail, not because of bad people, but because of bad information loops, bad feedback in the form of bad rules of behavior." Correcting this pattern and recovering from the "codependency" that it spawns compels one to experience the pain of his or her abandoned "inner child" (Bradshaw, 1988: 214).

Borrowing from Maslow's "hierarchy of needs," Bradshaw argues that the recovery of this inner child requires a three-stage process. First, the individual must "recover their disabled will," by handling his or her "self-indulging habits and addictions" (Bradshaw, 1988: 194). In this stage the individual is required to overcome the addictions initiated by their involvement in a dysfunctional family. Second, the individual must uncover his or her lost self, by "going back and uncovering the original pain that occurred as a result of our being abandoned" and "disenchanting" his or her childhood (Bradshaw, 1988: 210). Finally, the individual must discover his or her true self. This occurs as the individual undergoes a "spiritual awakening" by transcending the childlike ego that has been created by a dysfunctional family life.

The psychological code of marriage and family civility emergent in these eclectic therapeutic programs entails a particular way of organizing, accessing and responding to the types of verbal and nonverbal interactions that partners in a relationship or family members are expected to have with one another, as well as the types of emotions possessed by each individual. As with interactions in corporations, these strategies both rely on and construct particular notions of self-hood, appropriate emotional expression and correct and normal marital and family dynamics.[5] At the heart of this code of civility is a search for what Anthony Giddens (1991) has referred to as the "pure relationship." Such relationships place supreme importance on mutual self-disclosure, confession and appreciating the other's unique psychological composition (see Jamieson, 1999). Such pure relationships operate under the assumption that interpersonal marital and family conflicts and disagreements are in essence breakdowns in proper interpersonal communications. In this instance, disagreements can be corrected if family members can only find ways to open up their emotional worlds to the "communicative other." In this sense, "trust can be mobilised only by a process of mutual disclosure" (Giddens, 1991: 6).

Embedded in the psychological civility found in marriage and family counseling is an "injunction to participate in confessional discourse" (White, 1992: 11). Lack of participation or the unwillingness to participate is often viewed as a repression of the ability to express one's true inner feelings, or as "ineffective communication," and is itself viewed as a dysfunction that needs special therapeutic intervention. The reluctant participant is viewed as a threatening figure, who, in the words of one therapist, "may exhibit resistance, disrupt therapy sessions[,] . . . belittle the process, and lower other family members' motivation to participate in therapy" (Wierzbicki, 1999: 324). However, as Foucault (1980: 61–62) pointed out, confession is never an innocent act of voluntary disclosure but "unfolds within a power relationship, for one does not confess without the presence (or virtual presence) of a partner who is not simply the interlocutor but the authority who requires the confession, prescribes and appreciates it, and intervenes in order to judge, punish, forgive, console, and reconcile." Communicative and interactional deviance, whether in corporate or everyday life, becomes an opportunity to confess and correct the individual problems and dysfunctions seen to lie behind conflict and the breakdown of personal relationships. Confessing one's desires and needs, consequently, would become a means to render analyzable a deep truth about the individual's essential makeup.

CONCLUSION: PSYCHOLOGICAL CODES AND THE CONDUCT OF CONDUCT

The codes of civility introduced by psychology and allied professions into work and family life are powerful and pervasive. In particular psychologically inspired ways, these codes persuade employees to be expressive and cooperative, even if they have good reason not to be; marriage partners to communicate effectively even when perhaps they shouldn't; and families to engage in "quality time" even when there is something good on TV. In these situations a worker may be disciplined or ostracized for failing to participate in a "workplace sensitivity seminar," or a marriage may end because a partner is "unable to communicate." In short, these codes provide a language and style of interaction that compel us to be psychological in order to be accepted or be considered normal. Failing to be psychological in these instances is both an indication of emotional repression and incivility to others.

The codes of civility introduced by psychological knowledge have completely reshaped what Foucault (1988) referred to as the "conduct of conduct." By creating situations where others are to be observed, personal lives are to be delved into, and feelings are always to be communicated (see Tucker, 1999: 125), psychological codes of civility obligate one to perform in a manner psychologically appropriate to others. In doing so, they create a particular kind of modern ethical being, one who thinks and acts toward his or herself and others using the conceptual and practical frameworks provided by the knowledge and practices of psychology (see Rose, 1996b: 118). This new modern ethical being is, paradoxically, "obliged to be free" (Rose, 1990: 126). He or she is required, even mandated, to search for "inner resources," render up emotions and continuously make life decisions that are "emotionally healthy" (see chapter 8). In these inner resources are said to reside the means for freeing the psyche from the obstacles that hinder free expression and authentic living.

The prevalence of these codes of civility has ushered in what might best be described as "institutionalized psychological scripts," or "feeling rules." These scripts and rules provide a standard vocabulary, types and modes of expression and patterns of interaction that can be used to negotiate life at work or sustain relationships at home.[6] These scripts pay homage to the underlying emotional state of the person by elaborately attending to his or her "feelings" and inherent "emotional needs." The institutionalization of these psychological scripts allows for the "performances of modern psychological identities" (see Pfister, 1997b: 169). These performances enable people to see themselves and others as "psychological" and to "be psychological" in a number of settings. In other words, people are not necessarily "psychological" until they are persuaded or made to be so. Deep interiors, conflicting emotions, mental tendencies, psychic needs and other psychological characteristics only occur under very specific historical circumstances and in certain linguistic and organizational conditions and networks.

The psychological scripts created by the incorporation of psychological codes of civility require continuous "interaction rituals" or performances in order to be enacted and sustained. These scripts must be performed and reacted to for others, who are themselves seen as imbued with complex and deep interiors that also require great "ritual care" (see Goffman, 1967). Within the context of these codes, offending someone is no longer a matter of infringing on status hierarchies or betraying the moral boundaries between ingroup and outgroup, as in the historical instances described by Elias in the beginning of this chapter, but involves failure to provide the psychological attention necessary for others to sustain their own inherent emotionality. As Goffman (1967: 95) put it, "Many gods have been done away with, but the individual stubbornly remains as a deity of considerable importance." The contemporary psychological self requires a great deal of nurturing, or "little offerings," to sustain itself. The psychological codes of civility and scripts developed over the last century ensure that this nurturing will take place, by incorporating and institutionalizing psychological thinking and practices into a variety of everyday organizational and discursive activities. These codes have created—if not, in the words of one critic, a "compulsory niceness" (Snider, 1999: A64)—a situation where the proper manifestation of individual feelings and interpersonal communications increasingly become the new mandates and expectations of daily interactions.

The use of feeling rules or institutional psychological scripts has helped introduce what Alasdair MacIntyre (1981) has called an "emotivist ethic" into the decision making and judgments of everyday life. This ethic contends that "all moral judgments are nothing but expression of preference, expression of attitude or feeling" (MacIntyre, 1981: 11). Actions are to be evaluated not through rational method, for none is said to exist, or consensus, since none is possible, but on the basis of how they affect the "emotions or attitudes of those who disagree with one" (MacIntyre, 1981: 12). In such a moral environment the primary focus of concern is on the "emotional harm" done to individuals. In this situation the only personal or societal solutions to conflict available are therapeutically derived ones. Since there are thought to be no absolute moral foundations to legitimate actions, when decisions need to be made the decision maker must take care to guard the feelings of those who will be influenced. In this case a bifurcation is forged between the positions of the experts, such as managers and therapists, who view themselves as capable of rational, disinterested assessment, and the analyzed, who possess only subjective and relative emotions and feeling that need expression and resolution.

As these psychological scripts have grown in importance as fixtures of work and family life over the course of the last hundred years, they have fundamentally reshaped the way organizations and individuals think and act. The language of psychology has become that of organizational and family life. Today discourse at work is often indistinguishable from that of family therapy or on many TV talk shows. All harness a particular psychologically derived vocabulary to divulge and interpret actions and codes of conduct to assess and regulate behavior. Furthermore, these scripts provide standard vocabularies and procedures through which individuals, corporations and political operatives may "handle" or channel problems and challenges to their authority. Failure to invoke these scripts at work or at home is not only rude but, more importantly, violates the now sacred assumption that an emotional injury has occurred and the situation is in need of a psychological resolution.

NOTES

1. A German edition, *Psychologie und Wirtschaftsleben: Ein Beitrag zur angewandten Experimental-Psychologie*, had appeared a year earlier. Work had been conducted in psychology on advertising and selling prior to the publication of Muensterberg's book.

2. For instance, between 1968 and 1970 the U.S. Department of Labor spent almost $1.44 million "to teach sensitivity to its supervisors" (Dineen, 1996: 121).

3. Unions have generally considered such therapeutic approaches used by management as simply new strategies of worker control. Unions like the United Auto Workers argued that industrial psychologists were there to talk employees out of grievances (see Baritz, 1960: 165). However, this suspicion has not stopped unions from hiring their own behavioral specialists over the last forty years.

4. By the early 1990s there were some three thousand industrial/organizational psychologists in the United States, compared with around seventy-nine in 1943 (Katzell and Austin, 1992: 819). Of these some six hundred were in private and public organizations, over five hundred worked as full-time consultants and the remainder were in academia (Katzell and Austin, 1992: 822).

5. Several commentators have pointed out that the psychological imperative to create communicatively open and healthy marriages falls disproportionately upon women (see Benjamin, 1998).

6. The political and legal institutionalization of psychological codes of civility,

like their establishment in work and family relations, has been the outcome of a long, concentrated effort to introduce the field of psychology in law and politics. As early as 1908, the great "psychologist of all things," Hugo Muensterberg (1908: 194), had wondered why the "work of justice is carried out in the courts without every consulting the psychologist and asking him for all the aid which the modern study of suggestion can offer." Muensterberg (in Hale, 1980: 118) insisted that "to deny that the experimental psychologist has indeed possibilities of determining the 'truth-telling' process is just as absurd as to deny that the chemical expert can find out whether there is arsenic in a stomach or whether blood spots are human or animal origin." For Muensterberg everything from "police investigations to jury instructions required the assistance of a psychologist" (Wrightsman, 1999: 132). In 1979 the APA established the Office of General Counsel and the Committee on Legal Issues to establish a firm connection between psychology and the courts. One of the functions of these organizations is to determine whether psychological data can support positions in court cases. In such instances the groups prepare amicus curiae briefs for submission to the Supreme Court (Wrightsman, 1999: 154).

8

The Psychologically Examined Life: Issues, Healing, Closure and the Psychotherapeutic Self

ONE OF THE FIRST ACTS OF A COLONIZING FORCE WAS TO attempt to change the language of the people it colonized. Although those colonized often resorted to a Creole or patois to subvert this political and linguistic intrusion, the conquering force's language, nevertheless, often became the official language of the state, in which all "official business" and affairs of the state were to be conducted. Embedded in this colonizing act was not only the recognition that an official language shaped political identification but also the notion that changing the official language of a group dramatically altered the way people conducted their lives. In short, changing a language served to convert and resituate a group's practices and ways of thinking. As with religious conversation, in which it is not enough simply to change the sign on the church, new lexicons, modes of reasoning and interactional orders were institutionalized in order to realign collective action, redirect intersubjective meaning and shift political identification.

The psychological colonization of everyday life, however, has proceeded in a somewhat different manner.[1] Over the course of the last century, the modern vocabulary of mind and self has become filled with a host of psychologically derived concepts and classifications that did not exist in previous centuries. Terms such as "developmentally delayed," "positive reinforcement," "psychopath," "learning disabled," "paranoid," "encounter group," "phobia," "anal fixation," "codependency," and "enabler," to name but a few, have drifted from the confines of professional psychology and other "psy-fields" into the vocabulary of everyday life. Descriptions of these classifications fill the pages of psychology textbooks, self-help guides, parenting books and diagnostic manuals, as well as the banter of cocktail parties. Indeed, as we saw in the last chapter, many of these concepts and classifications have become so interwoven into everyday modes of interpretation and explanation that it is difficult to imagine thinking or acting without them. They have taken on a naturalness that is impossible or difficult to dislodge or "outthink" (see Soyland, 1994). We utilize them to explain everything from why we are unmotivated at our job to why a relationship failed, to why we did not receive a promotion. In this sense, psychology has perhaps not so much "colonized a pre-existing territory" as it has managed to "spread a particular way of understanding, judging and intervening over a wide surface of practices and issues" (Rose, 1996b: 58).

Evidence of the "psychological colonization" of everyday life can be found in national trend studies conducted over the last few decades. In a 1981 report, Veroff, Douvan and Kulka (1981) found a marked trend away from moral or material terminology toward psychological language in the period from the 1950s through the 1970s. Likewise, Yankelovich (1981) found indications of a move from a religiously based "giving/getting covenant" toward an increased preoccupation with psychological fulfillment during the 1970s and 1980s. These trends reveal a general "rewriting of the soul" (Hacking, 1995) throughout American culture. In this rewriting, folk and religious languages of the soul and its interiors have been replaced—or perhaps more accurately, reconfigured—into a psychological vocabulary of the self, at least within large segments of the population. This reconfiguration has been made possible by the introduction of a host of psychological therapies over the last century, ranging from the classic Freudian psychotherapy to Carl Rogers's client-centered therapy, to more recent approaches like eye movement desensitization and reprocessing (EMDR), all designed to construct or restore a stable, coherent and emotionally healthy self (see Giddens, 1991).

In the last chapter I argued that people are not psychological until they are made to be so. In other words, being psychological is something that happens only in specific places, under particular circumstances and in certain networks. Just as the psychological codes of civility discussed in the prior chapter created a realignment of the way relationships with others are enacted at home or work, psychological knowledge has created a number of new languages and technologies of the self.[2] This chapter expands on this point by examining how psychology, specifically its clinical and counseling branches, came to be the primary "spokesperson" of the mind and self and of some of the experiential and linguistic reconfigurations inspired by its rise to prominence. The first part of the chapter explores how clinical and counseling psychology arose to its current status in a space created by the complex political and cultural interplay between medicine and various "mind cure" movements in the late nineteenth and early twentieth centuries. This section traces the development of clinical and counseling psychology from an initial rejection of spiritualism and mind cures to their secularized return in the humanistic psychology associated with Abraham Maslow, Carl Rogers and counterculture therapeutical groups like Esalen. The next two sections briefly examine two seemingly unrelated areas where psychological concepts and language have recently made tremendous inroads—politics and death. The section on politics explores the alliance between the state and psychology that emerged in the wake of World War II and the resulting increase in the use of mandatory counseling to solve social and political problems. The next section traces the recent movement of psychological expertise into one of the last vestiges of religious authority—what has come to be known as grief, disaster or "mass trauma" counseling. I conclude the chapter with a discussion of how the movement of psychological knowledge into these and other areas has contributed to a particular subjectivizing of experience.

MIND CURES, PSYCHOANALYSIS AND THE BIRTH OF CLINICAL PSYCHOLOGY

In the United States, psychology's role in reformulating the self can be traced to a struggle among the established field of medicine, proponents of the new psychology and advocates of various mind-cure therapies that occurred in the late nineteenth and early twentieth centuries. During this time a number of groups to which William James (1961: 89) generally referred to as the "mind cure movement" began offering Americans advice on fixing their ailing bodies and spirits. Many of these groups, like the emerging discipline of psychology itself, were centered in Boston and became euphemistically referred to as the "Boston craze" (Dresser, 1919: 132). Borrowing from such earlier movements as Transcendentalism, Spiritualism and Mesmerism, these newer therapeutic movements responded to what was thought to be a spiritual and mental crisis that was sweeping an increasingly neurasthenic United States (see Beard, 1881). Although greatly varied in their approaches, most of these groups were united by the belief that physical aliments secretly masked deep-seated spiritual and psychic problems wrought by industrialization and modernization.

One of the first and most popular of these movements was the mind cure, developed in the 1860s by Phineas Quimby, a Portland, Maine clockmaker turned physician. An advocate of a "spiritual or true science," Quimby rejected previous mental therapies, particularly the French transplanted Mesmerism, as too unscientific to be trusted. He contended that "physical diseases are physical effects proceeding from mental states of unrest and discord" (Coleville, 1895: 76). Accordingly, Quimby sought to heal the body by employing a type of "mental therapy" to alter people's thinking. Quimby or a surrogate would first sit with a patient, in order to develop rapport. He would then enter a trancelike state in which he could view the "mental atmospheres" surrounding a patient (E. Taylor, 1999: 112). Once these atmospheres had been located, Quimby used a technique he referred to as "mental daguerreotyping" to infuse them with "mental healing fluids" (E. Taylor, 1999: 112). By the end of his career Quimby claimed to have treated over twelve thousand people using his mind-cure techniques. Included among his patients was Mary Baker Eddy, soon to be the founder of Christian Science, who proclaimed that Quimby "speaks as never man spoke and heals as never man healed since Christ" (in Caplan, 1998a: 73). She began a correspondence with Quimby that lasted until his death in 1866.

By the late 1880s, another important group, known as "New Thought," began to appear on the American cultural scene. Its underlying principle was that "thoughts are things"; if positive and properly directed, they could maintain or restore an individual's physical health and well-being. Like the mind-cure advocates and Christian Scientists, advocates of New Thought sought to "spread a knowledge of the fundamental principles that underlies healthy and harmonious living" (Dresser, 1919: 244). Promoters of New Thought, such as Henry Wood (1893: 55), accused religion, science and metaphysics of damaging "millions of sensitive and responsive souls." Medicine's exclusively somatic focus left many ailments untreated, while the eschatological determinism of traditional religions failed to grasp people's ability actively to change their situations. New Thought's manifesto declared that its purpose was "to teach the infinitude of the Supreme One; the Divinity of Man and his Infinite possibilities through the creative power of constructive thinking and obedience to the voice of the Indwelling Presence, which is a source of Inspiration, Power, Health and Prosperity" (in Griswold, 1934: 310). By the late 1880s, the New Thought movement had thousands of members and had established discussion clubs throughout the United States (Moskowitz, 1995: 65).

Another popular movement, formed at the Emmanuel Episcopal Church in Boston in 1906, also sought to connect the somatic and psychical. Unlike other therapies, however, the Emmanuel Movement sought to join the rigorous scientific principles of an emerging therapeutic psychology with religious values. Proponents argued that they were essentially saving both medicine and religion from groups like Christian Science and New Thought, which were sweeping the nation and threatening to undermine an emerging scientifically based psychotherapy (Cunningham, 1962: 50). Also unlike other approaches, the Emmanuel Movement was headed by two well-respected Boston ministers, Elwood Worcester and Samuel McComb, and was supported by a number of eminent Boston physicians. Worcester, the primary founder, had, prior to his theological training, obtained a Ph.D. in philosophy and psychology at Leipzig, where he studied with Wilhelm Wundt (Caplan, 1998b: 293). Worcester (in Caplan, 1998a: 306) claimed to have "learned from psychology the advantage of a scientific method in dealing with myself and with other men."

Worcester and McComb sought to use scientific principles in combination with religion-based therapy to unleash the power of the subconscious mind to heal physical ailments. In 1905, in a joint project with the physician Joseph Pratt at Massachusetts General Hospital, Worcester provided tuberculosis patients with "the approved modern method of combating consumption, plus discipline, friendship, encouragement and hope" (Worcester, McComb and Coriat, 1908: 1). The project proved so popular that Worcester began to institute an official counseling program, housed at the Emmanuel Church. In its first form the Emmanuel Movement set up a clinic, where doctors examined patients and Worcester and his associates held weekly health classes and offered private psychotherapy sessions. He soon began lecturing on this successful union of medicine and religion at churches and clubs throughout the country. By 1908 the movement had spread to many other large cities throughout the country and overseas. It had also attracted wide public attention through a series of articles written by Worcester for *Good Housekeeping* and *Ladies' Home Journal*. Also, it was bolstered by the publication of the group's manifesto, *Religion and Medicine: The Moral Control of Nervous Disorders* (Worcester, McComb and Coriat, 1908), cowritten with Isador Coriat, a leading neurologist. Within a few years *Religion and Medicine* became a best-seller, selling almost two hundred thousand copies (Caplan, 1998b: 297).

The emphasis of various therapeutic movements on the power of the mind to overcome bodily afflictions caught the attention of Williams James in the early 1880s.[3] In order to investigate the legitimacy of these movements, James, along with fellow psychologists and philosophers James Mark Baldwin, G. Stanley Hall, Joseph Jastrow, Christine Ladd-Franklin, George Fullerton and a number of other academics and professionals, formed the American Society for Psychical Research (ASPR) in 1885 (Coon, 1992: 144). Modeled after the British Society for Psychical Research, the American society set up specific committees to perform demonstrations and experiments to test the efficacy of such techniques as hypnotism, crystal gazing, clairvoyance, thought transference and automatic writing. Unlike many academics and physicians who rejected such mind cures outright, James (1960a: 59) contended that science should not "leave a great mass of human experience to take its chances between vague tradition and credulity on the one hand and dogmatic denial at long range on the other." It was up to psychical researchers "to study the matter with both patience and rigor" (James, 1960a: 59). After performing numerous experiments on the legitimacy of various techniques, James (1960b: 312) came to the conclusion that what such therapies revealed was not simply "human gullibility" but possibly a "genuine realm of natural phenomena." For James this new realm revealed the existence of an "extraconsciousness" as real and effective as that of the "upper consciousness" (James, 1960c: 34). It also revealed that some of the techniques, specifically light hypnosis, were effective ways to access and analyze this extraconsciousness.

One of the most important outcomes of the ASPR's committee work on hypnotism was the formation of what came to be referred to as the Boston School of Psychopathology. The school, consisting of James, G. Stanley Hall and a group of Boston-based neurologists, psychologists and psychiatrists, began to meet at the house of Morton Prince, a Tufts University professor of medicine and physician for nervous and mental diseases at the Boston City Hospital (Taylor,

1999: 165), to discuss patients and the possibilities offered by various mental-healing techniques (Caplan, 1998a: 98). The group began to explore ways to use hypnotism, suggestion and other mind therapies to treat mental conditions where no underlying organic cause was apparent. Of these techniques, Prince found the power of suggestion to be the most helpful to his patients. Often a cure could be achieved once a patient came to realize "how often unrelated mental and physical phenomena will resolve itself into a series of logical events, and law and order found to underlie the symptomatic tangle" (Prince, 1929: 335). Prince soon went on to found the *Journal of Abnormal Psychology*, in which to report the findings of this new approach to psychopathology (Burnham, 1967: 6).

The popularity of the various therapeutic groups, particularly the Emmanuel Movement, prompted an increased awareness of psychotherapy by many middle and upper-class Americans. Many came to accept the so-called psychogenic hypothesis that the mind was the harbinger of a subconscious that affected physical well-being. They also slowly came to see doctors and other professionals as people who could help with what were becoming known as "mental problems" and "mental adjustments." In retrospect, the Emmanuel Movement in particular served as a middle point in the secularization of therapy in the United States. It took the Emmanuel Movement, in words of the great popularizer of psychology H. Addington Bruce (1909: 32), "to galvanize them [physicians] into belated action." In a way reminiscent of the American Medical Association's recent reaction to the rapid growth of alternative medicine, the Emmanuel Movement shook medicine out of its exclusively somatic focus and forced physicians to move into the area of mental health. It also signaled to some within the young field of psychology that psychopathology and therapy should become areas of focus for the new discipline.

The work of the "mind-cure" movement and the like, as well as the Emmanuel project, prefaced the arrival of Sigmund Freud and Karl Jung at Clark University in September 1909. Indeed, without them the rapid popular acceptance of Freud in the United States would not have been possible (Caplan, 1998a). Immediately after Freud's appearance at Clark, a group of supporters fanned out through the country to spread the word of Freudian psychoanalysis to physicians and popular audiences (see Burnham, 1967: 134–137). One supporter, Ernest Jones, attended as many meetings of medical societies as possible to spread the word. Due in part to their efforts during the 1910s, Freudian psychoanalysis began to erode support for other mind therapies, particularly in the middle and upper classes. Writings about Freud and psychoanalysis began to replace those by generic mind-cure advocates in popular magazines and newspapers (Hale, 1971). Articles about Freud in publications such as *Ladies' Home Journal* and *Good Housekeeping* helped establish him as a household figure by 1917. By the 1920s, writings of mind cure advocates had almost completely disappeared from the public discourse on psychotherapy and mental health. Suddenly Freudianism was everywhere, and people, particularly in the upper classes and avante garde circles, were becoming Freudian. Describing the impact of psychoanalysis on the bohemian culture of the 1920s, Joseph Freeman (1936: 158), editor of *The New Masses*, wrote, "We began to have alarming dreams. . . . We talked all day long; we analyzed each other's dreams and became conscious of them. New fears developed. . . . We suffered from various 'complexes.' We concluded in turn that we were extroverts, introverts, Schizophrenics, paranoiacs and victims of *dementia praecox*."

Initially many psychologists dismissed Freud's theories as being "as relevant to their work as Mrs. Eddy's epistles" (Hornstein, 1992: 255). For these critics, particularly experimentalists like Edward Scripture at Yale and E.B. Titchener at Cornell, Freud's psychoanalysis represented a Europeanized version of the therapies they were fighting so hard to discredit or redirect. The experimental psychologist Christine Ladd-Franklin (1916: 374) warned that unless Freudian psychoanalysis could be stopped, "the prognosis for civilization is unfavorable." Other psychologists, however, openly embraced it, arguing that embedded in psychoanalysis was the weapon psychologists needed finally to redirect the public fascination with therapies like mind cure. Although highly critical of "attempts [by psychoanalysis] to strangle [science] from the inside," Knight Dunlap (1920: 8–9) contended that just as Christian Science and the various mind cures had forced medicine to change its exclusively somatic focus, psychoanalysis, "by compelling psychology to put its house in order, will eventually help in the development of the Scientific Psychology it aims to thrust aside." For proponents, psychoanalysis contained both a language and theoretical perspective for converting large sections of the population away from the earlier movements and toward a scientifically based psychotherapy. However, a political clash with psychiatry would soon make such enthusiasm for Freudian psychotherapy within psychology short-lived.

Interest within the new field of psychology for offering a

scientifically based therapy had been quietly gathering since James's efforts in the ASPR to investigate various mind cures scientifically, and the formation of the Boston School of Psychotherapy. However, many experimentalists thought that such a connection with psychotherapy would soil psychology's already fragile scientific reputation. Some argued that psychology needed first to supply general laws of the "normal mind" before it could begin to study and treat abnormality (see Lutz, 1991: 67). The situation began to change in the period between 1906 and 1909. During this time the *Journal of Abnormal Psychology* and *Psychological Clinic* were founded, and Hugo Muensterberg published his work *Psychotherapy*—in 1909, the same year as the arrival of Freud and Jung at Clark. In the preface to *Psychotherapy*, Muensterberg argued that the Emmanuel Movement and Christian Science should be viewed as "symptoms of transition" toward more scientific therapeutics (Muensterberg, 1909: x). He warned physicians that "scientific medicine should take hold of psychotherapeutics now or a most deplorable disorganization will set in, the symptoms of which no one ought to overlook to-day" (Muensterberg, 1909: x). Practicing this new psychotherapeutics required that physicians be trained in psychology. The time had come, Muensterberg (1909: ix) argued, "when every physician should systematically study psychology, the normal in the college years and abnormal in medical school." He warned physicians that "the only safe basis of psychotherapy is a thorough psychological knowledge of the human personality" (Muensterberg, 1909: 9).

After the publication of *Psychotherapy*, a concentrated effort began to make therapy an integral part of the rapidly expanding applied efforts of psychologists. By 1917 the therapeutic wing of psychology had grown strong enough to establish its own organization. That year a group of psychologists, borrowing the word "clinical" from Lightner Witmer's clinic in Philadelphia and the journal he founded, announced at the APA's annual meeting in Pittsburgh the formation of the American Association of Clinical Psychologists (AACP) (Blocher, 2000: 82). At its inception the group was worried about statements being made by the New York Psychiatrical Society limiting the role of clinical psychologists in psychotherapy, and about the virtual exclusion of psychologists from the recently established ninety-member National Committee of Mental Hygiene (Franz, 1917: 229). The clinicians finally joined the APA a few years later, when the APA agreed to pursue certification for clinicians.[4] By this time, however, psychoanalysis and psychopathology had become firmly incorporated into the field of medicine. Physicians had convinced many state legislatures that psychologists and other mental health professionals lacked the training and expertise to diagnose and treat mental disorders properly or to use Freudian psychoanalytical techniques.

The early relationship of clinical and counseling psychology with Freudian psychoanalysis proved to be both beneficial and harmful to the fledgling subfield of psychology. On the one hand, the advent of psychoanalysis had freed up a vast new clientele for psychological information and services by helping undermine public support for the various mind cures. It had also provided an expansive new vocabulary and technique for practicing a radically new and innovative form of psychology. On the other hand, psychologists' own therapeutic techniques, as well as places in which they could practice their craft, were being severely restricted by the more powerful field of medicine. Shortly after Freud's arrival in the United States, psychiatry had managed to seize control of psychotherapy and launched efforts to suppress clinical psychologists, blocking their certification and refusing them training in psychoanalytic institutes and societies. As the clinical psychologist Albert Ellis (1991: 28–29) described the situation, in the 1930s and '40s "almost all psychotherapy was psychoanalytic and practically all of the reputable analysts were psychiatrists. This was because, until about 1949, the psychoanalytic societies admitted very few psychologists for training; and most psychologists, like myself, who wanted to be analysts had to find unconventional analysts who would train them and help set them up in practice." From the 1920s until the 1940s, clinical and counseling psychologists were left to purvey their advice in child-guidance clinics, schools, colleges and universities and in industry—places outside the purview of the more powerful field of psychiatry.

Due in part to these political constraints, psychology's incorporation of Freudian psychoanalysis was initially selective at best. Psychology's unsettled relationship with psychoanalysis, however, defined the characteristics of the fledgling fields of clinical and counseling psychology and helped chart their future directions. Clinical psychology came to be defined as sorting through and testing psychotherapeutic concepts to determine which ones met psychologists' scientific standards, while counseling came to signify treating and helping those outside of the domain and influence of psychiatry. The relationship also shaped the direction of the larger discipline of psychology itself, by introducing a strong resentment toward Freudian psychoanalysis, which in turn fueled efforts by experimentalists to keep psychology "scientific." The condemnation of psychoanalysis for its amorphous and unmeasurable concepts also had the effect of turning many psychologists toward behaviorism.

Nonetheless, by the 1940s psychoanalysis had become "so popular that it threatened to eclipse psychology entirely" (Hornstein, 1992: 258). When people thought of psychology they often actually had psychotherapy in mind. The efforts of many APA members to forge an experimentalist reputation for their field seemed to be lost in the great tide of psychoanalysis occurring primarily outside of the field. Because psychologists were largely shut out of the practice of psychotherapy or were relegated to other "lesser" forms of therapy, clinical psychologists began to do what they did best—put psychoanalytical concepts to the experimental test. During the 1940s and '50s, hundred of studies were conducted using concepts taken from psychoanalytic theory. As a result of these studies psychologists came to the realization that they shared the commitment of psychoanalysis to psychic determinism and optimistic outlook, and they began reincorporating Freud into the conceptual repertoire of psychology (see Hornstein, 1992: 261).[5]

The secondary status of clinical and counseling psychology in the world of psychotherapy changed dramatically at the end of World War II. With vast government funding for counseling through the Disabled Veterans Rehabilitation Act and the GI Bill, the demand for clinical and counseling psychologists exploded. Suddenly the expensive and time-consuming psychoanalysis performed by psychiatrists could not keep pace with the sheer number of available patients. In order to meet the surging demand the Veterans Administration (VA) began to provide funds to train new clinical and counseling psychologists. With VA funding, the job description of psychologists began to change dramatically. No longer relegated to supporting positions, primarily in testing, the role of psychologists came to be redefined as involving diagnosis, research and therapy (see Garfield, 1991: 104). The VA programs allowed psychologists to treat patients and practice psychotherapy. It also increased the status of clinical psychologists by putting their salaries somewhat on a par with those of physicians (Blocher, 2000: 103). In response to these changing conditions, clinical and counseling psychologist began producing clinical and counseling psychologists in record numbers. A decade and a half after the end of World War II, they greatly outnumbered practicing psychiatrists ("Joint Report on the Relations between Psychology and Psychiatry," 1960).[6] Clinical psychologists also began the cost-effective process of converting individually oriented Freudian therapy to groups (Marx and Seldin, 1973: 41).

As clinical and counseling psychology rapidly gained new practitioners and popularity, many psychologists became disenchanted with the discipline's Freudian and behaviorist influences (see Ellis, 1991: 15). A "third force" began to coalesce around the works of Carl Rogers, Alfred Adler, Rollo May, Anthony Sutich and Abraham Maslow. These "humanistic psychologists" argued that the domination of psychology by psychoanalysis and behaviorism had caused the exclusion of what should be at the heart of psychology—the individual's search for authentic values by which to live (Karier, 1986: 9). The extreme positivism of experimental psychology and the expert-driven style of psychoanalytic therapy had stripped the field of its ability to offer people genuine advice on how to live productive and healthy lives. Rogers's (1951) classic work *Client-Centered Therapy: Its Current Practice, Implications, and Theory* "protestantized" therapy by introducing a new therapeutic technique that allowed clients to reflect and direct their own growth and recovery. For Rogers the key to therapy was for therapists to create a setting of "unconditional positive regard" that allowed for individual reflection and growth. Psychotherapy was to be an inner journey of discovery that would allow for a new, less pathological way of living.

In the view of Abraham Maslow, the discipline of psychology needed to be completely reinvented. In his view, "the study of the crippled, stunted, immature, and unhealthy specimens can yield only a crippled psychology and a crippled philosophy" (Maslow, 1954: 180). What was needed was a psychology that focused on the "fully growing and self-fulfilling human being" (Maslow, 1962: 4). This self-actualized being was "one whose inner nature expresses itself freely, rather than being warped, repressed, or denied" (Maslow, 1962: 4). Maslow maintained that people in modern societies suffered from an acute "value illness." Once society had produced a situation where the basic needs of people were met, it was time to focus on the ultimate in human potential, self-fulfillment and self-actualization. In Maslow's view, therapy should be about a search for "values, because ultimately the search for identity, is, in essence, the search for one's own intrinsic, authentic values" (Maslow, 1962: 166–167).

In the 1960s and early 1970s, the ideas of humanistic psychology began to intermingle with the political activities of the counterculture. Counterculture figures like Abbie Hoffman, who had been a student of Maslow at Brandeis University, incorporated humanistic psychology into the "Yippie" political movement (see Moskowitz, 2001: 205–208). Humanistic psychology also helped set the stage for the emergence of much broader approaches to psychological therapy. Known under such labels as "transpersonal psychology" and "the human potential movement," programs like sensitivity training, encounter groups, primal-scream therapy, psychodrama, Est and assertiveness training began rapidly to appear across the country. One of the most important of these programs was Esalen, a compound in Big Sur, California, "dedicated to exploring work in the humanities and sciences that furthers the full realization of the human potential" (www.esalan.org). Esalen held seminars and retreats on such topics as shamanism, holistic sexuality and creativity, using ideas borrowed from humanistic psychology and the human potential movement (see W. Anderson, 1983). By the early 1970s Esalen had become nationally known and was attracting some of the America's leading intellectuals and entertainers. By the mid-1970s, humanistic psychology's self-actualization had spawned a series of new therapeutic movement that eventually became grouped under the generic label of "self-help." Mixing psychological principles and often Eastern and Native American religions, these movements produced a number of best-selling books, reading clubs and encounter groups. In the 1970s books in the self-help genre accounted for 15 percent of all best-selling titles (Starker, 1989: 120). Likewise, by the mid-1980s over four hundred different types of psychotherapy were available (Kazdin, 1986).

In many ways, psychology's "third force" and the subsequent popular therapeutic movements it spawned, such as Esalen, marked a secularized return to the spiritual and existential concerns of the nineteenth century "mind cure" movements from which early psychiatrists and psychologists had fought so forcefully to escape. These approaches helped switch the language of psychotherapy from psychoanalytic concepts like fixation, Oedipal anxiety and ego function to such terms as self-actualization, choice and esthetics. The practice of therapy also changed from being didactic and directive to exploratory and client centered. This altered the role of the therapist from that of an expert who taught the patient insights into his or her life to a psychological guide who encouraged a client on voyages of self-discovery. Perhaps most importantly, however, the introduction of these new therapies changed the practice of psychotherapy from being a response to the neurotic and disturbed to an ordinary part of "normal" and "well adjusted" lives. This made therapy a "lifestyle issue" as much as a treatment for psychological problems. Therapy was a vehicle that enabled a person to live up to his or her potential. This change began to limit severely psychiatry's virtual monopoly over therapeutic intervention. Psychiatry, which had fought so hard to restrict the influence of spiritualists in the late nineteenth century and of clinical and counseling psychologists in the twentieth century, began to take a back seat to the virtual explosion of popular therapy spawned by clinical psychology.[7] With this development, psychology finally had its revenge—although this new psychology was one that few early clinical and counseling psychologists would have recognized or perhaps wanted.[8]

YOU NEED COUNSELING: MANDATING PSYCHOLOGICAL INTROSPECTION

The various popular therapies spawned by humanistic psychology made therapy and the therapeutic ethos centerpieces of many people's lives. In doing so it propelled psychological language and therapy into entirely new domains. Two of these new domains were the areas of politics and social policy. As early as 1930 Robert Yerkes (1930: 4), the director of psychological testing for the army during World War I, proclaimed that "the primary objective of legislation is effective regulation of human behavior in the interest of social welfare and progress." For Yerkes, legislation could provide a type of experimental laboratory wherein new policies and modes of social control could be tested. In this sense, government was conceived of as a "branch of human engineering which by manipulation of social behavior and its conditions" could create well-ordered lives (Yerkes, 1930: 4). Yerkes's statements reveal the nature of the relationship between psychology and politics that existed until the 1970s. This early relationship was marked by the contributions of psychologists to the testing, classification and sorting of people for the state's management or social-control efforts. The humanistic turn and subsequent therapeutic movements, however, brought an entirely new language and orientation to the relationship between psychology and politics.

Beginning in the 1970s, as counterculture figures familiar with humanistic psychology and Esalen encounters begin to move into the mainstream of American life, including government and universities, psychological introspection became incorporated into the workings of the state and social policy.[9] As this occurred, therapeutic concepts and practices came to be offered as solutions to the political and social ills facing governments and policy makers. In this process psychology's older social-control function and the human potential of the newer therapeutic movements begin to meld, producing mandatory counseling. In this new approach, therapy is officially mandated, through the legal and extralegal operations of such organizations as universities, social service agencies and churches, and through the larger interventionist efforts of what Andrew Polsky (1991) has called the "therapeutic state." In these instances psychological introspection is institutionalized as a legal or extralegal requirement levied upon persons served by various organizations.

This mandate may come from a court demand that a defendant receive counseling for drunk driving or spousal abuse. It may come from a social service agency that suspects child abuse or welfare fraud. It may even be instituted by universities or churches that demand mandatory counseling as a condition of return from an academic suspension or of permission to be married (see Gilbert and Sheiman, 1995). Whether instituted by a court, university, church or social service agency, this mandated introspection aims to "give recipients better psychological tools and stronger emotional resources" by which to conduct their lives (Polsky, 1991: 4). Their "failure," or in some cases even potential for failure, is seen as the result of some type of correctable personality flaw that can be overcome with proper psychological tools. Recipients of this type of mandatory therapy are required to "change how they rear their children, adopt different spending habits, find a new residence, maintain sexual abstinence, and more; refusal to comply can mean the breakup of a family or incarceration" (Polsky, 1991: 16).

The list of people targeted for mandatory counseling have included a motley assortment of groups, ranging from those filing for bankruptcy to those convicted of torturing cats, to school bullies to Little League parents. However, some of the most conspicuous examples of mandatory counseling come from the area of family planning and recent state efforts to develop more stringent marriage and divorce requirements. Gail Thoen, a certified marriage and family psychologist, has advocated one of the most extreme examples—she believes that "teachers and professionals in the mental heath field can and must help prevent the birth of unwanted children" (Thoen, 1985: 197). In order to ensure that "only qualified people have children," Thoen argues, there should be mandatory counseling sessions for all people wishing to have children (Thoen, 1985: 193). In these counseling sessions Thoen proposes to use "guided fantasy" and other therapeutic techniques to enable potential parents to envision their prospective lives as parents. This, she believes, would force them to come to terms with their possible future roles.

The issue of mandatory counseling has also become part of a "marriage movement" in many states. Louisiana, Arizona and (recently) Arkansas allow couples to opt for stricter "covenant marriages" that require counseling before the wedding and during marital problems and to establish tougher criteria for divorce (Otto, 1999: 1H). Officials hope that in time the now-optional program will become mandatory for all marriages. In 1998 Florida became the first state in the United States to require the teaching of marriage and relationships skills in all private and public schools. In other areas churches have begun adopting a "community marriage policy" that forces couples to complete a "marriage preparedness program" before a minister will agree to marry them. In Lenawee County, Michigan, a district judge, James Sheridan, in 1997 began mandating "premarital inventory tests, which identify areas of agreement and disagreement, and instruction in such things as conflict resolution for couples seeking a civil marriage in the county" (Otto, 1999: 1H). Diane Sollee, a marriage therapist and head of the Coalition for Marriage, Family and Couples Education, applauds this and other efforts and maintains that mandatory courses offered on such topics as "conflict resolution, constructive complaining and mutual appreciation" should be prerequisites for people attempting to obtain a marriage license in all states (Otto, 1999: 1H).

Cities in the United States have also begun using mandatory counseling programs in their efforts to fight various social problems. In Birmingham, Alabama, those arrested for any offense who test positive for an illicit drug are now forced to undergo mandatory counseling before being released (Greenberg, 1996). After the 1992 riots in Los Angeles, the city spent nearly six million dollars on counseling for members in the affected communities (Moskowitz, 2001: 4). In New York therapists trained in conflict resolution were recently called on to counsel people living in overcrowded, city-owned apartments (Moskowitz, 2001: 4). In Denver, mandatory counseling recently became instituted in the city's efforts to fight homelessness (Meadow, 1996: 4A). One aspect of the program requires homeless teenage mothers to participate in "parenting and independent living courses." Other parts require homeless individuals to receive counseling in managing a household before being allowed access to the city's temporary housing. Other cities, such as Boston, have begun to institute mandatory counseling for "out of control youth" and other delinquent populations (Burnett, 2000: 1A). In Kansas City, Missouri, officials have begun to use counseling as a way to end prostitution; Kevin Well, a counselor for Kansas City Corrective Training, Inc., has suggested that the city should move away from fining prostitutes and their clients and toward providing counseling and therapy (Berrios, 2000: B3).

Another group recently targeted for mandated counseling has been divorcing adults with children. Based on psychological research showing that children of divorce "exhibit more aggressive, impulsive, and antisocial behaviors, have more difficulties in their peer relationships, are less compliant with authority figures, and show more problem behaviors at school" (Kelly, 1993: 30), states such as Connecticut, Iowa, Utah and Vermont have made attendance in parenting classes a mandatory part of the divorce process for people with children (Arbuthnot and Gordon, 1997). Other states allow counties or others jurisdictions to enforce mandatory counseling. These programs include counseling and information on such issues as the impact of brainwashing the child, emotional responsibility, parenting skills and "postdivorce reaction of children" (Arbuthnot and Gordon, 1997: 349). Many of the mandatory programs use prepackaged video-based psychological materials, such as "SMILE" (Start Making It Livable for Everyone), "Don't Divorce the Children" and "Children in the Middle." After viewing the video, divorcing parents are required to complete "homework assignments" based on a guidebook accompanying the film. Once parents have completed the program, they are free to go forward with an actual court proceeding or mediation.

Mandatory counseling has also become a prominent means to handle public scandals. One of the most publicized instances occurred in January 2000, after John Rocker, a baseball player then on the Atlanta Braves, made several racist, anti-gay and anti-immigrant remarks in *Sports Illustrated*. Following the uproar created by the article, Bud Selig, commissioner of the National Baseball League, required Rocker to undergo psychological testing and counseling in order to determine his "psychological fitness" to continue in the game; once these requirements were completed he was allowed to return to playing baseball. Another recent example occurred in 1999 after a scandal involving missing documents and computers at the Los Alamos National Laboratory in New Mexico. As part of his solution to the mistakes at the laboratory, Bill Richardson (secretary of energy in the Clinton administration) recommended that those involved in the mishandling of a suspected Chinese spy at the laboratory receive mandatory counseling as part of their "punishment" (Pincus and Loeb, 1999: A04).

Prior to 1945, most people's direct exposure to psychologists would have occurred during the expansive psychological testing and classification performed during World Wars I and II or in schools or corporations. However, the new post–World War II governmental initiatives, such as the GI Bill and the Disabled Veterans Rehabilitation Act, introduced psychology and psychotherapy to an entirely new audience. In doing so they helped make therapeutic intervention a standard feature of the lives of not just the wealthy but many average Americans as well. Situated between the expensive and relatively small field of psychiatry and the disreputable arena of spiritualism and evangelism, psychologists were increasingly called upon by state and federal governments to provide relatively inexpensive services and contribute to ongoing efforts to manage risk (see Rose, 1996c).

The close relationship forged between the state and therapy has led to an increased use of psychological counseling techniques to aid government in solving problems and disposing of anomalous or problematic situations. As with psychologically based recovery movements and humanistic psychology, this officially sanctioned "moral therapy" attempts to connect "individual therapy with collective empowerment" (Feher, 1996: 86). Inequalities and social injustices are viewed as personal problems and, consequently, do not necessarily require political reform or mobilization but rather "coping strategies" and a "courage to heal." In this process a "therapeutocracy" (Habermas, 1987: 363) is constructed, wherein "politics is now an enterprise not of social change or even restoration, but of mass therapy" (Krauthammer, 1999: 3). In this therapeutocracy political and legal problems become reinterpreted in psychological terms, and social reform is couched in the same language as therapeutic recovery. This therapeutic solution "derives collective rights from the experience of pain ... and assigns a therapeutic mission to legal and political reform" (Feher, 1996: 86). For individuals this often takes the form of claiming emotional or psychological injury from various causes.[10] In the case of the legal system, punishment increasingly comes to involve counseling and therapy rather than jail or fines. As the state increasingly uses the accumulated moral authority of the various psy-fields to make decisions, policies are enacted not necessarily because they represent particular partisan interests but because they serve the psychological needs of certain segments of the citizenry.[11] In the end a situation develops, as Marcuse (1955: viii) argued in another context, in which "psychological categories become political categories."

GRIEF COUNSELING, HEALING AND THE DEVASTATED SELF

Just as psychological language and practices have become an integral part of politics and social policy over the last few decades, it has also recently begun to colonize one of the final outposts of religious authority, death and grieving (see Seale, 1998). Historically, people turned to religion for solace when a death or tragedy occurred. In recent years, however, psychologists and other mental health workers have come to dominate what critics have called the "grief industry." The vocabulary of grief, much like the vocabulary of politics, has now become thoroughly psychologized. Terms such as "coping," "recovery," "healing," "denial" and "the grieving process," all borrowed from psychotherapy, are now common means by which death and trauma are conceptualized and represented in everyday life.

Particularly evident in the psychological colonization of grief is the presence of psychologists and other mental health providers at disaster scenes. As a result of case studies of the long-term effects of disasters (see Lindemann, 1944; Titchener and Kapp, 1976; Erikson, 1976) and clinical work on "posttraumatic stress disorder" (Grinker and Spiegel, 1945), the treatment of large-scale community grief has become an important new area of expansion for clinical and counseling psychology. The practice of grief therapy, as it has become known, is largely based on the work of Harvard psychologist J. William Worden and his 1982 book *Grief Counseling and Grief Therapy: A Handbook for the Mental Health Practitioner*, as well as the seminars he conducts on grieving and recovery around the country. Worden (1982: 1) contends that as many as 15 percent of people experiencing psychological problems have what he terms "an unresolved grief reaction." The "facilitation" of this grief reaction requires the intervention of a trained mental health worker who will aid the person in the "four tasks of mourning"—accepting the reality of the loss, experiencing the pain of grief, adjusting to a new environment and withdrawing emotional energy (Worden, 1982: 11–16). Since its inception, the new subfield has responded to airline crashes, community disasters (like floods, tornados or hurricanes) and more recently to problems in schools (such as the death of a student or a school shooting) and the September 11 terrorist attacks.

Psychology's recent focus on grief has been instrumental in the growth of the new field of disaster mental health (DMH) and has led to the new professional designation of "disaster psychologist." DMH received its first official recognition in 1974, when the Disaster Relief Act provided funding to establish the Crisis Counseling Program. The act stipulated that funds managed by the Federal Emergency Management Agency could be used to support mental health services at disaster scenes (Jacobs, 1995: 544). In 1989 the American Red Cross fielded its first mental health team in response to Hurricane Hugo in South Carolina (Jacobs, 1995: 545). A year later the American Psychological Association agreed to provide funding for a training program in disaster mental health operated by the California Psychological Association (Jacobs, 1995: 545). In 1991 the APA signed a "statement of agreement" with the American Red Cross to develop further the field of disaster mental health (American Red Cross, 1991).

As a result of the alliance between the APA and the American Red Cross, efforts to establish and promote the field of disaster mental health became much more organized in the 1990s. During Operation Desert Storm in 1991, the American Psychological Association established a hotline for people to discuss the war with psychologists; the hotline received sixteen thousand calls (*Mental Health Weekly*, 1995: 6). The next year the APA developed the Disaster Response Network (DRN) to react to similar disasters and conflicts. The DRN created a network of some two thousand psychologists and other mental health workers throughout the country, ready to respond to mass disasters. Echoing Worden's work on individual grief, the organizers of the DRN maintain that disasters create an assortment of psychological needs for those affected. In their view, "if left untreated, these needs can develop into chronic problems that are disabling to people in both their professional and personal lives" (APA in Dineen, 1996: 230). Since its founding the DRN has responded to floods, earthquakes, bombings, airline crashes, and more recently, school shootings (*Mental Health Weekly*, 1995: 6).

After the Oklahoma City bombing in 1995, another toll-free psychological help-line was established, as part of larger efforts to manage the emotional trauma created by the atrocity. Sponsored by the APA, the American Red Cross and AT&T, the goal of the "Helping the Children to Heal" hotline was to "help restore a sense of security" in individuals affected by the bombing (*Mental Health Weekly*, 1995: 5). The hotline attempted, in the words of an APA spokesperson, to "turn this disaster into something productive for survivors so they don't feel that their loved ones died in vain" (American Psychological Association, 1995b). Six years later, upon the federal execution of the Oklahoma City bomber, counselors were again on the scene to offer solace to the families of victims. As part of the Oklahoma City counseling efforts, an organization calling itself the "Green Cross" was established to focus on the "long-term struggles to recovery" (Dineen, 1996: 228). The Green Cross set up training workshops that allowed individuals to be credentialed as "registered traumatologists."

One of the primary counseling strategies used in disaster mental health is known as the "critical incident stress debriefing" (CISD). Advocates of CISDs argue that community members and emergency personnel responding to emergencies can, if they do not receive intervention, develop posttraumatic stress disorder. In the debriefing for both counselors and community members, living victims of mass disasters are recast as "survivors" and are described as experiencing "signs of emotional and psychological strain," such as "short-term memory loss, confusion, difficulty setting priorities and making decisions" (Myers, 1994: 2). To limit these effects, disaster psychologists teach stress-reduction techniques and provide forums in which participants are encouraged to talk through their feelings. Gerard Jacobs (1994: A7), a psychologist and director of the Disaster Mental Health Institute at the University of South Dakota, describes the role of counselors: "We try to let them know that their reactions are normal[.] . . . [C]ounseling will ease workers through each day." After the shooting at Columbine High School in Colorado, a team of disaster counselors was sent in by the National Association of School Psychologists. The team used the debriefing technique as a means "to get people to open up, ask questions and unburden the psychical pain they are carrying around" (Feinberg in Labi, 1999: 70).

Grief counseling has also become a standard part of the response of schools and other community groups to various tragedies. Many schools have developed crisis-management plans utilizing a "crisis team" composed of area psychologists, social workers and clergy. When a crisis occurs, "students, staff members, community members, and the family of the deceased need assistance to cope with their feelings" (Page and Page, 1993: 274). School-based grief counseling is based on the assumption of developmental psychology that "the adolescent survivor will not have developed the skills to cope with death and needs assistance in the grieving process" (Carson and War-ren, 1995: 194). This being the case, grief counselors are needed to help initiate the "grief work" (Page and Page, 1993) that enables students to express better their feelings and begin the process of grieving.

Some grief counselors, such as Martha Oates (1988), have developed a scale to be used by tramatologists for determining the "expected degree of trauma" in particular tragedies. The scale calibrates community trauma into categories of "high," "moderate" and "low," in order to help the crisis team to respond in an appropriate manner. An incident is rated in severity on a scale of four to sixteen, on the basis of the popularity of the person killed, where the death took place and how the person died (Oates, 1988: 84–85). Oates also advises counselors on the importance of allowing time for "grief expressions" and the use of "helpful responses." In order to help with the "healing process," the counselor is advised to use phrases such as "I can see that you are hurting," "It is very hard to accept the death of someone close," and "I know—it just seems unbelievable," while avoiding such statements as "You will feel better tomorrow" (Oates, 1988: 92). She also suggests that students discuss the event in a group or write papers about their feelings in order to facilitate the "grieving process."

Ian Hacking (1998: 83) has observed that "one of the incidental hazards of being involved in a mass disaster in America is that you will now be descended upon by traumatologists who will track you down the rest of your life, to determine the long-term effects of the trauma upon your psyche." That is, this movement of psychological knowledge into yet another domain of everyday life marks an important transition in moral authority. As psychology colonizes more of everyday life, its particular means of representing situations become the common language people use to situate and understand critical events in their lives, such as death and dying. Disaster and death are increasingly becoming "psychological issues" that require, perhaps even demand, a "therapeutics of finitude" (Rose, 1990: 244). This type of therapeutics situates reactions to death and tragedy on a continuum between "pathological" and "normal," and envisions them as either the root of personal dysfunctions or as opportunities for "personal growth." In this moral transformation of death, psychology begins to replace religion as the conveyer of advice and solace in times of despair. Death, consequently, becomes reconfigured from a moral experience to a "psychological trauma" that requires therapeutic resolution.

CONCLUSION: PSYCHOLOGY AND THE SUBJECTIVIZING OF EXPERIENCE

In the late eighteenth century, the poet, novelist, and playwright Goethe (1962 [1792]: 312) predicted that society would eventually turn into "one huge hospital where everyone is everyone else's humane nurse." By the early twenty-first century, this vision of omnipresence of bodily affliction has taken a decidedly psychological turn. According to psychologists and psychiatrists, some twenty million Americans suffer from gambling addiction, eighty million have eating disorders, twenty-five million are thought to be love or sex addicts, ten million have borderline personality disorders and fifty million are said to suffer from depression and anxiety (Dineen, 1996: 210). All this diagnosing has been made possible by the vast expansion of psychological language and services in everyday life. In 1960, about 14 percent of Americans received some type of mental health service. Estimates from psychologists and psychiatrists during this time suggested that as many as 80 percent of the population had some type of mental illness that was in need of diagnosis (Gross, 1978: 6). By taking advantage of this "untapped market," psychologists and others in allied fields increased the number of Americans who had received a mental health service to 33 percent by 1990 (VandenBos, DeLeon and Belar, 1991: 442). By the mid-1990s that percentage had increased to almost 46 percent, according to an American Psychological Association telephone survey (Dineen, 1996: 19). Other accounts have found that the number of Americans seeking psychological services has increased as much as 1,000 percent since the 1950s (Justman, 1998: 139). In addition, each year some ten million Americans seek out psychological services (Dineen, 1996: 249). As a result of these trends, by the late 1990s there were some 650,000 counselors providing various forms of therapy throughout the United States (Chriss, 1999: 2).[12]

This "triumph of the therapeutic," as Philip Rieff (1966) referred to it, has contributed to a realignment of the way in which we experience, conceptualize and represent our lives. Specifically, psychology and other psy-fields have created a particular "subjectivization of experience" (see Rose, 1996b: 13). Through this subjectivization, thoughts and feelings come to be confined solely and exclusively to minds (see Taylor, 1989: 186). Minds are conceived of as independent, universal and foundational entities that house both the ability to self-actualize and the complex, idiosyncratic and sometimes troubled world of the self. The configuration of these minds is seen as identical—"everyone is expected to have private motives, everyone is expected to have social attitudes, everyone is expected to fall somewhere on the range of the distribution of intelligence" (Danziger, 1997: 185). In this sense psychology, as Stewart Justman (1998: 141) argues, "renders us alike" by "standardiz[ing] the portrayal of behavior." People are expected—and, under mandatory counseling, compelled—to have "psychological issues" in need of resolution or expression. Failing to do so is a sign of being out of touch with one's own psyche or "in denial" and is itself an indication of the need for therapeutic intervention.

Psychology's subjectivization of experience creates a number of taken-for-granted truths of contemporary life. The first of these truths is the notion of the "deep down." This is the place where pathology, or the true self, resides in wait of release through confession, therapy, cognitive recognition, "self-actualization" or perhaps a "primal scream." The language of deep interiors, found in such terms as "neurosis," "paranoia," "the unconscious," "repression" and "self-actualization," characterize a true or authentic self that lies buried beneath the vicissitudes of modern life. Psychological therapies, in their various forms, provide a particular vocabulary and set of accepted truths and therapeutic practices that are said to render these foundations of life "visible," in order to make them better or more genuine. In doing so, this "depth psychology" often mandates "an introspection more rigorous than that of the Puritans" (Matthews, 1988: 352). People are expected to probe continuously their lives for repressed memories, neuroses, unhappy childhoods or "unresolved grief," because in these factors is said to reside both the truth about the self and the material needed for recovery and healing.

Psychological knowledge also unleashes another great truth of contemporary life, a duality between the conscious and the unconscious. Arising from the movements like the "mind cure" and becoming solidified by Freudian psychoanalysis, this truism postulates a dichotomy between the subterranean world of desire, fear and other traits, and the surface domain of convention. As is the case with other divisions between appearance and reality, this psychological division invites expert interpretation and analysis, since only those "in the know" have access to this hidden world (see Feyerabend, 1999). In this process, experience comes to be viewed as a complex "interiority" with a manifest level of behavior and a latent level of cause. This, in turn, creates a particular "psychologization of the visual," wherein perception is no longer seen as a mirror of the world outside but as a complex outcome of internal psychological processes (Jay, 1996: 99; also see Crary, 1990).[13] Psychology, consequently, helps redefine "the limits of vision, and create new ways of acting upon that which is brought into view" (Rose, 1996b: 58–59). Indeed, this particular psychological orientation between depth and surface, inside and outside and the authentic and dramaturgical self sometimes characterizes what we call "modernity." One outcome of this orientation is that life becomes lived as a "psychodrama," where deep-seated emotions mingle with social obligations to direct continuously our conceptualizations of who we are, as well as our everyday activities.

In her comparative study of the manifestations of Freudianism in different countries, Edith Kurzweil (1989: 1) remarked that "every country creates the psychoanalysis it needs." The same may hold true of the broader area of psychotherapy. In the United States, the infusion of psychotherapy into everyday life was the result of a number of historical movements, political clashes and serendipitous outcomes. At one level, the large-scale twentieth-century expansion of clinical and counseling psychology amounted to a secularization and reformation of the generic "mind cure" movements of the nineteenth century. This secularization was the product of a complex political and cultural interplay among medicine, psychology and religion. In this process a continually shifting division of labor was forged that eventually assigned psychologists the powerful and influential role of "mental healers" and "confidants of the middle class." While the wealthy came to use the services of high-status and expensive psychiatrists and the poor often turned to fundamentalist religions, clinical and counseling psychologists became the middle way—cheaper than psychiatrists but more "modern" and respected than faith healers, religious figures or mystics. With its humanistic turn, however, psychology itself began to take on a quasi-religious form. As a result, clinical and counseling psychology did something that the field of psychiatry never quite managed to do—it made "normality" and "health" as much the focuses of psychological advice and help as pathology.

Psychology, of course, marks but one of the innumerable ways in which the world can be experienced. However, by the early twenty-first century, psychology and allied fields have so managed to rewrite the soul of religion into the mind and self of psychology as to make other modes of experience largely untenable or impossible (see Hacking, 1995). In doing so they have greatly transformed the way the world is experienced, contemplated and acted upon by large segments of the population. What people in previous centuries or other cultures saw as resulting from moral or religious violations, such as possession, spiritual frailty or moral indiscretions, modern psychologists and psychiatrists reveal to be in actuality outcomes of distinct underlying psychological states, syndromes and often treatable psychological disorders (see Foucault, 1965; Hacking, 1995). As this psychological perspective on the self became increasingly intertwined with governmental problem solving and decision making, and as it replaced religion's moral authority over grief and death, psychology became a new type of civil religion. Within this new civil religion, therapy became as much a staple of everyday life as medicine, and therapeutical solutions became standard means for solving all types of problems. This created, to rephrase Durkheim (1973 [1898]), a new type of religion, in which humans are both the worshipers and the god.

NOTES

1. If psychologists can indeed be classified as colonizers, they preferred to use more decentralized methods of indirect influence and control over their territories. As Danziger (1997: 85) has described the discipline, it has had a "tendency to annex new areas without being able to assimilate them."

2. In fact, it could be argued that even the division between the relational and the personal (or society and self) is part of an epistemic bifurcation inherited, at least in part, from psychological knowledge and its classifications. No doubt there are other sources of this bifurcation outside of the discipline of psychology.

3. James, himself a sufferer of neurasthenia, had earlier written to his father that he had been cured by "giving up the notion that all mental disorders had a physical base" (James in Lutz, 1991: 66).

4. Failure to keep this agreement, however, forced many clinicians and counselors to leave the APA in the 1930s to become members of the American Association for Applied Psychology. It was not until the mid-1940s, when a new arrangement was worked out, that the clinicians and counselors rejoined the ASA.

5. A 1954 survey conducted by the APA found that Freud was mentioned as the person who had influenced psychologists the most (Clark, 1957).

6. Within the APA, pressure by the growing number of clinical and counseling psychologists forced a reorganization of the association in the mid-1940s and a meeting in Boulder, Colorado, late in the decade to devise a new model of training clinical psychologists. Individual psychology departments were also forced to change their internal structures to place more emphasis on clinical training in order to obtain and maintain governmental funding (Ross, 1991: 220). In the late 1930s only a small percentage of psychologists were clinicians and counselors; by 1957, almost 40 percent of APA members were clinicians or counselors (Clark, 1957: 116). These

changes collectively marked a dramatic shift of the discipline from an experimental science to a profession.

7. This situation would begin to reverse itself with the growing influence of psychopharmacology in the 1980s and 1990s, particularly since insurance providers often prefer these faster and cheaper forms of therapeutic intervention.

8. The influence of humanistic styles of therapies has been eroded to some degree by the growing popularity of cognitive-behavioral therapy. Cognitive-behavioral therapy blends aspects of the older, more authoritarian forms of therapy, where the therapist serves as an expert coach, with the more collaborative approach used in client-centered therapy. As with the growth of psychopharmacology, the popularity of cognitive-behavioral therapy has been fueled by a preference among insurance companies for its goal-oriented approach and empirical focus. Indeed, its characteristics seem ideally suited to insurance companies and other agencies looking for the least expensive way to solve individual problems.

9. Therapeutic discourse is not reserved for mainstream politics. The manifesto of the Unabomber, Ted Kazinsky, decried the "demoralization, low self-esteem, inferiority feelings, defeatism, depression, anxiety, guilt, frustration, hostility" created by modern society (*New York Times*, 1995: A16).

10. As James Nolan (1999: 15) points out, so entwined is the language of psychology in contemporary moral discourse that "the most permissible way to object to therapeutically incited violations of individual liberty or parental authority is to make the victimized claim to have been psychologically or emotionally injured."

11. For example, after the elimination of affirmative action at the University of Texas, disgruntled students were asked to attend self-esteem workshops and other therapy sessions (Cloud, 1998: 4).

12. In addition to these more direct forms of psychological services, as of 1990 some fifteen million Americans also attended some five hundred thousand recovery groups, most of which utilized psychologically based models of recovery (M. Jones, 1990: 16).

13. Such subjectivization of experience can also be seen in an array of twentieth-century art and literature. James's "stream of consciousness" influenced a number of writers, including Virginia Woolf, James Joyce and Dorothy Richardson (Ryan, 1991: 1).

9

Conclusion: The Psychologization of the United States

THROUGHOUT THIS BOOK I HAVE TRIED TO ILLUSTRATE HOW over the course of the last century psychological categories and practices became "naturalized." As this happened, psychology, like other naturalized ideas and categories, "disappeared into infrastructure, into habit, into the taken for granted" (Bowker and Star, 1999: 319). Psychology's presence in schools, workplaces and homes is now an ordinary and seemingly indispensable feature of the cultural landscape. As a result of its presence we are now aware that there are children with varying IQ levels, that motivation can be enhanced through certain psychological techniques, that healthy marriages necessitate open communication, that people have certain psychological needs that require fulfillment, that aptitude can be gauged through psychological measurements and that self-esteem determines how we interact with others. Today, psychological knowledge and categories seem, to rephrase Aaron Cicourel (1964: 21), "intuitively right and reasonable because they are rooted in everyday life." As is the case for all types of naturalized knowledge, psychology is no longer a "fragile convention," as it clearly was in its early days. It now appears to be "founded in nature and therefore, in reason." As a result of this naturalization process, psychology is now "part of the order of the universe" and so "[is] ready to stand as the grounds of argument" (Douglas, 1986: 52).

However, today's naturalized status of psychological knowledge is how things look long after knowledge has settled—after fragile assertions have become crystallized into commonsense and institutional practices. Prior to this all that existed were weak and lonely opinions about how the mind works, how the self develops or what constitutes human nature. As we have seen throughout this work, psychology's transformation from a set of local and provisional opinions to a series of universal and natural truths was a long and complex process. In psychology's early history its concepts and principles were often ridiculed and marginalized by school principals who were skeptical of intelligence tests, corporate executives who questioned the benefit of hiring industrial psychologists, psychiatrists who doubted the diagnostic skill of clinical psychologists, philosophers who were critical of mental experimentation and the general public who often confused psychologists with spiritualists. However, by establishing a series of alliances with groups such as educators, industrialists and parents, and by using these connections to open up new domains for the flow of its knowledge, psychology managed over the course of several decades to make itself the central purveyor of knowledge about the mind and self. When this happened, psychological knowledge ceased to be a provisional human construct and disappeared into the known and the commonsensical. As such, its constructions no longer appear constructed.

In this concluding chapter I explore some of the factors that explain how psychological knowledge became naturalized and how the United States became "psychologized." In the first part of the chapter I review some of the reasons psychology became a successful knowledge form. Here I look at five factors that can be used to understand how psychological knowledge became both influential and natural. Next, I investigate what it means to "be psychological." As I argued in chapter 7, being psychological is something that happens only under certain circumstances and in particular places and networks. In this section I consider some of the defining features of being psychological, as well as some of the other "forms of being" that psychological experience marginalizes or obliterates. Finally, I conclude the chapter with a discussion of psychological knowledge's role in creating a different type of society by examining its contribution to the construction and constitution of modernity.

WHAT EXPLAINS PSYCHOLOGY'S SUCCESS?

Writing in the early 1930s the industrial psychologist Walter Bingham (1932a: v) claimed that "as a result of systematic observations of behavior and controlled experiments in laboratories, hospitals, industries, and schools," psychology had provided "new light on the reasons for what we do and think and feel." In doing so, psychology "[had] helped in freeing us from the entanglements of prejudice and of propaganda." For Bingham, as well as most other psychologists, psychology differed from past approaches "not that human nature has changed; but we know more about it, thanks to scientific method." (Bingham, 1932a: v). Although perhaps overly exuberant, Bingham's proclamations are not much different from what most psychologists and their supporters think today about psychology's accomplishments. In their view, by successfully utilizing and applying the methodology of the natural sciences, the discipline revolutionized and greatly advanced our understanding of the mind and self, as well as their various pathologies. As a result, psychology has been an integral part of the broader movement of the human sciences that has largely succeeded at supplanting the myths and superstitions of past opinions with the truth and reality of the modern behavioral sciences.

There is, however, another story told about psychology's historical accomplishments. In this account, psychological knowledge exhibits nothing but "experimental methods and conceptual confusion" (Wittgenstein, 1953: 232e). From this critical view, psychology is fragmented into numerous competing divisions and warring cliques; its knowledge is continuously challenged and undermined by other fields, such as medicine, sociology, biology and, more recently, computer science; its therapeutic wing is often the butt of jokes and social satire; and it is sometimes difficult to tell the difference between "pseudo" and "legitimate" practitioners. In short, in this view, psychology is a failed or "immature" discipline that has not delivered on its promise to provide a science of the mind and self.

Neither of these epistemologically inspired stories does justice to the contradictions and complexity found in the history of psychological knowledge. Beyond first impressions hides a highly successful knowledge form that has greatly revolutionized the way we think and act. It has done this not necessarily through adhering to a particular philosophy of science or by creating new material technologies but instead through the establishment of new "technologies of the self" (Foucault, 1988). These technologies of the self provide people with seemingly essential strategies for managing and conducting everyday life. Psychology succeeded not because it finally vanquished myth and superstition or because of its use of scientific methods but because of the confluence of its assembled alliances. As Latour (1999: 97) has pointed out, the success of a knowledge form is not dependent upon its ability to accurately capture reality but rather "the extent of its transformations, the safety of its connections, the progressive accumulations of its mediations, the number of interlocutors it engages, its ability to make nonhumans accessible to words, its capacity to interest and convince others, and its routine institutionalization of these flows." In this "nonepistemological" sense, psychology is clearly successful.

Reviewing the history of psychological knowledge in the United States over the last century, it is possible to identify five overlapping factors that explain its success: (1) its encompassing and heterogeneous network, (2) its loose organizational structure, (3) its ability to utilize existing neighboring networks to spread its ideas, (4) the ease of its transportability in material form, and (5) the recent convergence of a number of "psy" networks. First, if any knowledge form is to be successful, it must "incorporate a sufficiently broad theoretical vision, methods, and where relevant an inventory of techniques and instruments capable of sustaining research on a wide front of problems" (Lenoir, 1997: 56). As we have seen throughout this book, psychology easily fulfilled this requirement. Psychologists and their knowledge were not just relegated to laboratories or universities but were present in schools, corporations, courtrooms, disaster scenes, marriage retreats, talk shows, as well as in abstentia in self-help books, personality measures, intelligence tests and codes of civility. With such an encompassing and heterogeneous presence, psychology today is capable of quickly and easily deploying its knowledge creations to various locales. Indeed, it is difficult to find an area of life or an institution or organization that has not in some manner been shaped by its exposure to psychological concepts and methods.[1]

Such heterogeneity in application was given credence and justification by the idea that the mind is at the center of all activity—in James Cattell's (1893b: 779) words, "the center from which we start and to which we return." In this view, literally all human activities, from loving to working to dying, are seen as being produced by basic underlying internal mental processes assessable only by the investigatory techniques of psychology (see Rose, 1996b: 197). Buoyed by this belief, psychologists set out on a calculated quest to make the world psychological by getting others to also place the mind, and by extension psychology, at the center of their activities. They accomplished this by establishing alliances with various groups and organizations that could serve as conduits for the flow of psychological theories, measures and practices. Over time, as these alliances began to solidify into a somewhat stable network, psychology was able to utilize its well-established contacts to get the word out and to enhance its status as a purveyor of wisdom on the workings of the mind and the conduct of life. If psychological knowledge had not made itself a useful tool for groups within these alliances, it easily could have been relegated to the historical archives of unsuccessful ideas or scientific false starts. Likewise, if psychological knowledge had not become attached to and insinuated itself into the activities of various groups, it would have probably remained just another academic discipline.

The expansion of psychological knowledge is not merely a result of the size of the network that supports psychological ways of knowing, however. Psychological knowledge's strength is also buoyed by the variety of elements that make up its network. For instance, its strength and legitimacy is not just supported by other academics or professionals but is witnessed to and propagated by schoolteachers, grief counselors, magazine editors, TV commentators, social service workers, Oprah Winfrey and a host of other knowledge disseminators. People in these groups testify to the explanatory power of psychology even when no psychologists are present. In so doing they further spread the idea that the mind is at the center of all activity and that psychology can provide the answers to life's mysteries and problems. Likewise, psychological knowledge's efficacy is not given credence only by such textual creations as books and research articles, as is often the case in the humanities and some parts of the social sciences, but by such material entities as mazes, experimental hardware and thousands of psychological measures. These material entities give the knowledge durability, as well as a range and quality of influence, that would not be possible with texts alone. Use of these machines and measures also allows the knowledge to become "embodied" in particular psychologically oriented practices. Just as Western colonization took place because the invaders "arrived separately, each in his place and with his purity" (Latour, 1988b: 202), the psychologization of the United States occurred because of the rich variety of items found in psychology's network of support.

Psychological knowledge was simultaneously material, spiritual, applied, industrial, educational, civil, social and political—it was all things to all people.

Since psychological knowledge appeared almost concurrently on a number of fronts, resistance to one area of its application was not enough to doom the overall advancement of the knowledge. If psychology had appeared only in universities or public schools, competitors or enemies could have more easily contained its knowledge. However, because psychological knowledge appeared so rapidly in so many different places and in so many different forms, it was impossible to stop. The heterogeneity of psychology's network allowed psychological knowledge to circumvent more easily groups or organizations that stood in its way. For example, in the early twentieth century, when psychiatrists undertook legal maneuvers to block the certification of clinicians or their right to practice and use the word "psychotherapy," other avenues, particularly in the areas of education and industry, were available for the knowledge to flow into. If psychology had been limited to only one place from which to spread its ideas, it could have easily been forced into academic isolation or strangled by the legal and political efforts of the considerably more powerful field of psychiatry. However, since there were other alliances that could be called upon, the efforts of psychiatrists to block psychology's movement in one area represented only a temporary obstacle.

Such network heterogeneity was responsible for creating another important feature that helps explain psychology's success: a loose level of disciplinary control within the field. In fact, it could be argued that we are not dealing with one psychology at all but with many psychologies with their own "mini" associations, loops and networks. During its first few decades of existence psychology was a relatively small field experiencing rapid growth in membership. The only means for a fledgling organization to survive in such a high-growth situation is either to spread outward or collapse in on itself. In order for arrivals into the new field to distinguish themselves from others, they had to either fall in line with the central figures or move into new areas of inquiry. Since the number of people who could be accommodated in the universities and laboratories controlled by the central figures of psychology was relatively small, the only viable option for the majority of newcomers was to expand outward into new, more applied areas. This created a "structural crunch" where creativity was continually squeezed outward (Collins, 1999: 74–75). Such innovation was also fueled by the status competition present in most small, rapidly growing fields (see Whitley, 1984). In such a dense and highly competitive situation, it makes little sense to follow in the footsteps of those who have gone before. Instead, knowledge makers must give the impression of producing something that is "new and improved" if they are to get noticed or even merely survive as knowledge makers.

Ironically, however, the lack of disciplinary control spawned by these organizational characteristics partially explains psychology's success. Although groups such as the APA and most experimentalists sought to control strictly the type of people who could be called "psychologists" and the type of knowledge the discipline was to produce, they were never able to establish a monopoly on what would count as legitimate psychological knowledge. As a result, practitioners peddled all types of intellectual wares under the label of "psychology" throughout most of the twentieth century. This is, after all, a discipline that has housed everyone from people doing highly quantitative, timed experiments on rats and pigeons to individuals seeking to liberate humanity through self-actualization and movement therapy, and from scholars in elite university laboratories to celebrities appearing on games shows like *Hollywood Squares*. Such disciplinary malleability has enabled psychology to adapt quickly to changes brought by its emerging alliances with other groups. These groups expected that psychology would produce knowledge they could use within their own fields; had the founding figures maintained an oligarchic control over the field, psychology would have not been able to adapt to the changes brought about by its alliances. Although psychology was often condemned for being disorganized and unfocused, this lack of focus actually gave it the flexibility needed to remake itself continuously in the image of its allies. Ironically, it was because the discipline of psychology lacked complete control over its own knowledge and internal structure that it became so influential.[2] The organization of psychology was loose enough to allow for flexibility in application but tight enough to keep its name attached to its knowledge products as they moved from one area to another.[3]

Another factor that helps explain psychology's success is its ability to utilize existing networks to insinuate itself into the activities of these networks and to become an active participant in the way various groups and institutions solve their problems. As Gail Hornstein (1992: 261) remarked, "American psychology has always been distinguished by an uncanny ability to adapt itself to cultural trends as quickly as they emerge." For example, as soon as various manifestations of spiritualism began to make an impact on American culture, psychologists began offering advice in newspapers on the conduct of daily life; as quickly as schools sought new modes for organizing students, psychologists were there with IQ measures and developmental theory; and as soon as industries needed ways to manage large industrial workforces, psychologists appeared with personality tests and personnel advice. Such adaptability has given the impression that psychology merely fulfills the emergent epistemic needs of various groups and institutions. For instance, today it appears that the legal system needs mechanisms for determining sanity and competence to testify, and for calculating damages in lawsuits; schools need means for determining intelligence and for dealing with problematic and fidgety children; industries require ways to motivate and test the personalities of its workers; and groups like the American Red Cross want help in aiding survivors of mass disasters. In addition, individuals seem to need help raising their children, saving their marriages, recovering from addictions, getting along with coworkers, or overcoming grief. However, as I have tried to illustrate, this "needs-filling role" of psychology is not quite as straightforward as it might appear. While psychology has provided a number of groups the conceptual tools and methods to solve or rechannel some of their anomalies or problems, it did so less through the capacity to fulfill a preexisting need within those groups than the ability of psychologists to create a need in the first place. As we saw in earlier chapters, there were other knowledge producers that could have, under the right circumstances, also supplied knowledge to these groups, or these groups could have produced and housed their own indigenous knowledge. In other contexts, the so-called problems of these groups that required psychological intervention could have gone "unidentified" and unnoticed.

Psychology was able to create a widespread need for its knowledge products in two general ways. First, psychological terminology and methods were mobilized to make an area problematic. For instance, at the turn of the twentieth century psychology frequently criticized education for its unscientific pedagogy and ad hoc teaching methods. Such an "unpsychologized" educational system was portrayed as dangerous to a child's development and as an affront to the emerging modern way of life. Second, after it had destabilized an area by an assault of psychological terminology, the field offered psychological concepts and methods as a means to fix the problems. It turns out that teachers needed developmental theory to teach well, administrators needed intelligence tests to sort learners properly, parents needed psychological advice to bring up better children, mangers needed personality tests to produce more efficiently and disaster survivors needed direction in order to "grow" from their experiences. What psychology offered these groups was a way to simplify the complexity of their tasks by reducing their problems to remediable mental and psychological issues. In a psychological reading, the reasons for everything from masturbation to poor reading skills, to worker strikes, were underlying psychological mechanisms residing in each individual. Once authority figures in these areas employed psychological reasoning and practices, the problems of their organization would be solved. Groups utilizing psychological knowledge were merely responding to the inherent psychological needs and disposition of the individual.

Psychologists were also able to insinuate themselves into places where others had failed or refused to go, because of their cross-affiliations in a number of groups outside of academia. Psychologist were not just members of the APA or Titchener's Experimentalist Club but active participants in education groups, social reform movements, religious organizations, university departments of education, psychic research, the YMCA and the Children's Foundation, to name but a few. From positions in these groups, psychologists were able to create spaces in which psychological knowledge could flourish by convincing these groups of the centrality of psychology to their endeavors. The presence of psychologists in education groups, movie making, personnel selection, marriage counseling, self-help and a slew of other activities promoted psychological knowledge in areas into which other knowledge producers would not or could not go. While all knowledge-producing fields want to reduce the world to their own precepts, it is only active and well-connected ones that are capable of exporting their precepts to other domains. Psychology's exportation was made possible by the connections and cross-affiliations that it made with teachers, children, educational administrators, parents, athletes, the grief stricken, the insane and troubled over the course of the last century.

Part of psychology's success is attributable not only to creating entirely new alliances but to utilizing, and in some instances co-opting, existing networks in order to spread its ideas. In some cases, such as spiritualism, New Thought and the Emmanuel Movement, this meant essentially capturing a vast and already well-established network and, over time and with considerable effort, infusing, psychological frameworks and concepts into it, in some cases substituting them entirely.[4] In this instance, psychologists were able to utilize connections, particularly those established by William James and Elwood Wooster, to gain a presence in these movements. With a presence established, psychologists began to criticize these movements for their unscientific positions, at the same time offering more modern therapeutic alternatives. In other cases, utilizing existing networks meant developing "trading zones" where concepts and ideas could be exchanged. In the case of education, psychology was able to "trade" a number of conceptual tools and instruments that allowed education to "modernize," in exchange for the right to be considered important players in pedagogy and teacher training. However, involvement with these other networks forced a change within the network of psychology itself. Psychologists were compelled to redirect their knowledge strategies toward these existing networks in order to increase their range of influence within them. In order to endure the process, their own ideas, particularly their belief in the purity and revelatory power of experimentation, had to undergo a transformation.

As we saw in chapter 5, psychology's success is due to more than its human alliances and organization. Psychological knowledge has also succeeded because of the ease of its transportability in material form. While laboratory machines were important for establishing psychology's early organization and for illustrating its scientific focus to the public, it was the various measures offered by psychology that actually enabled the knowledge form to expand. Machines were much too bulky and complex technically to be easily transported from place to place. However, measures of personality, intelligence, aptitude, motivation, job satisfaction, employability, self-esteem and a host of other "psychological traits" could easily make the journey from site to site. Once "on location," the measures ensured that psychological notions of the mind and self would be continuously used within the area, as long as the measures were used. Consequently, psychologists were able to have their knowledge present even if they were not. However, in most cases psychologists were there as well. By insisting that amateurs or those who lacked formal training could not properly interpret the results and meanings of such measures, psychologists affirmed the need for their own services in areas where the measures had migrated. The measures were flexible enough to enjoy widespread use, but cryptic enough to require expert administration and interpretation.[5] Psychological measures were in essence "materialized" consultants. They presented psychological solutions by framing problems, issues and solutions in psychological terms. As such, psychological measures simultaneously spread the knowledge and helped to legitimate it.

A final factor that helps explain the success of psychology is the convergence of a number of different "psy" networks within the last few decades. The delimitations of this book may have given the mistaken impression that psychological knowledge is solely the product of the discipline of psychology, but it is perhaps better to see psychological knowledge, at least in the contemporary context, as the outcome of multiple, interlocking epistemic movements. While psychologists were undoubtedly the primary producer of psychological knowledge over the course of the last century, other groups, particularly psychiatrists, government bureaucrats, heads of foundations, social workers and to some extent religious leaders also produced and spread their own various psychological notions. For instance, today even most mainstream religious groups have incorporated some degree of psychological language and therapy into their spiritual practices.

This convergence of "psy" networks is particularly evident in the historical relationship between psychology and psychiatry. The two disciplines spent much of their early relationship fighting over certification, the use of psychotherapy and the true legacy of Freud. However, within the last few decades this relationship, although still sometimes raucous, particularly with regard to prescription-writing privileges, has become much more cooperative, particularly after a suitable division of labor was forged in the 1950s. For instance, clinical psychologists in their practices routinely use the *Diagnostic and Statistical Manual* categories developed and used by psychiatrists. Likewise, in their own activities psychiatrists often use measures developed by psychologists. In addition, other groups, such as social workers, management theorists, twelve-step groups, agency researchers and educators, although largely independent, produce reams of psychological knowledge every year. Such cooperation signals the merger of a number of "psy" organizations and groups, all contributing to the production and dissemination of psychological knowledge (see Rose, 1996a). What all of these disparate groups share is a psychological outlook—all seek to reduce phenomena and events to what they consider to be their basic, underlying mental or psychological dimensions. Psychological knowledge has, consequently, become much greater and larger than that produced by the discipline of psychology. Today the discipline of psychology is just one of the major players in the making of psychological knowledge. Indeed, today psychological knowledge would live on even if the discipline of psychology did not.

BEING PSYCHOLOGICAL

At first appearance it would seem not to matter much that psychology has produced all these concepts and techniques to guide everyday life. After all, psychological advice seems to be within our capacity to accept or reject. However, the matter is much more complex than this. The convergence of all the factors that explain psychology's success has produced a historically and culturally unique form of psychological existence, or being, one that is difficult simply to reject or ignore. As the historian J.T. Jackson Lears (1981) described it, to "be psychological" in the early part of the twentieth century was to be "hip" and glamorous. It was to grasp and incorporate into one's identity and repertoire of action the energy and contradictions of modern life. To be psychological then was to engage in a particular way of being, even if one was not directly aware of the findings of the emerging fields of psychiatry or psychology (see Lears, 1981: 56). To be psychological today, long after the knowledge and practices of psychology have become commonplace, is to be normal and civil. It is to conduct life in the way it is supposed to be conducted and to treat one's self and other selves with due emotional deference. Just as blowing one's nose on a shirt, once an accepted practice in the West, has become the epitome of bad manners, acting toward others without regard to their "interpersonal dynamics," "emotional needs" or complex and multilayered psychological interiors is today a sign of uncouthness and incivility.

This transformation of psychological knowledge into an active component of everyday life speaks to the fact that psychology has today become much more than a static body of knowledge. It is, rather, best seen as a series of techniques based in and directed by an underlying psychological ontology. For most people living in the West today, psychological knowledge seems to capture basic, inherent aspects of what it means to be human. Today "we have come to think, judge, console, and reform ourselves according to psychological norms of truth" (Rose, 1996b: 96). Such psychological categories and concepts as self-esteem, psychological development and self-realization seem to mirror and report a reality residing within each of us. When we talk about and represent our lives, these concepts seem to tap into the way things really are, or perhaps could be. Psychological concepts seem useful, even commonsensical means of expressing to others how our minds and selves work or why we feel the way we do. However, the inevitability of utilizing psychological concepts and frameworks in everyday life speaks less to their inherent epistemological truthfulness than to the success and proliferation of the vast network of psychology. As this historical examination has tried to show, the content of psychological knowledge could have been otherwise or not existed at all. An examination of the history of psychology reveals many once important concepts or frameworks that have either fallen out of favor or have been recast. Psychology's complex history also reveals that the places where psychological knowledge traveled could have easily been blocked, or they could have been colonized by other knowledge forms, such as sociology or biology. If this had occurred, the various psychological concepts that seem so necessary for describing who we are today would be simply unthinkable.

In the early 1960s, Abraham Maslow (1962) argued that it was time for the establishment of a "psychology of being." What Maslow's argument failed to capture was that by that time "being" was already well on its way to becoming psychological. In this sense, psychology can be seen as transforming what Paul Feyerabend (1999) referred to as the "richness of being" into the "abstractions" of the discipline of psychology. Today the presence of psychological knowledge permits us to employ certain psychological techniques and to engage in particular forms of action. In other words, it allows us to describe and act toward people and in ordinary situations in particular psychological ways. For example, as detailed in earlier chapters, the concepts of self-esteem and self-actualization force us to look at the self as a reservoir of potentiality; the self is either full of this potential or is in need of replenishment. Such concepts make us attentive to fostering the self through a continuous application of psychological techniques. Other concepts, such as "psychological development," permit us to see others and ourselves as occupying particular emotional and cognitive planes. Psychological tests show us where we reside relative to others and where we "should be"—and would be, if we were "normal." Clinical psychologists, in turn, help us achieve this normality, as identified by the tests. In addition, such terms as "the healing process," "recovery," and "closure" structure our understanding of tragedy as a psychological obstacle, which, like substance addiction, can be overcome only by psychological techniques. When we use these concepts in dinner conversation, seek out therapy or read a child-care manual, we are participating in and reproducing a particular psychological construction of human nature. This "psychologism" portrays everyone everywhere as possessing the same psychological characteristics. Variations among people are seen as matters of level and degree rather than differences in kind. Thus people in other cultures are shaped by the same underlying traits that affect people in the West, although they may explain and represent them differently. Psychology argues that they too have varying levels of self-esteem, anxiety and latent hostility, although they, like a psychologically unaware Westerner, may not recognize it yet. Psychology, consequently, helps to construct a particular universal notion of "human nature," which it then claims to capture and describe.

The extensive use of psychological concepts also produces a "psychologization of the mundane" (Rose, 1990: 244). In this process, ordinary "life events," such as childbirth, marriage, moving or acquiring a new job, become recast as psychological events. These ordinary life events are seen as the harbingers of basic underlying psychological states—such as anxiety, denial, fear or repression—that need identification, expression and often intervention and treatment. People must learn to be in tune with their complex psychological traits in order to understand why they do what they do or why others do what *they* do. In order to ensure that these potentially dangerous underlying psychological traits do not upset the balance of everyday life, people must be taught "coping strategies" by which they may "work on themselves" and experience "personal growth." Such attention attaches people to an ongoing and never-ending "project of identity" (Rose, 1996b: 196). They must work diligently in order to make their selves "fulfilled" and "emotionally healthy." In addition to awareness of their own psychological traits, people also need vigilance with regard to their interactions with others. If individual selves are reservoirs of potentially threatening or disrupting psychological characteristics, so too are relationships with spouses, friends, children and coworkers. Without monitoring and intervention, these interpersonal relationship may become "unhealthy" and "dysfunctional," threatening the fabric of marriage, the profitability of a corporation or the emotional balance of children.

It is possible, of course, to explain "mental states" or "behavior" without referring to psychological concepts or without reducing all things to the mind. We could possess and use radically different epistemic arrangements of mind, self and society or introduce completely new elements into the arrangement. We could have a childhood without "child development." We could have failure without "fear of success." We could feel without "emotional intelligence." In short, we could get along perfectly well without self-esteem, delusional, emotional disorders or most other psychological concepts. We could also, under dramatically different circumstances and with involvement with different networks, rediscover the religious language of the soul or the romantic discourse of transcendentalism or invoke the language of biological or sociological determinism. In short, there are a myriad of other ways of being and means of representing being that are not psychological in origin, although they are becoming increasingly difficult to imagine.[6]

It is better to see psychological being not as an inevitable part of human existence but as an outcome of the workings of particular networks. In this sense, being psychological is similar to "having" electricity or cable television—one only has it if one is plugged into the right network (see Latour, 1987). Being psychological, like having a soul, attention deficit disorder, karma or tuberculosis, is possible only within the confines of a particular network that links people and objects together in a particular system of meaning and a network of practice. Once established, this network begins to take on a life of its own, generating its own rules, structure and culture. If someone steps outside of the network that supports a particular mode of being— whether the mode happens to be psychological, Buddhist or Baptist— or is enrolled in another network, he or she possesses, and is, something entirely different.

The above is not meant to suggest that psychological knowledge and activities are not useful. Without doubt, being psychological allows people a degree of respect and personal freedom. It helps construct, explain and legitimize particular feelings and emotions. It also provides some degree of destigmatization for those with mental disorders and establishes the care of mind and self as centerpieces of existence and well-being—at least, this is the way things look like from within the network of psychology. In this sense, psychology today is more akin to a "life philosophy," or common sense, than a formal brand of knowledge. We use it to situate ourselves, understand our failures and orient our lives. There are undoubtedly many different forms of being that would be much worse. However, this should not obscure the modes of experience that being psychological disallows. However positive a cultural attitude being psychological seems compared with those of the past, it could also be seen as destroying or marginalizing other aspects of existence. For example, psychological being, with its emphasis on the scientific representation of mind and self, obliterates the romantic view of the self (see Gergen, 1991). Words such as "passion," "genius" and "depth" lose their meaning when converted to or replaced by psychological concepts. If psychology provides a rich and expansive vocabulary of mind, self and relationships, it also robs us of other ways of being that could be equally as rewarding. It would be impossible to know the full extent of these ways of being, however, unless we were immersed in the networks that support them.

PSYCHOLOGY AND THE MAKING OF MODERN SOCIETY

Our current framing of self and society is largely the epistemic product of nineteenth and twentieth-century psychology and the social sciences. Psychology and the social sciences helped magnify and naturalize an existing philosophical bifurcation between individuals "over here" and society "over there." This bifurcated ontology created a situation in which we talk about humans as possessors of particular traits, characteristics, desires and needs, and societies as made up of structures, cultures, organizations and ideologies. The story of their interrelationship is then told in either of two ways. Either individual characteristics or desires constitute the larger society (e.g., behaviorism, Freudianism or exchange theory), or societies' rules and structures work to make the individual (e.g., structuralism, functionalism or systems theory). As a result of this bifurcated ontology, psychological accounts begin with selves and minds already in place, while sociologically inspired accounts of knowledge most often start with the assumption that society is "always already there." In the psychological version, selves and minds are driven by their own unique structures and characteristics. Individual characteristics, such as low self-esteem, paranoia or levels of intelligence, work to make the individual and ultimately the society in which he or she lives. In the sociological version, society, like the natural world, is governed by its own unique laws and rules. These laws and rules, in turn, determine the composition and flow of knowledge and culture. Confining social forces, such as class dynamics, gender hierarchies, racial divisions and societal evolution, all work to shape and mold the context and content of the knowledge that is produced within a given society.

However, as I argued in chapter 1, it would be a mistake to contend that conventional sociological accounts are sufficient for explaining the content of psychology. Explaining something as heterogeneous as American psychology requires new epistemic frameworks. What the traditional sociology of knowledge ignores as it works to show so thoroughly how society shapes knowledge is that society, like minds and selves, must also be made. Society, like knowledge itself, is the result of the convergence and cooperation of a multitude of local practices. It is the name we give to the innumerable practices and things after they have congealed into recognizable and nominal patterns. In this sense, both the meaning and composition of the social varies depending on the network doing the sorting, assembling and naming. Just as knowledge continuously moves and changes, so too does society, as the practices, alliances and networks that constitute it shift.

The common account of knowledge found in the sociology of knowledge also ignores the multitudes of initially local activities and practices that went into the making of what we call "modernity." Modernity is often thought of as the outcome of a series of macro-level changes occurring in Western society over the last five hundred years or so. Within this account, industrialism, capitalism, rationalization, the forced division of labor and other massive social changes created an entirely new sociocultural environment, one unlike any that existed before. With the advent of this new environment, a boundary was forever drawn between the traditional and modern worlds. However, modernity can perhaps best be thought of as less a uniform state of social and cultural development that sweeps aside tradition than as a concept used to provide a post hoc description of these multitudes of local practices. Modernity and modernization are, consequently, not so much things that happen to a society as they are things that accumulate into particular orientations and forms of action that are knowable and identifiable only after the fact. In this sense, "it is the sorting that makes the times, not the times that make the sorting" (Latour, 1993: 76). In other words, historical epochs do not determine how things are organized; rather, the way things become organized and who does the organizing determine the names and meanings given to historical periods.

With this understanding of modernity as a theoretical backdrop, it is possible to rethink the contribution of psychological knowledge to the remaking of society and the creation of modernity. Psychology is best seen not as an outcome of societal modernization, as both its critics and proponents often characterized it, but as one of the components that constitutes the assemblage now thought of as modernity. Psychology was not simply a response to modern life or an outcome of the rationalization of society but an important part of modernity's constitution. Psychology added to all the other forces that made up modernity in the United States and throughout the world and, in the process, modified the meaning of society. In this new psychologized society "reality becomes ordered according to a psychological taxonomy, and abilities, personalities, attitudes and the like become central to the deliberations and calculations of social authorities and psychological theorists alike" (Rose, 1996b: 60).

Psychology contributed to the construction of modernity, at least in part, by rearranging and displacing some of society's previous actors. With the rise of psychological knowledge, spiritualists became relegated to the margins of advice giving, mental philosophers were discredited and replaced in the university, introspection was replaced by experimentation and lay interpretations of a person's character were replaced by formal "personality measures." As part of this displacement, psychology became linked with the accomplishments of other knowledge workers in such fields as economics, physics, political science, biology and medicine. Just as economists were constructing the "rational consumer," sociologists were assembling "modern society" and physicians were founding the "biomedical model," psychologists were at work making the "self" and "mind."

Psychology was, consequently, a key part of the rearrangement of people and things that constituted modernity. In this rearrangement, existing entities were renamed and realigned into new configurations, and new conceptual categories were formed in which people and things were placed. In this sense, "societies are displaced and reformed with and through the very contents of science" (Latour, 1983: 154). Without psychology's efforts to modernize the mind and self, the thing that we call modernity would undoubtedly look different and operate very differently. For example, it is hard to imagine marketing strategies today without the leverage provided by psychological behaviorism. Likewise, it is difficult to envision the confessional talk show without psychotherapy and the self-actualization movement. It is also impossible to picture the workings of today's public schools and the training of teachers without the input of developmental and cognitive psychology. Without psychological knowledge's presence, there would be no test of intelligence, no self-actualization, no school counseling and no parenting manuals, or perhaps these items would have been constructed by other groups, in very different forms. In turn, without these psychological innovations, courts would lack the means of determining sanity, schools would have no resources for sorting students and couples would be without a vocabulary of inter-personal relations (or perhaps these groups would utilize the representations and practices of other groups). In other words, without the presence of psychological knowledge, some of the elements that compose the "modern world" would be very different. Psychology was an integral part of the multitudes of linkages that created the fragile but coherent and purposive whole so familiar to us. If society is the name given to things once they have settled at least temporarily into a nameable form, however, even that name is open to ongoing and competing explanations and terminologies.

One important misconception that stands in the way of our understanding of psychology's contribution to the constitution of modern society is a tendency to see modernity and psychology as inevitable universal trends or as all-encompassing forms of being. However, just as not all people are modern, not all people are psychological. In this sense, universality too must be constructed (see Lenoir, 1997: 18). In our own time both modernity and psychological knowledge exist only in wide patches spread across time and space—although these patches are increasingly global and tend to be in powerful locales, such as courts, hospitals and schools. For most people being psychological is a local and temporal matter; it occurs only at certain places and points in the day and during particular segments of life, as they move in and out of psychological networks. In fact, as was evident in chapter 8, many of the ways we think about the self are more hybrids of religious, folk and psychological frameworks than of a purely and uniquely psychological nature. In some instances being psychological is inevitable, as in the case of mandatory therapy or employee testing. In other cases it is something that is drawn upon voluntarily in order to make sense of particular situations and orient our lives, as in marriage counseling or parenting manuals. In most circumstances, however, it is an automatic response to particular events, as with emotivism or codes of civility. Such a distribution leaves gaps where psychological knowledge is not present or is "in remission." However, as psychological knowledge has expanded over the course of the last century, the spaces where psychological knowledge is not present have become fewer and fewer. As a result, the times and places we spend outside of psychologically influenced networks are increasingly rare.

It is also important to remember that a knowledge form lasts only as long as its network of support endures. All established knowledge forms face ongoing threats from other entrenched groups or from upstarts who want to reduce the world to their own concepts, measures and representations or to migrate into an existing area. As Randall Collins (1999: 876) has pointed out, "Conflict over the attention space is a fundamental social fact about intellectuals." Although well entrenched in schools, courtrooms and counseling centers, psychological knowledge has begun to show signs of erosion in some quarters as other networks of knowing challenge it. Such instability may signal the unraveling of psychology's vast network or merely a brief and fleeting regionalized revolt against its authority. Whatever the case, the history of psychology indicates that any new group that wishes to establish its own knowledge form has a long and arduous road ahead of it.

Finally, as I argued in chapter 1, in order to understand the complexities of the relationship between psychological knowledge and society, as well as knowledge and society in general, it is more beneficial and less contradictory to see psychological knowledge and society as simultaneous co-constructions rather than essential and distinct. Indeed, all dichotomies, such as those between society and the individual, culture and nature and truth and rhetoric, are not essential, naturally occurring categories but, in the words of Stephan Fuchs (2001: 104), "social devices of description and explanation." Consequently, it is important to see "solutions to the problem of knowledge [as] solutions to the problem of social order" (Shapin, 1988: 539). Constructing psychological knowledge also means building a particular associational entity or collectivity that views and acts in accordance with certain ideas and within certain constraints. In other words, psychological knowledge once constructed, offers an alternative form of a possible society (see Woolgar, 1994: 11). Therefore, society does not make people psychological; society itself is composed of the epistemic products of the field of psychology. In other words, the society we now inhabit is partially the outcome of the workings of psychological knowledge. Likewise, the individual is not in possession of a psychological mind or self until he or she is made to be so. Just as societies that practice ancestor worship or witchcraft are quite different from those that do not, a society with psychological knowledge and practices is considerably different from a society without them. The actants that were mobilized to build psychological knowledge into widespread truths about the mind and self are also responsible for building a particular social order or arrangement. While this knowledge was being formed, many other agents were also being mobilized to construct other truths and social arrangements—indeed, "unknowns" and "societies" are constantly under construction. What we call "society," "history," and "knowledge" are the outcomes of those historical and ongoing constructions.

NOTES

1. Even writing itself has been subjected to the psychological gaze. For example, E. Bergler (1950) contended in *The Writer and Psychoanalysis* that all writing is essentially neurotic, an attempt to substitute the flow of words for disrupted flow of mother's milk.

2. Of course, within the discipline this created conflict between purists and populists, experimentalists and clinicians, and humanists and positivists. This conflict was diffused, in part, by creating a multitude of sections (now fifty-five of them) within the APA.

3. As I argued in chapter 2, disciplines with overly commodified knowledge forms can easily lose control of their epistemic products to outsiders. Psychology and psychiatry managed to wrestle control of mental therapeutics from mind-cure advocates only to have this new control eroded by "New Age" therapies in the late twentieth century.

4. As we saw in chapter 8, these groups infused their own ideas into psychology as well.

5. In many cases, only certified psychologists are allowed to use and interpret the results of various tests and measures. Their use is limited to psychologists not because of their inherent difficulty but due to psychology's ability to establish legal and institutional rules that demand that the tests be applied only by psychologists.

6. Over the last two centuries a number of writers have sought to overcome the inherent dualism between the self and society found in most psychological and social scientific accounts. For example, in 1885 Ludwig Gumplowicz (in Fleck, 1979 [1935]: 46–47) argued that "the greatest error of individualistic psychology is the assumption that a person thinks. . . . What actually thinks within a person is not the individual himself but his social community. The source of his thinking is not within himself but is his social environment and the very social atmosphere he 'breathes.'" A few decades later Wittgenstein (1953: 61e) echoed this view in *Philosophical Investigations*, when he asked that we "try not to think of understanding as a 'mental process' at all . . . but ask [ourselves]: in what sort of case, in what kind of circumstances, do we say, 'Now I know how to go on,'" when, that is, the formula has occurred to me?" More recently, in his book *Against Essentialism* Stephan Fuchs (2001: 124) argued that "'wants' and 'beliefs' are not internal states or attributes of personal minds, but result from observations and self-observations." What these positions reveal are other

ways to think about personhood and thinking, radically different from the one supplied by psychology. However, to think in this way is not to turn toward the truth of personhood or society but to step into other, somewhat weaker knowledge networks.

Appendix: A Few Important Dates in the History of American Psychology

The dates included here are generally limited to the themes discussed throughout the book. Some dates are taken from Warren Street's (1994) *A Chronology of Noteworthy Events in American Psychology*. Others come from sources cited throughout the text.

1860   Gustav Fechner publishes volume 1 of *Elements of Psychophysics* in Germany.

1874   Wilhelm Wundt publishes *Principles of Physiological Psychology* in Germany.

1878   G. Stanley Hall became the first person to earn a Ph.D. in psychology from an American university.

1879   Wilhelm Wundt establishes the first psychological laboratory in Leipzig, Germany.

1883   G. Stanley Hall establishes the first psychological laboratory in the United States, at Johns Hopkins University.

1885   William James establishes a small laboratory at Harvard University based on a demonstration laboratory for his course in physiological psychology.
        The American Society for Psychical Research is founded.

1887   The *American Journal of Psychology* is launched by G. Stanley Hall.
        John Dewey publishes his book *Psychology*.

1889   G. Stanley Hall became the first president of Clark University.

1890   William James's title at Harvard University is changed to "professor of psychology."
        William James's *Principles of Psychology* is published.
        The term "mental test" is used in an article written by James Cattell.

1891   William James delivers the first of his ten lectures entitled "Talks to Teachers." The talks will be published in 1899.

1892   James Baldwin publishes *Psychology Applied to the Art of Teaching*.

The American Psychological Association (APA) is organized at Clark University.

The first meeting of the APA is held at the University of Pennsylvania.

G. Stanley Hall establishes the National Association for the Study of Children.

Hugo Muensterberg and Joseph Jastrow supervise a psychology exhibit at the World's Columbia Exposition in Chicago.

1893   Edmund C. Sanford's *Course in Experimental Psychology* is published.

The journal *Psychological Review* is first published.

1894   The National Education Association establishes a Child Study Department at the urging of G. Stanley Hall.

James Cattell uses a mental test on students entering Columbia College and the Columbia School of Mines.

1895   E.W. Scripture publishes *Thinking, Feeling, Doing*, one of psychology's first widely sold books.

1896   Lightner Witmer establishes the first psychological clinic at the University of Pennsylvania.

1897   William James's title is changes back to "professor of philosophy."

G. Stanley Hall is invited to speak at the first gathering of the National Congress of Mothers.

1902   Teachers College at Columbia establishes a Department of Educational Psychology directed by Edward Thorndike.

1904   E.B. Titchener organizes a club for experimentalists that later will become known as the Society of Experimental Psychologists.

G. Stanley Hall publishes his multivolume book *Adolescence*.

Psychologists set up a public exhibit at the St. Louis World's Fair.

1905   In France, Alfred Binet and Theodore Simon publish results of a new test to measure intelligence.

1906   Morton Prince establishes the *Journal of Abnormal Psychology*.

Henry Goddard becomes director of the Vineland Laboratory, at the Vineland Training School in New Jersey.

The Emmanuel Movement is formed in Boston. The movement seeks to blend scientific principles of therapeutical psychology with religious values.

Edward Thorndike publishes his influential *The Principles of Teaching Based on Psychology*.

1907   The Binet-Simon scale of general intelligence based on mental age is developed.

1909   Sigmund Freud and Carl Jung visit the United States.

1910   Edward Thorndike establishes the *Journal of Educational Psychology*.

Grace Kent and Aaron Rosanoff publish results of word-association tests comparing "normals" and subjects with mental pathologies.

1911   Applicants for membership in the APA are now required to provide copies of their published research.

1913   John B. Watson delivers a lecture entitled "Psychology as the Behaviorist Views It" at Columbia University.

Hugo Muensterberg publishes *Psychology and Industrial Efficiency*.

1916   Lewis Terman publishes *The Measurement of Intelligence*.

1917   The Iowa Child Welfare Research Station is established.

The Stanford-Binet Intelligence Test is published.

The first pen-and-paper personality test is developed, by Robert Woodworth, to test American recruits in World War I.

The U.S. War Department begins using intellectual (alpha) and physical (beta) tests developed by Robert M. Yerkes. Over two million alpha tests will be given.

The American Association of Clinical Psychologists is founded; the association will become the APA Section of Clinical Psychology two years later.

1919   Walter Dill Scott opens the Scott Company to sell testing materials and advice to companies.

1920   The National Research Council sponsors a conference to ease the volatile relationship between psychiatry and psychology.

Membership in the APA reaches almost four hundred.

1921   The Psychological Corporation is incorporated.

Hermann Rorschach's book *Psychodiagnostik* introduces his inkblot method of personality testing.

Psychologists at Columbia release the results of a series of psychological experiments performed on Babe Ruth.

1923   The term "school psychologists" is first used in print, in an article written by R.B.W. Hunt.

1924   Sigmund Freud appears on the cover of *Time* magazine.

1926   The magazine *Children, a Magazine of Parents* (later known as *Parents Magazine*) is first published.

1927   Elton Mayo and his associates begin a study of industrial workers at Western Electric Company's Hawthorne plant near Chicago.

1928   J.B. Watson publishes *Psychological Care of Infant and Child.*

1931   Walter Bingham's radio series *Psychology Today* is first aired on nearly fifty NBC-affiliated radio stations.

1932   Dorothy Yates warns the public of the dangers of "pseudo-psychology' in her book *Psychological Racketeers.*

1933   The Bernreuter Personality Inventory is published.

1939   The National Council on Family Relations is formed.

1940   The National Research Council appoints an Emergency Committee in Psychology to mobilize psychologists for World War II.

1942   Starke Hathaway and J.C. McKinley first publish the Minnesota Multiphasic Personality Inventory.

1943   The Disabled Veterans Rehabilitation Act is passed. The act begins to change the role of clinical psychologists in therapy.

1945   Connecticut becomes the first state to allow psychologists to be certified or licensed.

1946   The physician Benjamin Spock publishes *The Commonsense Book of Baby and Child Care.*

1949   The Boulder scientist-practitioner model for clinical psychologist is established at a conference in Boulder, Colorado.

1951   Carl Rogers publishes *Client-Centered Therapy.*

1954   Abraham Maslow publishes *Motivation and Personality.*

1955   The psychologist Dr. Joyce Brothers becomes the first woman to win the game show *The $64,000 Question.*

1958   Title V of the National Defense Education Act provides funds to increase school testing, counseling and guidance services.

1962   A U.S. court of appeals rules that psychologists are acceptable as expert witnesses.

The *Journal of School Psychology* is founded.

The Esalen Institute is formed in Big Sur, California. Over the years the institute will become an important center for the human potential movement and humanistic psychology.

1967   *Psychology Today* is first published.

1968   The National Association of School Psychologists is formed.

New Jersey passes a law allowing insurance companies to cover psychological services.

1969   The children's program Sesame Street is first aired. Psychologist Edward Palmer leads the program's research and evaluation team.

1973   A conference at Vail, Colorado, endorses a professional model for training clinical psychologists.

1974   The APA opens a public information office.

1976   The Health Insurance Association endorses "freedom of choice" legislation in every state. The legislation calls for allowing direct insurance payments to clinical psychologists.

1982   The Association for Media Psychology is founded. The association later becomes Division 46 of the APA.

The APA airs its first television public-service messages.

William Worden publishes *Grief Counseling and Grief Therapy*; the book helps launch grief counseling and will contribute to the growth of disaster mental health.

1983   The APA purchases *Psychology Today* for $3.8 million; the periodical will be sold in 1988 after losing money.

1986   The National Council for Self-Esteem is formed.

1987   The California Task Force to Promote Self-Esteem and Personal Responsibility is formed.

1988   APA members who feel that the organization no longer represents the interest of experimental and academic psychologists form the America Psychological Society.

1989   The American Red Cross fields its first mental health team in response to Hurricane Hugo.

1991   The APA establishes a hotline for people to discuss the Gulf War.

1992   The APA establishes the Disaster Response Network to coordinate responses to disasters.

References

Abbott, Andrew. 1988. *The System of Professions: An Essay on the Division of Expert Labor*. Chicago: University of Chicago Press.

———. 2001. *Chaos of Disciplines*. Chicago: University of Chicago Press.

Adams, Grace. 1928. "The Decline of Psychology in America." *American Mercury* (December): 450–454.

———. 1931. *Psychology: Science or Superstition?* New York: Covici Friede.

———. 1934. "The Rise and Fall of Psychology." *Atlantic Monthly* (January): 82–92.

Adelman, Howard, and Linda Taylor. 2000. "Shaping the Future of Mental Health in the Schools." *Psychology in the Schools* 37: 49–60.

Adler, Helmut. 1994. "The European Influence on American Psychology: 1892 and 1942." Pp. 113–122 in H. Adler and R. Rieber (eds.), *Aspects of the History of Psychology in America: 1892–1992*. New York: New York Academy of Sciences.

Allport, Floyd, and Gordon Allport. 1921. "Personality Traits: Their Classification and Measurement." *Journal of Abnormal and Social Psychology* 16: 6–40.

American Psychological Association. 1892a. "Proceedings of the American Psychological Association: Preliminary Meeting" (www.yorku.ca/dept/psych/classics/APA/prelim.htm).

———. 1892b. "Proceedings of the American Psychological Association: First Annual Meeting" (www.yorku.ca/dept/psych/classics/APA/meeting1.htm).

———. 1912. "Proceedings of the Twentieth Annual Meeting of the A.P.A." *Psychological Bulletin* 9: 41–92.

———. 1947. "Recommended Graduate Training Program in Clinical Psychology." *American Psychologist* 2: 539–558.

———. 1954. "Psychology, Psychiatry, and Legislation in New York." *American Psychologist* 9: 160–164.

———. 1995a. *Current Major Field of APA Members by Employment Status: 1995.* Washington, D.C.: American Psychological Association.

———. 1995b. "Responding to Oklahoma City's Needs." *APA Monitor* (June): 22, 26.

American Red Cross. 1991. *Statement of Understanding between the American Psychological Association and the American National Red Cross* (Document no. 4468). Washington, D.C.: American Red Cross.

Amsterdamska, Olga. 1987. "Intellectuals in Social Movements: The Experts of Solidarity." Pp. 213–245 in S. Blume, J. Bunders, L. Leydesdorff and R. Whitley (eds.), *The Social Direction of Public Sciences, Sociology of the Sciences Yearbook.* Boston: D. Reidel.

Andersen, Robin. 1995. *Consumer Culture and TV Programming.* Boulder, Colo.: Westview Press.

Anderson, Walter. 1983. *The Upstart Spring: Esalen and the American Awakening.* Reading, Mass.: Addison Wesley.

Arbuthnot, Jack, and Donald Gordon. 1997. "Divorce Education for Parents and Children." Pp. 341–364 in L. Vandecreek, S. Knapp and T. Jackson (eds.), *Innovations in Clinical Practice: A Source Book.* Sarasota, Fla.: Professional Resources Press.

Aries, P. 1962. *Centuries of Childhood: A Social History of Family Life.* Translated by R. Baldick. New York: Alfred A. Knopf.

Arthur, Winfred, Jr., and Ludy Benjamin. 1999. "Psychology Applied to Business." Pp. 98–115 in A. Stec and D. Bernstein (eds.), *Psychology: Fields of Application.* Boston: Houghton Mifflin.

Ashbaugh, E.J. 1919. "The Organization and Function of a Bureau of Research." *School and Society* 9: 577–584.

Ashmore, Malcolm. 1989. *The Reflexive Thesis: Wrighting the Sociology of Scientific Knowledge.* Chicago: University of Chicago Press.

Bachelard, George. 1984 [1934]. *The New Scientific Spirit.* Translated by A. Goldhammer. Boston: Beacon Press.

Baldwin, James M. 1893. *Elements of Psychology.* New York: Henry Holt.

———. 1895. *Mental Development in the Child and the Race.* New York: Macmillan.

———. 1902 (ed.). *Dictionary of Philosophy and Psychology.* New York: Macmillan.

Baritz, Loren. 1960. *The Servants of Power: A History of the Use of Social Science in American Industry.* Middletown, Conn.: Wesleyan University Press.

Barkley, Russell. 1990. *Attention-Deficit Hyperactivity Disorder: A Handbook for Diagnosis and Treatment.* New York: Guilford Press.

Barnes, Barry. 1995. *The Elements of Social Theory.* Princeton, N.J.: Princeton University Press.

Barnhill, Laurence. 1979. "Healthy Family Systems." *Family Coordinator* 28: 94–100.

Barthes, Roland. 1976. *Sade Fourier Loyola.* Translated by R. Miller. New York: Hill and Wang.

Baumeister, Roy (ed.). 1993. *Self-Esteem: The Puzzle of Low Self-Regard.* New York: Plenum Press.

Beard, George. 1881. *American Nervousness: Its Causes and Consequences.* New York: Putnam.

Beck, Ulrich. 1992. *Risk Society: Towards a New Modernity.* Translated by M. Ritter. London: Sage.

Becker, Howard S. 1963. *Outsiders: Studies in the Sociology of Deviance.* New York: Free Press.

————. 1982. *Art Worlds.* Berkeley: University of California Press.

Becvar, R.J., and D.S. Becvar. 1982. *Systems Theory and Family Therapy: A Primer.* Washington, D.C.: University Press of America.

Bell, H.M. 1935. *The Theory and Practice of Personal Counseling with Special Reference to the Adjustment Inventory.* Stanford, Calif.: Stanford University Press.

Bell, Paul, Robert Digman and James McKenna. 1995. "Should Psychologists Obtain Prescribing Privileges?" *Professional Psychology Research and Practice* 26: 371–376.

Ben-David, Joseph, and Randall Collins. 1966. "Social Factors in the Origins of a New Science: The Case of Psychology." *American Sociological Review* 31: 451–465.

Benjamin, Ludy. 1986. "Why Don't They Understand Us? A History of Psychology's Public Image." *American Psychologist* 41: 941–946.

Benjamin, Ludy, and William Bryant. 1997. "A History of Popular Psychology Magazines in America." Pp. 585–593 in W. Bringmann, H. Luck, R. Miller and C. Early (eds.), *A Pictorial History of Psychology.* Chicago: Quintessence.

Benjamin, Orly. 1998. "Therapeutic Discourse, Power and Change: Emotion and Negotiations in Marital Conversations." *Sociology* 32: 771–793.

Benjamins, James. 1950. "Changes in Performance in Relation to Influences upon Self-Conceptualization." *Journal of Abnormal and Social Psychology* 45: 473–480.

Bergler, E. 1950. *The Writer and Psychoanalysis.* Garden City, N.Y.: Doubleday.

Bernreuter, Robert. 1933. "The Theory and Construction of the Personality Inventory." *Journal of Social Psychology* 4: 387–405.

Berrios, Jerry. 2000. "Counselor Offers Advice on Ousting Prostitution." *Kansas City Star*, February 29: B3.

Bettelheim, Bruno. 1988. *A Good Enough Parent: A Book on Child-Rearing.* New York: Vintage Books.

Bijker, W., T. Hughes and T. Pinch (eds.). 1987. *The Social Construction of Technological Systems.* Cambridge, Mass.: MIT Press.

Bills, Robert. 1953. "Rorschach Characteristics of Persons Scoring High and Low in Acceptance of Self." *Journal of Consulting Psychology* 17: 36–38.

Binet, Alfred, and T. Simon. 1916. *The Development of Intelligence in Children.* Translated by E. Kite. Baltimore: Williams and Wilkins.

Bingham, Walter. 1932a. "Forward." Pp. v–vi in W. Bingham (ed.), *Psychology Today: Lectures and Study Manual.* Chicago: University of Chicago Press.

————. 1932b. "Making Work Worth While." Pp. 35–36, 262–271 in W. Bingham (ed.), *Psychology Today: Lectures and Study Manual.* Chicago: University of Chicago Press.

Bird, Graham. 1991. "Humanistic Understanding and Physiological Explanation in the Principles." *British Journal of Psychology* 82: 195–203.

Birnbaum, Lucille. 1955. "Behaviorism in the 1920's." *American Quarterly* 7: 15–30.

Bjerre, Andreas. 1927. *The Psychology of Murder: A Study in Criminal Psychology.* New York: Longmans, Green.

Blake, R.R. 1948. "Some Quantitative Aspects of *Time Magazine*'s Presentation of Psychology." *American Psychologist* 3: 124–126.

Blakeslee, Alton. 1952. "Psychology and the Newspaper Man." *American Psychologist* 7: 91–94.

Blocher, Donald. 2000. *The Evolution of Counseling Psychology*. New York: Springer.

Bloor, David. 1976. *Knowledge and Social Imagery*. London: Routledge and Kegan Paul.

———. 1978. "Polyhedra and the Abominations of Leviticus." *British Journal for the History of Science* 39: 245–272.

———. 1983. *Wittgenstein: A Social Theory of Knowledge*. London: Macmillan.

Blumenthal, Arthur. 1994. "Joseph Jastrow: Pioneer Psychologist Facing the 'Administrative Peril.'" Pp. 79–89 in H. Adler and R. Rieber (eds.), *Aspects of the History of Psychology in America: 1892–1992*. New York: New York Academy of Sciences.

Borell, Merriley. 1993. "Training the Senses, Training the Mind." Pp. 244–261 in W.F. Bynum and R. Porter (eds.), *Medicine and the Five Senses*. Cambridge: Cambridge University Press.

Boring, Edwin. 1923. "Intelligence as the Tests Test It." *New Republic*, June 6: 35–37.

———. 1942. *Sensation and Perception in the History of Experimental Psychology*. New York: Appleton-Century-Crofts.

———. 1950. *A History of Experimental Psychology*. New York: Appleton-Century-Crofts.

———. 1967. "Titchener's Experimentalists." *Journal of the History of the Behavioral Sciences* 3: 315–325.

Bouhoutsos, Jacqueline. 1990. "Media Psychology and Mediated Therapeutic Communication." Pp. 54–72 in G. Gumpert and S. Fish (eds.), *Talking to Strangers: Mediated Therapeutic Communication*. Norwood, N.J.: Ablex.

Bourdieu, Pierre, Jean-Claude Chamboredon and Jean-Claude Passeron. 1991. *The Craft of Sociology: Epistemological Preliminaries*. Translated by R. Nice. New York: Walter de Gruyter.

Bourdieu, Pierre. 1977. "The Economics of Linguistic Exchanges." *Social Science Information* 16: 645–668.

———. 1984. *Distinctions: A Social Critique of the Judgment of Taste*. Translated by R. Nice. Cambridge, Mass.: Harvard University Press.

Bourhis, R., S. Roth and G. MacQueen. 1989. "Communication in the Hospital Setting: A Survey of Medical and Everyday Language Use amongst Patients, Nurses and Doctors." *Social Science and Medicine* 28: 339–346.

Bowker, Geoffrey, and Susan L. Star. 1999. *Sorting Things Out: Classification and Its Consequences*. Cambridge, Mass.: MIT Press.

Bradshaw, John. 1988. *Bradshaw On: The Family, A Revolutionary Way of Self-Discovery*. Deerfield Beach, Fla.: Health Communications.

Branden, Nathaniel. 1969. *The Psychology of Self-Esteem: A New Concept of Man's Nature*. Los Angeles: Nash.

———. 1984. "In Defense of Self." *Association of Humanistic Psychology Perspectives* 8/9: 12.

Bray, D.W., R.J. Campbell and D.L. Grant. 1974. *Formative Years in Business: A Long-Term Study of Managerial Lives*. New York: Wiley.

Bregman, Elsie. 1922. "A Scientific Plan for Sizing Up Employees." *System* (June): 696–698, 762–763.

Briggs, Dorothy. 1970. *Your Child's Self-Esteem: The Key to His Life*. Garden City, N.Y.: Doubleday.

Brock, B.W., and C.P. Barnard. 1992. *Procedures in Marriage and Family Therapy*. 2nd ed. Boston: Allyn and Bacon.

Brodbeck, Arthur, and Howard Perlmutter. 1954. "Self-Dislike as a Determinant of Market Ingroup-Outgroup Preferences." *Journal of Psychology* 38: 271–280.

Broderick, Carlfred, and Sandra Schrader. 1981. "The History of Professional Marriage and Family Therapy." Pp. 5–35 in A. Gurman and D. Kniskern (eds.), *Handbook of Family Therapy*. New York: Brunner/Mazel.

Brookover, W.B. 1949. "Sociology of Education: A Definition." *American Sociological Review* 14: 407–415.

Brotemarkle, R.A. (ed.). 1931. *Clinical Psychology: Studies in Honor of Lightner Witmer*. Philadelphia: University of Pennsylvania Press.

Brothers, Joyce. 1989a. "The Shows That'll Make You Feel Better." *TV Guide*, July 29: 12–15.

———. 1989b. "Why We Need to Laugh." *TV Guide*, November 11: 18–20.

———. 1990. "How TV Adds Spice to Your Life." *TV Guide*, February 10: 13–14.

Brown, JoAnne. 1992. *The Definition of a Profession: The Authority of Metaphor in the History of Intelligence Testing, 1890–1930*. Princeton, N.J.: Princeton University Press.

Bruce, H. Addington. 1908. "Insanity and the Nation." *North American Review* 187: 70–79.

———. 1909. "Mental Healing of To-day." *Outlook*, September 4: 32.

———. 1910. "Bending the Twig." *American Magazine* 69: 690–695.

———. 1911. "New Ideas in Child Training." *American Magazine* 72: 286–294.

———. 1915. "The Fears of Childhood." *Good Housekeeping* 61: 451–457.

Bruer, John. 1999. *The Myth of the First Three Years: A New Understanding of Early Brain Development and Lifelong Learning*. New York: Basic Books.

Bruner, Jerome, and Gordon Allport. 1940. "Fifty Years of Change in American Psychology." *Psychological Bulletin* 47: 757–776.

Buchanan, Roderick. 1994. "The Development of the Minnesota Multiphasic Personality Inventory." *Journal of the History of the Behavioral Sciences* 30: 148–161.

Buchner, Edward F. 1903. "A Quarter Century of Psychology in America, 1878–1903." *American Journal of Psychology* 14: 666–680.

Buckley, Kerry. 1982. "The Selling of a Psychologist: John Broadus Watson and the Application of Behavioral Techniques to Advertising." *Journal of the History of the Behavioral Sciences* 18: 207–221.

Bunn, Geoffrey. 1997. "The Lie Detector, Wonder Woman and Liberty: The Life and Work of William Moulton Marston." *History of the Human Sciences* 10: 91–119.

Burbank, Luther. 1905. "Cultivate Children Like Flowers." *Elementary School Teacher* 6: 457–460.

Buri, John, Peggy Kirchner and Jane Walsh. 1987. "Familial Correlates of Self-Esteem in Young American Adults." *Journal of Social Psychology* 127: 583–588.

Burnett, James. 2000. "Boston's Anti-Crime Efforts Something to Believe in: Area Delegation Will Travel There to Learn More about It." *Milwaukee Journal Sentinel*, May 22: 1A.

Burnham, John. 1967. *Psychoanalysis and American Medicine, 1894–1918.* New York: International Universities Press.

———. 1974. "The Struggle between Physicians and Paramedical Personnel in American Psychiatry, 1917–41." *Journal of the History of Medicine* 29: 93–106.

———. 1987. *How Superstition Won and Science Lost: Popularizing Science and Health in the United States.* New Brunswick, N.J.: Rutgers University Press.

Burnham, William. 1926. *The Normal Mind: An Introduction to Mental Hygiene and Hygiene of School Instruction.* New York: D. Appleton.

Buros, Oscar (ed). 1953. *The Fourth Mental Measurements Yearbook.* Highland Park, N.J.: Gryphon Press.

———(ed.). 1970. *Personality Tests and Reviews.* Highland Park, N.J.: Gryphon Press.

Burt, Cyril. 1927. *The Measurement of Mental Capacities.* Edinburgh: Oliver and Boyd.

Butcher, James, and Edwin Megargee. 1989. *Minnesota Multiphasic Personality Inventory-2.* Minneapolis: University of Minnesota Press.

Butt, D.S., and D.W. Fiske. 1968. "Comparison of Strategies in Developing Scales for Dominance." *Psychological Bulletin* 70: 505–519.

California Task Force to Promote Self-Esteem and Personal and Social Responsibility. 1990. *Toward a State of Self-Esteem.* Sacramento: California State Department of Education.

Calkins, Mary. 1915. "The Self in Scientific Psychology." *American Journal of Psychology* 26: 495–524.

Camfield, Thomas. 1973. "The Professionalization of American Psychology, 1870–1917." *Journal of the History of the Behavioral Sciences* 9: 66–75.

Camic, Charles, and Yu Xie. 1994. "The Statistical Turn in American Social Science: Columbia University, 1890–1915." *American Sociological Review* 59: 773–805.

Canguilhem, Georges. 1980. "What Is Psychology?" *I and C* 7: 37–50.

Caplan, Eric. 1998a. *Mind Games: American Culture and the Birth of Psychotherapy.* Berkeley: University of California Press.

———. 1998b. "Popularizing American Psychotherapy: The Emmanuel Movement, 1906–1910." *History of Psychology* 1: 289–314.

Capshew, James H. 1992. "Psychologists on Site: A Reconnaissance of the Historiography of the Laboratory." *American Psychologist* 47: 132–142.

———. 1999. *Psychologists on the March: Science, Practice and Professional Identity in America, 1929–1969.* New York: Cambridge University Press.

Carbaugh, D. 1988. *Talking America: Cultural Discourses on Donahue.* Norwood, N.J.: Ablex.

Career Track. N.D. *Conquering Workplace Negativity.* Shawnee Missions, Kans.

Carpenter, C.R., R.T. Lennon and E.J. Shoben. 1957. "Suggestions for Public Relations." *American Psychologist* 12: 218.

Carson, John. 1993. "Army Alpha, Army Brass, and the Search for Army Intelligence." *Isis* 84: 278–309.

Carson, Judy, and Barbara Warren. 1995. "An Investigation of the Grief Counseling Services Available in the Middle Schools and High Schools in the State of Mississippi." *Omega* 30: 191–204.

Cattell, James McKeen. [1888] 1947. "The Psychological Laboratory at Leipsic." Pp. 7–20 in A.T. Poffenberger (ed.), *James McKeen Cattell: Man of Science.* Lancaster, Penna.: Science Press.

———. 1890. "Mental Tests and Measurements." *Mind* 15: 373–381.

———. 1893a. "Mental Measurement." *Philosophical Review* 2: 316–332.

———. 1893b. "The Progress of Psychology." *Popular Science Monthly* 43: 779–785.
———. 1898. "Professor Muensterberg on 'The Danger from Experimental Psychology.'" *Psychological Review* 5: 411–413.
———. 1903. "A Statistical Study of Eminent Men." *Popular Science Monthly* 57: 359–377.
———. 1904. "The Conceptions and Methods of Psychology." *Popular Science Monthly* 58: 176–186.
———. 1922. The First Year of the Psychological Corporation. Unpublished Manuscript.
———. 1923. "The Psychological Corporation." *Annals* 110: 166.
———. 1978 [1895]. "The Progress of Psychology as an Experimental Science." Pp. 53–64 in Ernest Hilgard (ed.), *American Psychology in Historical Perspective: Addresses of the Presidents of the American Psychological Association, 1892–1977.* Washington, D.C.: American Psychological Association.
Chapman, Paul D. 1988. *Schools as Sorters: Lewis M. Terman, Applied Psychology, and the Intelligence Testing Movement, 1890–1930.* New York: New York University Press.
Charney, Nicolas. 1967a. "Editorial." *Psychology Today* 1 (1): 5.
———. 1967b. "Editorial." *Psychology Today* 1 (2): 5.
Choquet, Marie, Viviane Kovess and Nathalie Poutignat. 1993. "Suicidal Thoughts among Adolescents: An Intercultural Approach." *Adolescence* 28: 649–659.
Chriss, James. 1999. "Introduction." Pp. 1–29 in J. Chriss (ed.), *Counseling and the Therapeutic State.* New York: Aldine de Gruyter.
Cicourel, Aaron. 1964. *Method and Measurement in Sociology.* New York: Free Press.
Claparede, Edouard. 1911. *Experimental Pedagogy and the Psychology of the Child.* Translated by M. Louch and H. Holman. New York: Longmans, Green.
Clark, K.E. 1957. *America's Psychologists: A Survey of a Growing Profession.* Washington, D.C.: American Psychological Association.
Clarke-Stewart, K.A. 1978. "Popular Primers for Parents." *American Psychologist* (April): 359–369.
Cloud, Dana. 1998. *Control and Consolation in American Culture and Politics: Rhetoric of Therapy.* Thousand Oaks, Calif.: Sage.
Cohen, Louis. 1954. "Level-of-Aspiration Behavior and Feelings of Adequacy and Self-Acceptance." *Journal of Abnormal and Social Psychology* 49: 84–86.
Cohen, Ronald. 1985. "Child-Saving and Progressivism, 1885–1915." Pp. 273–309 in J. Hawes and N.R. Hiner (eds.), *American Childhood: A Research Guide and Historical Handbook.* Westport, Conn.: Greenwood Press.
Coleville, W.J. 1895. "The Ethics of Mental Healing." *Metaphysical Magazine* 1: 73–82.
Collins, Harry. 1985. *Changing Order: Replication and Induction in Scientific Practice.* London: Sage.
Collins, Randall. 1999. *The Sociology of Philosophies: A Global Theory of Intellectual Change.* Cambridge, Mass.: Harvard University Press.
Coon, Deborah. 1992. "Testing the Limits of Sense and Science: American Experimental Psychologists Combat Spiritualism, 1880–1920." *American Psychologist* 47: 143–151.
Coopersmith, Stanley. 1967. *The Antecedents of Self-Esteem.* San Francisco: W.H. Freeman.
Cooter, R., and S. Pumfrey. 1994. "Separate Spheres and Public Places: Reflections

on the History of Science Popularization and Science in Popular Culture." *History of Science* 32: 237–267.

Costner, Herbert. 1980. *The Changing Folkways of Parenthood: A Content Analysis.* New York: Arno Press.

Courtis, Stuart. 1925. "Data on Ability-Grouping from Detroit." *Twenty-Fourth Yearbook*, part 2. Bloomington, Ind.: Public School.

Crampton, C. Ward. 1908. *Anatomical and Physiological Age.* New York: Bobbs-Merrill.

Crary, Jonathan. 1990. *Techniques of the Observer: On Vision and Modernity in the Nineteenth Century.* Cambridge, Mass.: MIT Press.

Crockenberg, Susan, and Barbara Soby. 1989. "Self-Esteem and Teenage Pregnancy." Pp. 125–164 in A. Mecca, N. Smelser and J. Vasconcellos (eds.), *The Social Importance of Self-Esteem.* Berkeley: University of California Press.

Cunningham, Raymond. 1962. "The Emmanuel Movement: A Variety of American Religious Experience." *American Quarterly* 14: 48–63.

Dahlstrom, W. Grant. 1985. "The Development of Psychological Testing." Pp. 64–114 in G. Kimble and K. Schlesinger (eds.), *Topics in the History of Psychology,* vol. 2. Hillsdale, N.J.: Lawrence Erlbaum Associates.

Dahlstrom, W. Grant and Leona Dahlstrom. 1980. "Section I: Original Scale Development." Pp. 3–6 in W.G. Dahlstrom and L. Dahlstrom (eds.), *Basic Readings on the MMPI: A New Selection on Personality Measurement.* Minneapolis: University of Minnesota Press.

Danziger, Kurt. 1979. "The Positivist Repudiation of Wundt." *Journal of the History of the Behavioral Sciences* 15: 205–230.

———. 1990. *Constructing the Subject: Historical Origins of Psychological Research.* New York: Cambridge University Press.

———. 1997. *Naming the Mind: How Psychology Found Its Language.* London: Sage.

Darnton, Robert. 1968. *Mesmerism and the End of Enlightenment.* Cambridge, Mass.: Harvard University Press.

Delcato, C.H. 1959. *The Treatment and Prevention of Reading Problems.* Springfield, Ill.: Charles C. Thomas.

De Man, Paul. 1971. *Blindness and Insight: Studies in the Rhetoric of Contemporary Criticism.* New York: Oxford University Press.

Deming, W. Edwards. 1986. *Out of the Crisis.* New York: Cambridge University Press.

———. 1993. *The New Economics for Industry, Government, Education.* Cambridge, Mass.: MIT Center for Advanced Engineering Study.

Dennis, Paul. 1989. "'Johnny's a Gentleman, but Jimmie's a Mug: Press Coverage during the 1930s of Myrtle McGraw's Study of Johnny and Jimmy Woods." *Journal of the History of the Behavioral Sciences* 25: 356–370.

———. 1991. "Psychology's First Publicist: Addington Bruce and the Popularization of the Subconscious and Power of Suggestion Before World War I." *Psychological Reports* 68: 755–765.

Dennis, Wayne, and Edwin G. Boring. 1952. "The Founding of the APA." *American Psychologist* 7: 95–97.

Derrida, Jacques. 1976. *Of Gramatology.* Translated by G. Spivak. Baltimore: Johns Hopkins University Press.

Dewey, John. 1887. *Psychology.* New York: Harper and Brothers.

———. 1926. "Dewey on Interest." Pp. 575–576 in C. Skinner, I. Gast, and H. Skinner (eds.), *Readings in Educational Psychology*. New York: D. Appleton.

———. 1978 [1899]. "Psychology and Social Practice." Pp. 65–79 in Ernest Hilgard (ed.), *American Psychology in Historical Perspective: Addresses of the Presidents of the American Psychological Association, 1892–1977*. Washington, D.C.: American Psychological Association.

Diagnostic and Statistical Manual of Mental Disorders. 4th ed. 1994. Washington, D.C.: American Psychiatric Association.

Dickson, W.J. 1950. "The Hawthorne Plan of Personnel Counseling." Pp. 133–138 in A.H. Brayfield (ed.), *Readings in Modern Methods of Counseling*. New York: Appleton-Century-Crofts.

DiMaggio, Paul, and W.W. Powell. 1983. "The Iron Cage Revisited: Institutional Isomorphism and Collective Rationality in Organizational Fields." Pp. 63–82 in W. Powell and P. DiMaggio (eds.), *The New Institutionalism in Organizational Analysis*. Chicago: University of Chicago Press.

Dineen, Tana. 1996. *Manufacturing Victims: What the Psychology Industry Is Doing to People*. Montreal: Robert Davies.

Dinkmeyer, Don, and Gary McKay. 1973. *Raising a Responsible Child: Practical Steps to Successful Family Relationships*. New York: Simon and Schuster.

Dollinger, S.S., and M.H. Thelen. 1978. "Children's Perceptions of Psychology." *Professional Psychology* 9: 117–126.

Douglas, Mary. 1984 [1966]. *Purity and Danger: An Analysis of the Concepts of Pollution and Taboo*. London: Arc Paperbacks.

———. 1986. *How Institutions Think*. Syracuse, N.Y.: Syracuse University Press.

Drake, Lewis. 1946. "A Social IE Scale for the MMPI." *Journal of Applied Psychology* 30: 51–54.

Dresser, Horatio. 1919. *A History of the New Thought Movement*. New York: Thomas Y. Crowell.

Dukes, Richard, and Barbara Lorch. 1989. "Concept of Self, Mediating Factors and Adolescent Deviance." *Sociological Spectrum* 9: 301–319.

Dunlap, Knight. 1912. "The Case against Introspection." *Psychological Review* 19: 404–413.

———. 1920. *Mysticism, Freud and Scientific Psychology*. St. Louis: C.V. Mosby.

Dunn, Lloyd (ed.). 1980. "Preface," A. Binet and T. Simon, in *The Development of Intelligence in Children*. Nashville, Tenn.: Williams. Pp. v–viii.

Dunnett, M.D. 1962. "Personnel Management." *Annual Review of Psychology* 13: 285–314.

Dunwoody, S., and B. Scott. 1982. "Scientists as Mass Media Sources." *Journalism Quarterly* 59: 52–59.

Dunwoody, S., and M. Ryan. 1985. "Scientific Barriers to the Popularization of Science in the Mass Media." *Journal of Communication* 35: 26–42.

Durkheim, Emile. 1965. *The Elementary Forms of the Religious Life*. Translated by J.W. Swain. London: Allen and Unwin.

———. 1973 [1898]. "Individuals and the Intellectuals." Pp. 43–57 in R. Bellah (ed.), *Emile Durkheim: On Morality and Society*. Chicago: University of Chicago Press.

Eagle, Carol, and Carol Coleman. 1993. *All That She Can Be*. New York: Simon and Schuster.

Eastman, D. 1958. "Self Acceptance and Marital Happiness." *Journal of Consulting Psychology* 22: 95–99.

Edward, Allen. 1970. *The Measurement of Personality Traits by Scales and Inventories*. New York: Holt, Rinehart and Winston.

Eisenberg, Arlene, Heidi Murkoff and Sandee Hathaway. 1994. *What to Expect: The Toddler Years*. New York: Workman.

Elias, Norbert. 1978. *The History of Manners: The Civilizing Process*, Vol. 1. New York: Pantheon Books.

Ellis, Albert. 1991. "My Life in Clinical Psychology." Pp. 1–37 in C. Walker (ed.), *The History of Clinical Psychology in Autobiography*, Vol. 1. Pacific Grove, Calif.: Brooks/Cole.

Ellis, Havelock. 1890. *The Criminal*. London: Walter Scott.

———. 1910. *Studies in the Psychology of Sex*, Vol. 1. Philadelphia: F.A. Davis.

Empey, L.T. 1978. *American Delinquency: Its Meaning and Construction*. Homewood, Ill.: Dorsey Press.

Erikson, Kai. 1976. *Everything in Its Path: Destruction of Community in the Buffalo Creek Flood*. New York: Simon and Schuster.

Ewen, S. 1988. *All Consuming Images: The Politics of Style in Contemporary Culture*. New York: Basic Books.

"Excerpts from Manuscript Linked to Suspect in 17-Year Series of Bombings." 1995. *New York Times* August 2: A16.

Fagan, Thomas. 1986. "The Historical Origins and Growth of Programs to Prepare School Psychologists in the United States." *Journal of School Psychology* 24: 9–22.

Faludi, Susan. 1991. *Backlash: The Undeclared War against American Women*. New York: Crown.

Fearing, Franklin. 1947. "Psychology and the Films." *Hollywood Quarterly* 2: 118–121.

Fechner, Gustav. 1966 [1860]. *Elements of Psychophysics*, Vol. 1. Translated by H. Adler. New York: Holt, Rinehart and Winston.

Feher, Michel. 1996. "Empowerment Hazards: Affirmative Action, Recovery Psychology and Identity Politics." *Representations* 55: 84–91.

Ferguson, Leonard. 1952. *Personality Measurement*. New York: McGraw-Hill.

Fernberger, Samuel. 1932. "The American Psychological Association: A Historical Summary, 1892–1930." *Psychological Bulletin* 29: 1–89.

Feyerabend. Paul. 1999. *Conquest of Abundance: A Tale of Abstraction versus the Richness of Being*. Chicago: University of Chicago Press.

Fisher, Dorothy C. 1916. *Self-Reliance: A Practical and Informal Discussion of Methods of Teaching Self-Reliance, Initiative, and Responsibility to Modern Children*. Indianapolis: Bobbs-Merrill.

Fleck, Ludwik. 1979 [1935]. *Genesis and Development of a Scientific Fact*. Translated by F. Bradley and T. Trenn. Chicago: University of Chicago Press.

Fortune. 1998. "Escape from the Cult of Personality Tests." *Fortune* 137 (5): 80–84.

Foster, Robert. 1937. "Servicing the Family through Counseling Agencies." *American Sociological Review* 2: 764–770.

Foucault, Michel. 1965. *Madness and Civilization: A History of Insanity in the Age of Reason*. Translated by R. Howard. New York: Vintage Books.

———. 1972. *The Archaeology of Knowledge*. Translated by A.M. Sheriden. New York Pantheon Books.

———. 1979. *Discipline and Punish: Birth of the Prison*. Translated by A. Sheridan. New York: Vintage Press.

———. 1986. "Of Other Spaces." *Diacritics* 16: 22–27.

———. 1988. "Technologies of the Self." Pp. 16–49 in L. Martin, H. Gutman and P. Hutton (eds.), *Technologies of the Self*. Amherst: University of Massachusetts Press.

Franz, Shepherd. 1917. "Activities of Clinical Psychologists." *Psychological Bulletin* 14: 224–229.

Fredman, Norman, and Robert Sherman. 1987. *Handbook of Measurements for Marriage and Family Therapy*. New York: Brunner/Mazel.

Freeman, Joseph. 1936. *An American Testament: A Narrative of Rebels and Romantics*. New York: Farrar and Rinehart.

Freeman, M.J. 1953. "Medical Acceptance of the Clinical Psychologist in Private Practice." *American Psychologist* 8: 88–89.

Friedman, Neil. 1967. *The Social Nature of Psychological Research: The Psychological Experiment as a Social Interaction*. New York: Basic Books.

Fuchs, Alfred. 1998. "Psychology and 'The Babe.'" *Journal of the History of the Behavioral Sciences* 34: 153–165.

———. 2000. "Contributions of American Mental Philosophers to Psychology in the United States." *History of Psychology* 3: 3–19.

Fuchs, Stephan, and Steven Ward. 1995. "What Is Deconstructionism, and Where and When Does It Take Place? Making Facts in Science; Building Cases in Law." *American Sociological Review* 59: 481–500.

Fuchs, Stephan. 1992. *The Professional Quest for Truth: A Social Theory of Science and Knowledge*. Albany: State University of New York Press.

———. 1993. "Three Sociological Epistemologies." *Sociological Perspectives* 36: 23–44.

———. 1996. "The New Wars of Truth: Conflict over Science Studies as Differential Modes of Observation." *Social Science Information* 35: 307–326.

———. 2001. *Against Essentialism: A Theory of Culture and Society*. Cambridge, Mass.: Harvard University Press.

Furumoto, Laurel. 1988. "Shared Knowledge: The Experimentalists, 1904–1929." Pp. 94–113 in J. Morawski (ed.), *The Rise of Experimentation in American Psychology*. New Haven, Conn.: Yale University Press.

Galison, Peter. 1997. *Image and Logic: A Material Culture of Microphysics*. Chicago: University of Chicago Press.

Galton, Francis. 1879. "Psychometric Experiments." *Brain* 2: 147–162.

Garfield, Sol. 1966. "Clinical Psychology and the Search for Identity." *American Psychologist* 21: 342–352.

———. 1991. "A Career in Clinical Psychology." Pp. 87–123 in C. Walker (ed.), *The History of Clinical Psychology in Autobiography*, Vol. 1. Pacific Grove, Calif.: Brooks/Cole.

Garrett, Henry. 1932. "Psychology Today: A Brief Introduction for Radio Listeners." Pp. 5–28 in W. Bingham (eds.), *Psychology Today: Lectures and Study Manual*. Chicago: University of Chicago Press.

Geertz, Clifford. 1973. *The Interpretation of Cultures*. New York: Basic Books.

Geraghty, Mary. 1994. "Helping People Cope with Disaster." *Chronicle of Higher Education*, September 21: A7.

Gerbner, George. 1961. "Psychology, Psychiatry and Mental Illness in the Mass Media: A Study of Trends, 1900–1959." *Mental Hygiene* 45: 89–93.

Gergen, Kenneth. 1991. *The Saturated Self: Dilemmas of Identity in Contemporary Life*. New York: Basic Books.

Gerow, Josh (ed.). 1988. *Time: Psychology 1923–1988*. New York: Time.

Giddens, Anthony. 1991. *Modernity and Self-Identity: Self and Society in the Late Modern Era*. Stanford, Calif.: Stanford University Press.

Gieryn, Thomas. 1983. "Boundary-Work and the Demarcation of Science from Non-Science: Strains and Interests in Professional Ideologies of Scientists." *American Sociological Review* 48: 781–795.

Gilbert, Steven, and Judith Sheiman. 1995. "Mandatory Counseling of University Students: An Oxymoron?" *Journal of College Student Psychotherapy* 9: 3–21.

Gillespie, Richard. 1993. *Manufacturing Knowledge: A History of the Hawthorne Experiments*. New York: Cambridge University Press.

Gilman, Sander. 1988. *Disease and Representation: Images of Illness from Madness to AIDS*. Ithaca, N.Y.: Cornell University Press.

Gladding, Samuel. 1998. *Family Therapy: History, Theory, and Practice*. 2nd ed. Upper Saddle River, N.J.: Prentice Hall.

Goddard, Henry H. 1910. "Four Hundred Feeble-Minded Children Classified by the Binet Method." *Journal of Psycho-Asthenics* 15: 17–30.

———. 1928. *School Training of Gifted Children*. Yonkers, N.Y.: World.

Goffman, Erving. 1967. *Interaction Ritual: Essays on Face-to-Face Behavior*. Garden City, N.Y.: Anchor Books.

Goethe, Johann Wolfgang von. 1962 [1792]. *Italian Journey 1786–1788*. Translated by W.H. Auden and E.B. Mayer. San Francisco: North Point Press.

Goldberg, Lewis. 1971. "A Historical Survey of Personality Scales and Inventories." Pp. 293–336 in P. McReynolds (ed.), *Advances in Psychological Assessment*. Palo Alto, Calif.: Science and Behavior Books.

Gomart, Emilie and Antoine Hennion. 1999. "A Sociology of Attachment: Music Amateurs, Drug Users." Pp. 220–247 in J. Law and J. Hassard (eds.), *Actor Network Theory and After*. Oxford: Blackwell.

Goodwin, C. James. 1985. "On the Origins of Titchener's Experimentalists." *Journal of the History of the Behavioral Sciences* 21: 383–389.

Gottman, J., H. Markman, C. Notarius and J. Gonso. 1976. *The Couple's Guide to Communication*. Champaign, Ill.: Research Press.

Gottman, John, and Nan Silver. 1999. *The Seven Principles for Making Marriage Work*. New York: Crown.

Graff, M., and T.N. Clair. 1973. "Requirements for Certification of School Psychologists: A Survey of Recent Trends." *American Psychologist* 28: 704–705.

Graham, John. 1987. *The MMPI: A Practical Guide*. 2nd ed. New York: Oxford University Press.

Gray, John. 1992. *Men Are from Mars, Women Are from Venus: A Practical Guide for Improving Communication and Getting What You Want in Your Relationship*. New York: HarperCollins.

Gray, Susan. 1963. *The Psychologist in the Schools*. New York: Holt, Rinehart and Winston.

Greenberg, Josh. 1996. "U.S. Funds Drug Treatment Experiment." *Los Angeles Times*, July 4, 1996: A16.

Griffin, Christine. 1997. "Representations of the Young." Pp. 17–25 in J. Roche and S. Tucker (eds.), *Youth in Society: Contemporary Theory, Policy and Practice*. London: Sage.

Grinder, Robert. 1981. "The 'New' Science of Education: Educational Psychology in Search of a Mission." Pp. 354–366 in F. Farley and N. Gordon (eds.), *Psychology and Education: The State of the Union*. Berkeley: McCutchan.

Grinker, Roy, and John Spiegel. 1945. *Men under Stress*. New York: McGraw-Hill.

Griswold, Alfred. 1934. "New Thought: A Cult of Success." *American Journal of Sociology* 40: 309–318.

Gross, Martin. 1978. *The Psychological Society*. New York: Random House.

Gross, Paul, and Norman Levitt. 1994. *Higher Superstition: The Academic Left and Its Quarrels with Science*. Baltimore: Johns Hopkins University Press.

Grossack, M. 1954. "Some Negro Perceptions of Psychologists: An Observation on Psychology's Public Relations." *American Psychologists* 9: 188–189.

Grunwald, Bernice, and Harold McAbee. 1998. *Guiding the Family: Practical Counseling Techniques*. 2nd ed. Philadelphia: Accelerated Development.

Guest, L. 1948. "The Public's Attitudes toward Psychologists." *American Psychologist* 3: 135–139.

Guinn, Stephen. 1991. "Psychological Testing." Pp. 63–81 in C. Hansen and K. Conrad (eds.), *A Handbook of Psychological Assessment in Business*. New York: Quorum Books.

Habermas, Jürgen. 1979. *Communication and the Evolution of Society*. Boston: Beacon Press.

———. 1987. *The Theory of Communicative Action*, Vol. 2. Translated by T. McCarthy. Boston: Beacon Press.

Hacking, Ian. 1983. *Representing and Intervening: Introductory Topics in the Philosophy of Natural Science*. Cambridge: Cambridge University Press.

———. 1986. "Making Up People." Pp. 222–236 in T. Heller, M. Sosna and D. Wellbery (eds.), *Reconstructing Individualism: Autonomy, Individuality, and the Self in Western Thought*. Stanford, Calif.: Stanford University Press.

———. 1992. "The Self-Vindication of the Laboratory Sciences." Pp. 29–64 in A. Pickering (ed.), *Science as Practice and Culture*. Chicago: University of Chicago Press.

———. 1995. *Rewriting the Soul: Multiple Personality and the Science of Memory*. Princeton, N.J.: Princeton University Press.

———. 1998. *Mad Travelers: Reflections on the Reality of Transient Mental Illnesses*. Charlottesville: University of Virginia Press.

———. 1999. *The Social Construction of What?* Cambridge, Mass.: Harvard University Press.

Haggerty, M.E. 1921. "Intelligence and Its Measurement: A Symposium." *Journal of Educational Psychology* 12: 212–216.

Hale, Matthew. 1980. *Human Science and Social Order: Hugo Muensterberg and the Origins of Applied Psychology*. Philadelphia: Temple University Press.

Hale, N.G. 1971. *Freud and Americans: The Beginnings of Psychoanalysis in the United States, 1876–1917.* New York: Oxford University Press.

Hall, G. Stanley. 1891. "Editorial." *Pedagogical Seminary* 1 (June): 121.

———. 1894. *Addresses and Proceedings of the National Education Association.*

———. 1969 [1904]. *Adolescence,* Vols. 1 and 2. New York: Arno Press.

———. 1926. "The Ideal School." Pp. 713–714 in C. Skinner, I. Gast and H. Skinner (eds.), *Readings in Educational Psychology.* New York: D. Appleton.

———. 1965. *Health, Growth and Heredity.* New York: Teachers College Press.

Hall, Leslie. 1992. "Forbidden by God, Despised by Men: Masturbation, Medical Warnings, Moral Panic, and Manhood in Great Britain, 1850–1950." Pp. 293–315 in J. Fout (ed.), *Forbidden History: The State, Society and the Regulation of Sexuality in Modern Europe.* Chicago: University of Chicago Press.

Hall, Winfield S. 1924. "The Adolescent Period; Its Problems, Regimen and Hygiene." Pp. 300–324 in M.V. O'Shea (ed.), *The Child: His Nature and His Needs.* Valparaiso, Ind.: Children's Foundation.

Hally, Carolyn, and Robert Pollack. 1993. "The Effects of Self-Esteem, Variety of Sexual Experience, and Erotophilia on Sexual Satisfaction in Sexually Active Heterosexuals." *Journal of Sex Education and Therapy* 19: 183–192.

Hamachek, Don. 1992. *Encounters with the Self.* 4th ed. New York: Harcourt Brace Javanovich.

Hanson, F. Allan. 1993. *Testing Testing: Social Consequences of the Examined Life.* Berkeley: University of California Press.

Hardyment, Christina. 1983. *Dream Babies: Three Centuries of Good Advice on Childcare.* New York: Harper and Row.

Harper, Robert. 1950. "The First Psychological Laboratory." *Isis* 41: 158–161.

Hart, Louise. 1987. *The Winning Family: Increasing Self-Esteem in Your Children and Yourself.* New York: Dodd, Mead.

Hathaway, Starke, and J.C. McKinley. 1940. "A Multiphasic Personality Schedule (Minnesota): I. Construction of the Schedule." *Journal of Psychology* 10: 249–254.

———.1943. *MMPI Manual.* Minneapolis: University of Minnesota Press.

Havemann, Ernest. 1957. *The Age of Psychology.* New York: Simon and Schuster.

Hazelton, Deborah. 1991. *Solving the Self-Esteem Puzzle.* Dearfield Beach, Fla.: Health Communications.

Healy, William. 1915. *Honesty: A Study of the Causes and Treatment of Dishonesty among Children.* Indianapolis: Bobbs-Merrill.

Hearnshaw, Leslie S. 1987. *The Shaping of Modern Psychology.* New York: Routledge and Kegan Paul.

Heckscher, Charles. 1994. "Defining the Post-Bureaucratic Type." Pp. 25–28 in C. Heckscher, Charles and A. Donnelon (eds.). 1994. *The Post-Bureaucratic Organization.* Thousand Oaks, Calif.: Sage.

Hepner, Harry. 1938. *Human Relations in Changing Industry.* New York: Prentice Hall.

Herman, Ellen. 1995. *The Romance of American Psychology: Political Culture in the Age of Experts.* Berkeley: University of California Press.

Hersch, Patricia. 1988. "On Screen: Thirtysomething Therapy." *Psychology Today* (October): 62–64.

Hildreth, Gertrude. 1930. *Psychological Services for School Problems*. Yonkers, N.Y.: World Book.

Hilgard, Ernest. 1978. "Introduction: The American Psychological Association and Its Presidents." Pp. 3–15 in E. Hilgard (ed.), *American Psychology in Historical Perspective: Addresses of the Presidents of the American Psychological Association, 1892–1977*. Washington, D.C.: American Psychological Association.

———. 1987. *Psychology in America: A Historical Survey*. New York: Harcourt Brace Jovanovich.

Hirschauer, Stefan. 1991. "The Manufacture of Bodies in Surgery." *Social Studies of Science* 21: 279–319.

Hochberg, Julian. 1979. "Sensation and Perception." Pp. 89–142 in E. Hearst (ed.), *The First Century of Experimental Psychology*. Hillsdale, N.J.: Lawrence Erlbaum Associates.

Horne, Herman. 1904. *Philosophy of Education*. New York: Macmillan.

———. 1906. *The Psychological Principles of Education: A Study in the Science of Education*. New York: Macmillan.

Hornstein, Gail. 1988. "Quantifying Psychological Phenomena: Debates, Dilemmas, and Implications." Pp. 1–34 in J. Morawski (ed.), *The Rise of Experimentation in American Psychology*. New Haven, Conn.: Yale University Press.

———. 1992. "The Return of the Repressed: Psychology's Problematic Relationship with Psychoanalysis, 1909–1960." *American Psychologist* 47: 254–263.

Hudson, Henry. 1893. *The Law of Psychic Phenomena: A Working Hypothesis for the Systematic Study of Hypnotism, Spiritualism, Mental Therapeutics, etc.* Chicago: A.C. McClung.

Hunt, Alan. 1998. "The Great Masturbation Panic and the Discourses of Moral Regulation in Nineteenth- and Early Twentieth-Century Britain." *Journal of the History of Sexuality* 8: 575–615.

Hutt, R.B.W. 1923. "The School Psychologist." *Psychological Clinic* 15: 48–51.

Humm, D.G., and G.W. Wadsworth. 1935. "The Humm-Wadsworth Temperament Scale." *American Journal of Psychiatry* 92: 163–200.

Impare, James, and Barbara Plake (eds.). 1998. *The Thirteenth Mental Measurements Yearbook*. Lincoln: University of Nebraska Press.

Jacobs, Gerard. 1994. "Helping People Cope with Disaster." *Chronicle of Higher Education*, September 12: A7.

———. 1995. "The Development of a National Plan for Disaster Mental Health." *Professional Psychology: Research and Practice* 26: 543–549.

James, William. 1890. *The Principles of Psychology*. New York: Henry Holt.

———. 1892. "A Plea for Psychology as a 'Natural Science.'" *Philosophical Review* 1: 146–153.

———. 1952 [1890]. *Principles of Psychology*. Chicago: Encyclopedia Britannica.

———. 1960a. "Address by the President." Pp. 58–63 in G. Murphy and R. Ballou (eds.), *William James on Psychical Research*. New York: Viking Press.

———. 1960b. "The Last Report: The Final Impressions of a Psychical Researcher." Pp. 309–325 in G. Murphy and R. Ballou (eds.), *William James on Psychical Research*. New York: Viking Press.

———. 1960c. "What Psychical Research Has Accomplished." Pp. 25–47 in G. Murphy and R. Ballou (eds.), *William James on Psychical Research*. New York: Viking Press.

———. 1961. *The Varieties of Religious Experience: A Study in Human Nature.* New York: Collier Books.

———. 1962 [1899]. *Talks to Teachers on Psychology and to Students on Some of Life's Ideals.* New York: Dover.

Jamieson, Lynn. 1999. "Intimacy Transformed? A Critical Look at the 'Pure Relationship.'" *Sociology* 33: 477–494.

Jastrow, Joseph. 1886. "Popular Psychology." *Science* 7: 106–108.

———. 1893. "The Section of Psychology." Pp. 50–60 in M.P. Hardy (ed.), *Official Catalogue: World's Columbia Exposition.* Chicago: W.B. Conkey.

———. 1900. *Fact and Fable in Psychology.* Boston: Houghton Mifflin.

———. 1901. "Some Currents and Undercurrents in Psychology." *Psychological Review* 8: 1–26.

———. 1908. "The Versatility of Psychology." *Dial* 38–41.

———. 1928. *Keeping Mentally Fit: A Guide to Everyday Psychology.* New York: Greenberg.

Jay, Martin. 1996. "Modernism and the Specter of Psychologism." *Modernism/Modernity* 3: 93–111.

Jenkins, Richard. 1954. "Understanding Psychiatrists." *American Psychologist* 9: 617–620.

Jerome, F. 1986. "Media Resource Service: Getting Scientists and the Media Together." *Impact of Science on Society* 36: 373–376.

Johnson, Ann. 1995. "Constructing the Child in Psychology: The Child-as-Primitive in Hall and Piaget." *Journal of Phenomenological Psychology* 26: 35–57.

"Joint Report on the Relations between Psychology and Psychiatry." 1960. *American Psychologist* 15: 198–200.

Jolly, Hugh. 1986. *Hugh Jolly Book of Child Care: The Complete Guide for Today's Parents.* London: Unwin.

Joncich, Geraldine. 1968. *The Sane Positivist: A Biography of Edward L. Thorndike.* Middletown, Conn.: Wesleyan University Press.

Jones, Ernest. 1920. *Treatment of Neuroses.* London: Bailliere, Tindall and Cox.

Jones, M. 1990. "The Rage for Recovery." *Publishers Weekly*, November 23: 16–24.

Judd, Charles. 1925. "The Curriculum: A Paramount Issue." Pp. 805–811 in *Addresses and Proceedings of the Sixty-third Annual Meeting of the National Education Association.* Washington, D.C.: National Education Association.

Judd, Daniel, and Richard Winder. 1995. "The Psychology of Quality." *Total Quality Management* 6: 287–291.

Jung, Carl. 1910. "The Association Method." *American Journal of Psychology* 31: 219–269.

Justman, Stewart. 1998. *The Psychological Mystique.* Evanston, Ill.: Northwestern University Press.

Kant, Immanuel. 1970 [1786]. *Metaphysical Foundations of Natural Science.* Translated by J. Ellington. Indianapolis: Bobbs-Merrill.

Kantor, J.R. 1979. "Psychology: Science or Nonscience." *Psychological Record* 29: 155–163.

Karier, Clarence. 1986. *Scientists of the Mind: Intellectual Founders of Modern Psychology.* Urbana: University of Illinois Press.

Katz, Elihu. 1999. "Theorizing Diffusion: Tarde and Sorokin Revisited." *Annals of the American Academy of Political and Social Science* 566: 144–155.

Katz, Elihu, and Paul Lazarsfeld. 1955. *Personal Influence: The Part Played by People in Mass Communications*. Glencoe, Ill.: Free Press.

Katzell, Raymond, and James Austin. 1992. "From Then to Now: The Development of Industrial-Organizational Psychology in the United States. *Journal of Applied Psychology* 77: 803–835.

Kazdin, A.E. 1986. "Comparative Outcome Studies of Psychotherapy: Methodological Issues and Strategies." *Journal of Consulting and Clinical Psychology* 54: 95–105.

Kelly, J. 1993. "Current Research on Children's Post-Divorce Adjustment: No Simple Answers." *Family and Reconciliation Courts Review* 31: 29–49.

Kent, Grace, and Aaron Rosanoff. 1910. "A Study of Association in Insanity." *American Journal of Insanity*. 67: 37–96, 317–390.

Kersey, Katharine. 1983. *The Art of Sensitive Parenting: The 10 Keys to Raising Confident, Competent, and Responsible Children*. Washington, D.C.: Acropolis Books.

Kett, Joseph. 1977. *Rites of Passage: Adolescence in America 1790 to the Present*. New York: Basic Books.

Kilpatrick, W.H. 1922. "Coercion and Learning." *Journal of Educational Method* 1: 182–189.

King, Irving. 1914. *The High School Age*. Indianapolis: Bobbs-Merrill.

Kitcher, Philip. 1993. *The Advancement of Science: Science without Legend, Objectivity without Illusions*. New York: Oxford University Press.

Klausner, Samuel. 1953. "Social Class and Self-Concept." *Journal of Social Psychology* 38: 201–205.

Knorr-Cetina, Karin and Michael Mulkay (eds.). 1983. *Science Observed: Perspectives on the Social Study of Science*. London: Sage.

Knorr-Cetina, Karin. 1981. *The Manufacture of Knowledge: An Essay on the Constructivist and Contextual Nature of Science*. Oxford: Pergamon Press.

———. 1999. *Epistemic Cultures: How the Sciences Make Knowledge*. Cambridge, Mass.: Harvard University Press.

Krauthammer, Charles. 1999. "Politics as Therapy Has Gone too Far." *Buffalo News*, February 22: 3B.

Krohn, William. 1891. Facilities in Experimental Psychology in the Colleges of the United States. Washington, D.C.: n.p.

Kuhn, Thomas. 1962. *The Structure of Scientific Revolutions*. Chicago: University of Chicago Press.

Kuo, Z.Y. 1924. "A Psychology without Heredity." *Psychological Review* 31: 427–448.

Kusch, Martin. 1995. *Psychologism: A Case Study in the Sociology of Philosophical Knowledge*. London: Routledge.

———. 1999. *Psychological Knowledge: A Social History and Philosophy*. London: Routledge.

Kurzweil, Edith. 1989. *The Freudians: A Comparative Perspective*. New Haven, Conn.: Yale University Press.

L'Abate, Luciano. 1981. "Skill Training Programs for Couples and Families." Pp. 631–661 in A. Gurman and D. Kniskern (eds.), *Handbook of Family Therapy*. New York: Brunner/Mazel.

Labaree, David. 1997. *How to Succeed in School without Really Learning: The Credentials Race in American Education*. New Haven, Conn.: Yale University Press.

Labi, Nadya. 1999. "The Grief Brigade." *Time* 153 (19), May 17: 69–70.

Ladd, George T. 1894. "President's Address before the New York Meeting of the American Psychological Association." *Psychological Review* 1: 1–21.

———. 1899. "On Certain Hindrances to the Progress of Psychology in America." *Psychological Review* 6: 121–133.

Ladd-Franklin, Christine. 1916. " Letter to the Editor." *Nation* 103: 373–374.

LaFollette, Marcel. 1990. *Making Science Our Own: Public Images of Science 1910–1955.* Chicago: University of Chicago Press.

Lagemann, Ellen C. 2000. *An Elusive Science: The Troubling History of Educational Research.* Chicago: University of Chicago Press.

Landy, Frank. 1992. "Hugo Muensterberg: Victim or Visionary?" *Journal of Applied Psychology* 77: 787–802.

———. 1993. "Early Influences on the Development of Industrial/Organizational Psychology." Pp. 83–118 in T. Fagan and G. VandenBos (eds.), *Exploring Applied Psychology: Origins and Critical Analysis.* Washington, D.C.: American Psychological Association.

Latour, Bruno. 1983. "Give Me a Laboratory and I Will Raise the World." Pp. 141–170 in K. Knorr-Cetina and M. Mulkay (eds.), *Science Observed: Perspectives on the Social Study of Science.* London: Sage.

———. 1987. *Science in Action.* Cambridge, Mass.: Harvard University Press.

———. 1988a. "Comments on 'The Sociology of Knowledge about Child Abuse.'" *Nous* 22: 67–69.

———. 1988b. *The Pasteurization of France.* Cambridge, Mass.: Harvard University Press.

———. 1991. "Technology Is Society Made Durable." *Sociological Review Monograph* 38: 103–131.

———. 1993. *We Have Never Been Modern.* Cambridge, Mass.: Harvard University Press.

———. 1996. *Aramis, or the Love of Technology.* Cambridge, Mass.: Harvard University Press.

———. 1999. *Pandora's Hope: Essays of the Reality of Science Studies.* Cambridge, Mass.: Harvard University Press.

Latour, Bruno, and Steve Woolgar. 1986. *Laboratory Life: The Construction of Scientific Facts.* 2nd ed. Princeton, N.J.: Princeton University Press.

Lavelle, Louis. 1998. "Hirers Peeking into Corners of the Mind: Use of Psychology Test Is Rising." *Record,* July 8: B01.

Law, John. 1986. "On Power and Its Tactics: A View from the Sociology of Knowledge." *Sociological Review* 34: 1–37.

Law, John, and John Whittaker. 1988. "On the Art of Representation: Notes on the Politics of Visualization." Pp. 160–183 in G. Fyfe and J. Law (eds.), *Picturing Power: Visual Depiction and Social Relations.* London: Routledge.

Lawson, Hilary. 1985. *Reflexivity: The Postmodern Predicament.* La Salle, Ill.: Open Court.

Leacock, Stephen. 1924. "A Manual of the New Mentality." *Harpers* (March): 471–480.

Leahey, Thomas. 2000. *A History of Psychology.* 5th ed. Upper Saddle River, N.J.: Prentice Hall.

Lears, T.J. Jackson. 1981. *No Place of Grace: Antimodernism and the Transformation of American Culture 1880–1920.* New York: Pantheon Books.

———. 1983. "From Salvation to Self-Realization: Advertising and the Therapeutic Roots of the Consumer Culture, 1880–1930." Pp. 3–38 in R.W. Fox and T.J.J. Lears (eds.), *The Culture of Consumption: Critical Essays in American History, 1880–1980*. New York: Pantheon Books:

Leary, David. 1979. "Wundt and After: Psychology's Shifting Relations with the Natural Sciences, Social Sciences and Philosophy." *Journal of the History of the Behavioral Sciences* 15: 231–241.

———. 1982. "Immanuel Kant and the Development of Modern Psychology." Pp. 17–42 in W. Woodward and M. Ash (eds.), *The Problematic Science: Psychology in Nineteenth-Century Thought*. New York: Praeger.

———. 1987. "Telling Likely Stories: The Rhetoric of the New Psychology, 1880–1920." *Journal of the History of the Behavioral Sciences* 23: 315–331.

Lenoir, Timothy. 1997. *Instituting Science: The Cultural Production of Scientific Disciplines*. Stanford, Calif.: Stanford University Press.

Leplin, Jarrett (ed.). 1984. *Scientific Realism*. Berkeley: University of California Press.

Lesser, Gerald. 1976. "Applications of Psychology to Television Programming: Formulation of Program Objectives." *American Psychologist* 31: 135–136.

Levanway, Russell. 1955. "The Effects of Stress on Expressed Attitudes toward Self and Others." *Journal of Abnormal and Social Psychology* 50: 225–226.

Levine, Murray, and Adeline Levine. 1970. *A Social History of Helping Services: Clinic, Court, School, and Community*. New York: Meredith.

Levine, Murray, and J. Wishner. 1977. "The Case Records of the Psychological Clinic at the University of Pennsylvania." *Journal of the History of the Behavioral Sciences* 13: 59–66.

Lewis, Robert, and Hugh Petersen. 1974. *Human Behavior: An Introduction*. New York: Ronald Press.

Lindemann, E. 1944. "Symptomatology and Management of Acute Grief." *American Journal of Psychiatry* 101: 141–148.

Littman, Richard. 1979. "Social and Intellectual Origins of Experimental Psychology." Pp. 39–86 in E. Hearst (ed.), *The First Century of Experimental Psychology*. New York: Lawrence Erlbaum Associates.

Loomans, Diane. 1991. *The Lovables in the Kingdom of Self-Esteem*. Tiburon, Calif.: H.J. Kramer.

Lowell, Frances. 1922. "An Experiment in Classifying Primary Grade Children by Mental Age." *Journal of Applied Psychology* 6: 276–290.

Lowenstein, L.F. 1989. "Homicide: A Review of Recent Research." *Criminologist* 13: 74–89.

Lundy, Frank. 1992. "Hugo Muensterberg: Victim or Visionary?" *Journal of Applied Psychology* 77: 787–802.

Lutz, Tom. 1991. *American Nervousness, 1903: An Anecdotal History*. Ithaca, N.Y.: Cornell University Press.

Lynch, Michael. 1985. *Art and Artifact in Laboratory Science: A Study of Shop Work and Shop Talk in a Research Laboratory*. London: Routledge and Kegan Paul.

———. 1991. "Pictures of Nothing? Visual Construals in Social Theory." *Sociological Theory* 9: 1–21.

Lyotard, Jean-Francois. 1984. *The Postmodern Condition: A Report on Knowledge*. Minneapolis: University of Minnesota Press.

MacIntyre. Alasdair. 1981. *After Virtue: A Study in Moral Theory*. Notre Dame, Ind.: University of Notre Dame Press.

Madigan, Robert, Susan Johnson and Patricia Linton. 1995. "The Language of Psychology: APA Style as Epistemology." *American Psychologist* 50: 428–435.

Maher, Brendan, and Winifred Maher. 1979. "Psychopathology." Pp. 561–621 in E. Hearst (ed.), *The First Century of Experimental Psychology*. Hillsdale, N.J.: Lawrence Erlbaum Associates.

Malone, Dumas (ed.). 1934. *Dictionary of American Biography*, Vol. 7. New York: Charles Scribner's Sons.

Manis, Melvin. 1955. "Social Interaction and the Self Concept." *Journal of Abnormal and Social Psychology* 51: 362–370.

Maranhao, Tullio. 1986. *Therapeutic Discourse and Socratic Dialogue*. Madison: University of Wisconsin Press.

Marcuse, Herbert. 1955. *Eros and Civilization*. New York: Vintage Books.

Marston, William. 1928. *Emotions of Normal People*. New York: Harcourt, Brace.

———. 1936. *You Can Be Popular*. New York: Home Institute.

———. 1939. *March On! Facing Life with Courage*. New York: Doubleday, Doran.

Marx, John, and Joseph Seldin. 1973. "Crossroads of Crisis: I. Therapeutic Sources and Quasi-Therapeutic Functions of Post-Industrial Communes." *Journal of Health and Social Behavior* 14: 39–50.

Maslow, Abraham. 1942. "Self-Esteem (Dominance Feeling) and Sexuality in Women." *Journal of Social Psychology* 16: 259–294.

———. 1954. *Motivation and Personality*. New York: Harper and Row.

———. 1962. *Toward a Psychology of Being*. New York: D. Van Nostrand.

Matthews, Fred. 1988. "The Utopia of Human Relations: The Conflict-Free Family in American Social Thought, 1930–1960." *Journal of the History of the Behavioral Sciences* 24: 343–362.

Matza, David. 1969. *Becoming Deviant*. Englewood Cliffs, N.J.: Prentice Hall.

May, Rollo. 1953. "Legislation in Various States: New York." *American Psychologist* 8: 579.

Maynard, Douglas. 1982. "Defendant Attributes in Plea Bargaining: Notes on the Modeling of Sentencing Decisions." *Social Problems* 29: 347–360.

Mayo, Elton. 1933. *The Human Problem of an Industrial Civilization*. New York: Macmillan.

———. 1937. "What Every Village Knows." *Survey Graphic* 26: 695–698.

McCall, Robert, and S. Holly Stocking. 1982. "Between Scientists and Public: Communicating Psychological Research through the Mass Media." *American Psychologist* 37: 985–995.

McKeach, Wilbert. 1953. "Legislation in Various States: Michigan." *American Psychologist* 8: 578.

McNally, Richard. 1999. "AEMDR and Mesmerism: A Comparative Historical Analysis." *Journal of Anxiety Disorders* 13: 225–236.

McMurry, Robert. 1944. *Handling Personality Adjustment in Industry*. New York: Harper and Brothers.

Mead, Margaret. 1942. *And Keep Your Powder Dry*. New York: Morrow.

Meadow, James. 1996. "Breaking the Homeless Cycle: Advocates See Progress in Transitional Housing, Counseling Even Though Numbers May Be Higher." *Denver Rocky Mountain News*, July 21: 4A.

Mehan, H. 1986. "The Role of Language and Language of Role in Institutional

Decision Making." Pp. 140–163 in S. Fisher and A.D. Todd (eds.), *Discourse and Institutional Authority: Medicine, Education and Law*. Norwood, N.J.: Ablex.

Mehan, H., A. Hertweck and J.L. Meihls. 1986. *Handicapping the Handicapped: Decision Making in Students' Educational Careers*. Stanford, Calif.: Stanford University Press.

Melidonis, G.G., and B.H. Bry. 1995. "Effects of Therapist Exception Questions on Blaming and Positive Statements in Families with Adolescent Behavior Problems." *Journal of Family Psychology* 9: 451–457.

Menninger, Karl. 1947. "Psychology and Psychiatry." *American Psychologist* 2: 139–140.

Mental Health Weekly. 1995. "Hundreds Call Children's Hotline to Talk about Bombing." *Mental Health Weekly*, July 10: 5–6.

Menzies, K. 1921. *Autoerotic Phenomena in Adolescence: An Analytical Study of the Psychology and Psychopathology of Onanism*. New York: Paul B. Hoeber.

Mercer, Jane. 1973. *Labeling the Mentally Retarded: Clinical and Social Systems Perspectives on Mental Retardation*. Berkeley: University of California Press.

Meredith, Christabel. 1916. *The Educational Bearings of Modern Psychology*. Boston: Houghton Mifflin.

Meyer, John. 1988. "The Social Construction of the Psychology of Childhood: Some Contemporary Processes." Pp. 47–65 in E. Hetherington, R. Lerner and M. Perlmutter (eds.), *Child Development in Life-Span Perspective*. Hillsdale, N.J.: Lawrence Erlbaum Associates.

Meyers, John, and Brian Rowan. 1977. "Institutionalized Organizations: Formal Structure as Myth and Ceremony." *American Journal of Sociology* 83: 340–363.

Michael, Mike. 1996. *Constructing Identities: The Social, the Nonhuman and Change*. London: Sage.

Miller, G.A. 1969. "Psychology as a Means of Promoting Human Welfare." *American Psychologist* 24: 1063–1075.

Miller, Peter, and Nikolas Rose. 1994. "On Therapeutic Authority: Psychoanalytical Expertise under Advanced Liberalism." *History of the Human Sciences* 7: 29–64.

Miller, S., E.W. Nunnally and D. Wackman. 1975. *Alive and Aware: Improving Communication in Relationships*. Minneapolis: Interpersonal Communications Program.

Miles, Walter, Weston Bousfield and Marion Bills. 1953. "Legislation in Various States: Connecticut." *American Psychologist* 8: 572.

Miner, Burt G. 1904. "The Changing Attitude of American Universities toward Psychology." *Science* 20 (505): 299–307.

Minuchin, Salvador. 1974. *Families and Family Therapy*. Cambridge, Mass.: Harvard University Press.

Monroe, Walter. 1950. *Encyclopedia of Education Research*. Rev. ed. New York: Macmillan.

Moore, R. Laurence. 1977. *In Search of White Crows: Spiritualism, Parapsychology and American Culture*. New York: Oxford University Press.

Moran, Joseph. 1989. "Newspaper Psychology: Advice and Therapy." *Journal of Popular Culture* 22: 119–127.

Moran, Joseph, and Barbara Moran. 1990. "Psychology Today: Recasting the Popular Image of a Profession." *Journal of American Culture* 13: 109–115.

Morawski, Jill, and Gail Hornstein. 1991. "Quandary of the Quacks: The Struggle for Expert Knowledge in American Psychology, 1890–1940." Pp. 106–133 in J. Brown and D. van Keuren (eds.), *The Estate of Social Knowledge*. Baltimore: Johns Hopkins University Press.

Morawski, Jill. 1986. "Psychologists for Society and Societies for Psychologists: SPSSI's Place among Professional Organizations." *Journal of Social Issues* 42: 111–126.

Morgan, C.D., and H. Murray. 1935. "A Method for Investigating Fantasies." *Archives of Neurology and Psychiatry* 34: 289–306.

Moskowitz, Eva. 1995. "The Therapeutic Gospel: Religious Medicine and the Birth of Pop Psychology, 1850–1910." *Prospects* 20: 57–86.

———. 2001. *In Therapy We Trust: America's Obsession with Self-Fulfillment*. Baltimore: Johns Hopkins University Press.

Moyer, Diane. 1995. "An Opposing View on Prescription Privileges for Psychologists." *Professional Psychology Research and Practice* 26: 586–590.

Muensterberg, Hugo. 1893. "Psychological Laboratory at Harvard University." Available: www.psyclassics.yorkca/Muster/lab.

———. 1908. *On the Witness Stand*. Garden City, N.Y.: Doubleday and Page.

———. 1909. *Psychotherapy*. New York: Moffat, Yard.

———. 1913. *Psychology and Industrial Efficiency*. Boston: Houghton Mifflin.

———. 1916. *The Photoplay: A Psychological Study*. New York: D. Appleton.

Mussen, Paul, and Mary Jones. 1957. "Self-Conceptions, Motivations, and Interpersonal Attitudes of Late- and Early-Maturing Boys." *Child Development* 28: 243–256.

Myers, Charles, and F.C. Bartlett. 1911. *A Text-Book of Experimental Psychology with Laboratory Exercises*. New York: Longmans, Green.

Myers, Diane. 1994. *Disaster Response and Recovery: A Handbook for Mental Health Professionals*. Washington, D.C.: U.S. Department of Health and Human Services.

Myers, Lewis. 1924. "Preface." P. v in M.V. O'Shea (ed.), *The Child: His Nature and His Needs*. Valparaiso, Ind.: Childrens Foundation.

Napoli, Donald S. 1981. *Architects of Adjustment: The History of the Psychological Profession in the United States*. Port Washington, N.Y.: Kennikat Press.

National Research Council. 1943. *Psychology for the Fighting Man*. New York: Penguin Books.

Neubauer, John. 1992. *The Fin-de-Siecle Culture of Adolescence*. New Haven: Yale University Press.

New York Psychiatrical Society. 1917. "Activities of Clinical Psychologists." *Psychological Bulletin* 14: 224–225.

Nichols, H. 1893. "The Psychological Laboratory at Harvard." *McClure's* 1: 399–409.

Nichols, William. 1992. *The AAMFT: Fifty Years of Marital and Family Therapy*. Washington, D.C.: American Association of Marriage and Family Therapy.

Nolan, James. 1999. "Acquiescence or Consensus? Consenting to Therapeutic Pedagogy." Pp. 107–129 in J. Chriss (ed.), *Counseling and the Therapeutic State*. New York: Aldine de Gruyter.

Nudelman, Franny. 1997. "Beyond the Talking Cure: Listening to Female Testimony on the Oprah Winfrey Show." Pp. 297–315 in J. Pfister and N. Schnog (eds.), *Inventing the Psychological: Toward a Cultural History of Emotional Life in America*. New Haven, Conn.: Yale University Press.

Nussbaum, Emily. 2000. "Inside the Love Lab: A Research Psychologist Goes Pop." *Lingua Franca* (March): 25–32.

Oates, Martha. 1988. "Responding to Death in Schools." *TACD Journal* 16: 83–96.

O'Donnell, John. 1979. "The Clinical Psychology of Lightner Witmer: A Case Study of Institutional Innovation and Intellectual Change." *Journal of the History of the Behavioral Sciences* 15: 3–17.

———. 1985. *Origins of Behaviorism: American Psychology, 1870–1920*. New York: New York University Press.

O'Shea, Harriet. 1953. "Legislation in Various States: Indiana." *American Psychologist* 8: 576–577.

O'Shea, Michael. 1920a. *First Steps in Child Training*. Chicago: Frederick J. Drake.

———. 1920b. *The Trend of the Teens*. Chicago: Frederick J. Drake.

———. 1920c. *Faults of Childhood and Youth*. Chicago: Frederick J. Drake.

———. 1920d. *Everyday Problems in Child Training*. Chicago: Frederick J. Drake.

———. (ed.). 1924. *The Child: His Nature and His Needs*. Valapariso, Ind.: Childrens Foundation.

———. 1929. *Newer Ways with Children*. New York: Greenberg.

Otto, Mary. 1999. "High Cost of Divorce Driving New State Efforts to Strengthen Marriage." *Buffalo News*, February 21: 1H.

Overstreet, H.A. 1949. *The Mature Mind*. New York: W.W. Norton.

Page, R., and T. Page. 1993. *Fostering Emotional Well-Being in the Classroom*. Boston: Jones and Bartlett.

Palmer, Edward. 1976. "Applications of Psychology to Television Programming: Program Execution." *American Psychologist* 31: 137–138.

Parker, Gail. 1973. *Mind Cure in New England: From the Civil War to World War I*. Hanover, N.H.: University Press of New England.

Patterson, Donald. 1923. "A Note on Popular Pseudo-Psychological Beliefs." *Journal of Applied Psychology* 7: 101–102.

Peale, Norma V. 1952. *The Power of Positive Thinking*. New York: Prentice Hall.

Pearce, K. 1988. "ABC Series Getting in Touch with Audiences' Feelings." *Channels* (February): 12.

Pearl, David. 1954. "Ethnocentrism and the Self Concept." *Journal of Social Psychology* 40: 138–147.

Peck, Janice. 1995. "TV Talk Shows as Therapeutic Discourse: The Ideological Labor of the Televised Talking Cure." *Communication Theory* 5: 58–81.

Perera, Thomas, and Edward Haupt. 2001. "Museum of the History of Reaction Time Research." Available: http://www.chss.monclair.edu/psychology/museum/mrt.html.

Perloff, R.S., and L.S. Perloff. 1977. "The Fair: An Opportunity for Depicting Psychology and for Conducting Behavioral Research." *American Psychologist* 32: 220–229.

Peterson, D.R. 1968. *The Clinical Study of Social Behavior*. New York: Appleton-Century-Crofts.

Peyrot, Mark. 1995. "Psychological Testing and Forensic Decision Making: The Properties-in-Use of the MMPI." *Social Problems* 42: 574–586.

Pfister, Joel. 1997a. "On Conceptualizing the Cultural History of Emotional and Psychological Life in America." Pp. 17–59 in J. Pfister and N. Schnog (eds.), *Inventing the Psychological: Toward a Cultural History of Emotional Life in America*. New Haven, Conn.: Yale University Press.

———. 1997b. "Glamorizing the Psychological: The Politics of Performances of Modern Psychological Identities." Pp. 167–213 in J. Pfister and N. Schnog (eds.), *Inventing the Psychological: Toward a Cultural History of Emotional Life in America*. New Haven, Conn.: Yale University Press.

Phillips, Beeman. 1990. *School Psychology at a Turning Point*. San Francisco: Jossey-Bass.

Piaget, Jean. 1929. *The Child's Conception of the World*. Translated by J. and A. Tomlinson. New York: Harcourt, Brace.

Pincus, Walter, and Vernon Loeb. 1999. "Los Alamos Actions May Take Months; Lab Must Follow University's Procedures." *Washington Post*, August 31: A04.

Pipher, Mary. 1994. *Reviving Ophelia: Saving the Selves of Adolescent Girls*. New York: Ballantine Books.

Pollack, Robert, and Margaret Brenner. 1969. "Editors' Introduction." Pp. ix–xiv in R. Pollack and M. Brenner (eds.), *The Experimental Psychology of Alfred Binet*. New York: Springer.

Polsky, Andrew. 1991. *The Rise of the Therapeutic State*. Princeton, N.J.: Princeton University Press.

Poovey, Mary. 1998. *A History of the Modern Fact: Problems of Knowledge in the Sciences of Wealth and Society*. Chicago: University of Chicago Press.

Poponoe, Paul. 1946. "Biography." Pp. 487–488 in A. Rothe (ed.), *Current Biography*. New York: H.W. Wilson.

Popplestone, John, and Marion McPherson. 1984. "Pioneer Psychology Laboratories in Clinical Settings." Pp. 196–272 in J. Brozek (ed.), *Explorations in the History of Psychology in the United States*. Lewisburg, Penna.: Bucknell University Press.

Porter, Theodore. 1994. "Objectivity as Standardization: The Rhetoric of Impersonality in Measurement, Statistics, and Cost-Benefit Analysis." Pp. 197–237 in A. Megil (ed.), *Rethinking Objectivity*. Durham, N.C.: Duke University Press.

Powers, Francis, T.R. McConnell, William C. Trow, Bruce Moore and Charles Skinner. 1938. *Psychology in Everyday Living*. Boston: D.C. Heath.

Price, Derek de Solla. 1986. *Little Science, Big Science and Beyond*. New York: Columbia University Press.

Prilleltensky, Issaac. 1994. *The Morals and Politics of Psychology: Psychological Discourse and the Status Quo*. Albany: State University of New York Press.

Prince, Morton. 1929. *Clinical and Experimental Studies in Personality*. Cambridge, Mass.: Sci-Art.

Psychology Today. 2000. "Work." *Psychology Today* 32 (3): 14.

Putnam, Hilary. 1994. "Sense, Nonsense and the Senses: An Inquiry into the Powers of the Human Mind." *Journal of Philosophy* 91: 445–517.

Raimy, Victor. 1949. "Self Reference in Counseling Interviews." *Journal of Consulting Psychology* 12: 153–163.

Reckless, Walter, Simon Dinitz and Barbara Kay. 1957. "The Self Component in Potential Delinquency and Potential Non-Delinquency." *American Sociological Review* 22: 566–570.

Reed, Edward. 1997. *From Soul to Mind: The Emergence of Psychology from Erasmus Darwin to William James*. New Haven, Conn.: Yale University Press.

Reisman, John. 1991. *A History of Clinical Psychology*. 2nd ed. New York: Hemisphere.

Remmers, H.H. 1944. "Psychology: Some Unfinished Business." *Psychological Bulletin* 41: 713–724.

Reynolds, W.M., and N. Sundberg. 1976. "Recent Research Trends in Testing." *Journal of Personality Assessment* 40: 228–233.

Rhees, David. 1979. "A New Voice for Science: Science Service under Edwin E. Slosson, 1921–29." Master's thesis, Chapel Hill: University of North Carolina.

Rieff, Philip. 1966. *Triumph of the Therapeutic: Uses of Faith after Freud.* New York: Harper and Row.

Roethlisberger, Fritz, and William Dickson. 1939. *Management and the Worker: An Account of a Research Program Conducted by the Western Electric Company, Hawthorne Works, Chicago.* Cambridge, Mass.: Harvard University Press.

Rogers, Arthur. 1958. "The Self Concept in Paranoid Schizophrenia." *Journal of Clinical Psychology* 14: 365–366.

Rogers, Carl, and Rosalind Dymond (eds.). 1954. *Psychotherapy and Personality Change.* Chicago: University of Chicago Press.

Rogers, Carl. 1951. *Client-Centered Therapy: Its Current Practice, Implications, and Theory.* New York: Houghton Mifflin.

Rorschach, Hermann. 1942 [1921]. *Psychodiagnostics.* Translated by P. Lemkau and B. Kronenberg. New York: Grune and Stratton.

Rorty, Richard. 1979. *Philosophy and the Mirror of Nature.* Princeton, N.J.: Princeton University Press.

———. 1991. *Objectivity, Relativism, and Truth.* New York: Cambridge University Press.

Rose, Nikolas. 1985. *The Psychological Complex: Psychology, Politics, and Society in England, 1869–1939.* London: Routledge and Kegan Paul.

———. 1990. *Governing the Soul: The Shaping of the Private Self.* London: Routledge.

———. 1996a. "Power and Subjectivity: Critical History and Psychology." Pp. 103–124 in C. Graumann and K. Gergen (eds.), *Historical Dimensions of Psychological Discourse.* Cambridge: Cambridge University Press.

———. 1996b. *Inventing Our Selves: Psychology, Power, and Personhood.* Cambridge: Cambridge University Press.

———. 1996c. "Psychiatry as Political Science: Advanced Liberalism and the Administration of Risk." *History of the Human Sciences* 9: 1–23.

Rosenberg, Morris. 1965. *Society and the Adolescent Self-Image.* Princeton, N.J.: Princeton University Press.

Ross, Alan. 1991. "Memories and Reflections." Pp. 183–224 in C. Walker (ed.), *The History of Clinical Psychology in Autobiography*, Vol. 1. Pacific Grove, Calif.: Brooks/Cole.

Ross, Dorothy. 1972. *G. Stanley Hall: The Psychologist as Prophet.* Chicago: University of Chicago Press.

Ruckmick, Christian. 1912. "The History and Status of Psychology in the United States." *American Journal of Psychology* 23: 522–531.

———. 1926. "Development of Laboratory Equipment in Psychology in the United States." *American Journal of Psychology* 37: 582–592.

Russell, William. 1932. "The Place of the American Psychiatric Association in Modern Psychiatric Organization and Progress." *American Journal of Psychiatry* 12: 1–18.

Ryan, A.M., and P.R. Sackett. 1987. "A Survey of Individual Assessment Practices by I/O Psychologists." *Personnel Psychology* 40: 455–488.

Ryan, Judith. 1991. *The Vanishing Subject: Early Psychology and Literary Modernism.* Chicago: University of Chicago Press.

Sandoval, Jonathan. 1993. "The History of Interventions in School Psychology." *Journal of School Psychology* 31: 195–217.

Sanford, Edmund. 1893. "Some Practical Suggestions on the Equipment of a Psychological Laboratory." *American Journal of Psychology* 5: 429–438.

———. 1898. *A Course in Experimental Psychology.* Boston: D.C. Heath.

Satir, Virginia. 1967. *Conjoint Family Therapy.* Palo Alto, Calif.: Science and Behavior Books.

Schnack, George. 1953. "Comment." *American Psychologist* 8: 593–594.

Schnog, Nancy. 1997. "On Inventing the Psychological." Pp. 3–16 in J. Pfister and N. Schnog (eds.), *Inventing the Psychological: Toward a Cultural History of Emotional Life in America.* New Haven, Conn.: Yale University Press.

Schumm, W.R., S.R. Bollman and A.P. Jurich. 1981. "Dimensionality of the Relationship Inventory: An Urban Replication with Married Couples." *Psychological Reports* 48: 51–56.

Scripture, E.W. 1895. *Thinking, Feeling, Doing.* New York: Chautaugua-Century Press.

———. 1916. "Reaction Time in Nervous and Mental Diseases." *Journal of Medical Science* 62: 698–719.

Seale, Clive. 1998. *Constructing Death: The Sociology of Dying and Bereavement.* New York: Cambridge University Press.

Seashore, Carl. 1942. *Pioneering in Psychology.* Iowa City: University of Iowa Press.

Shapin, Steven. 1988. "Following Scientists Around." *Social Studies of Science* 18: 533–550.

———. 1994. *A Social History of Truth: Civility and Science in Seventeenth-Century England.* Chicago: University of Chicago Press.

Shapin, Steven, and Simon Schaffer. 1985. *Leviathan and the Air-Pump: Hobbes, Boyle, and the Experimental Life.* Princeton, N.J.: Princeton University Press.

Sharma, S.L. 1956. "Some Personality Correlates of Changes in Self-Esteem under Conditions of Stress and Support." *Journal of Education and Psychology* 14: 154–165.

Shiff, Eileen. 1987. *Experts Advise Parents: A Guide to Raising Loving, Responsible Children.* New York: Delacorte Press.

Shostrom, Everett. 1975. *Manual, Caring Relationship Inventory.* San Diego, Calif.: Educational and Industrial Testing Service.

Simonds, Wendy. 1992. *Women and Self-Help Culture: Reading between the Lines.* New Brunswick, N.J.: Rutgers University Press.

Sklar, Robert. 1979. "Prime-Time Psychology." *American Film* (March): 59–63.

Sleeter, Christine. 1986. "Learning Disabilities: The Social Construction of a Special Education Category." *Exceptional Children* 53: 46–54.

Smith, Laurence. 1981. "Psychology and Philosophy: Toward a Realignment, 1905–1935." *Journal of the History of the Behavioral Sciences* 17: 28–37.

Smith, Roger, and David Schroeder. 1980. "Psychology for the Public: A Content Analysis of Psychology Today." *Professional Psychology* (April): 228–235.

Smith, Timothy. 1997. "Punt, Pass and Ponder the Questions: In the N.F.L., Personality Tests Help Teams Judge Draftees." *New York Times*, April 20: 11.

Snider, Alvin. 1999. "Stifling the Naysayer in an Age of Compulsory Niceness." *Chronicle of Higher Education*, May 7: A64.

Snyder, T.D., C. Hoffman and C. Geddes. 1997. *Digest of Educational Statistics 1997.* Washington, D.C.: U.S. Department of Education.

Sokal, Michael, Audrey Davis and Uta Merzbach. 1976. "Laboratory Instruments in the History of Psychology." *Journal of the History of the Behavioral Sciences* 12: 59–64.

Sokal, Michael. 1987. "James McKeen Cattell and Mental Anthropometry: Nineteenth-Century Science and Reform and the Origins of Psychological Testing." Pp. 21–45 in M. Sokal (ed.), *Psychological Testing and American Society*. New Brunswick, N.J.: Rutgers University Press.

Song, Elaine. 2001. "Jury Awards $1.5 Million over Stress Disorder." *Legal Intelligencer*, March 23: 1.

Soyland, A.J. 1994. *Psychology as Metaphor*. London: Sage.

Spector, Paul. 2000. *Industrial and Organization Psychology: Research and Practice*. 2nd ed. New York: Wiley.

Spillman, Jutta, and Lothar Spillman. 1993. "The Rise and Fall of Hugo Muensterberg." *Journal of the History of the Behavioral Sciences* 29: 322–338.

Spock, Benjamin. 1946. *The Common Sense Book of Baby and Child Care*. New York: Duell Sloan Pearce.

Star, Susan Leigh, and James Griesemer. 1989. "Institutional Ecology, 'Translations' and Boundary Objects: Amateurs and Professionals in Berkeley's Museum of Vertebrate Zoology, 1907–39." *Social Studies of Science* 19: 397–420.

Stark, Rodney, and William S. Bainbridge. 1980. "Networks of Faith: Interpersonal Bonds and Recruitment to Cults and Sects." *American Journal of Sociology* 85: 1376–1395.

Stark, Rodney. 1997. *The Rise of Christianity: How the Obscure, Marginal Jesus Movement Became the Dominant Religious Force in the Western World in a Few Centuries*. San Francisco: HarperCollins.

———. 1999. "Micro Foundations of Religion: A Revised Theory." *Sociological Theory* 17: 264–289.

Starker, Steven. 1989. *Oracle at the Supermarket*. New Brunswick, N.J.: Transaction.

Starr, Paul. 1982. *The Social Transformation of American Medicine*. New York: Basic Books.

Stearns, Carol, and Peter Stearns. 1986. *Anger: The Struggle of Emotional Control in America's History*. Chicago: University of Chicago Press.

Stearns, Peter. 1988. "Anger and American Work: A Twentieth-Century Turning Point." Pp. 123–149 in C. Stearns and P. Stearns (eds.), *Emotion and Social Change: Toward a New Psychohistory*. New York: Holmes and Meier.

Steere, Geoffrey. 1968. "Freudianism and Child-Rearing in the Twenties." *American Quarterly* 20: 759–767.

Steinem, Gloria. 1992. *Revolution from Within: A Book of Self-Esteem*. Boston: Little, Brown.

Steiner, Lee. 1953. "Figures on Charlatanism." *American Psychologist* 8: 708.

Sterrett, J. MacBride. 1909. "The Proper Affiliation of Psychology: With Philosophy or the Natural Sciences?" *Psychological Review* 16: 85–106.

Stewart, Lynn. 1993. "Profile of Female Firestarters: Implications for Treatment." *British Journal of Psychiatry* 163: 248–256.

Stille, Alexander. 1998. "The Betrayal of History." *New York Review of Books* 45 (10): 15–20.

Stoppard, Miriam. 1983. *Dr. Miriam Stoppard's Baby Care Book*. London: Dorling Kindersey.

Stotland, Ezra, and Alvin Zander. 1958. "Effects of Public and Private Failure on Self-Evaluation." *Journal of Abnormal and Social Psychology* 56: 223–229.

Stratton, George M. 1903. *Experimental Psychology and Its Bearing upon Culture*. New York: Macmillan.

Strauss, A.A., and N.C. Kephart. 1955. *Psychopathology and Education of the Brain-Injured Child*. New York: Grune and Stratton.

Strauss, A.A., and L.E. Lehtinen. 1963. *Psychology and Education of the Brain-Injured Child*. New York: Grune and Stratton.

Street, Warren. 1994. *A Chronology of Noteworthy Events in American Psychology*. Washington D.C.: American Psychological Association.

Strickland, Charles, and Andrew Ambrose. 1985. "The Baby Boom, Prosperity, and the Changing Worlds of Children, 1945–1963." Pp. 533–585 in J. Hawes and N.R. Hiner (eds.), *American Childhood: A Research Guide and Historical Handbook*. Westport, Conn.: Greenwood Press.

Strong, Charles. 1891. "A Sketch of the History of Psychology among the Greeks." *American Journal of Psychology* 4: 177–197.

Sweetland, Richard, and David Keyser (eds.). 1986. *Tests: A Comprehensive Reference for Assessment in Psychology, Education, and Business*. 2nd ed. Kansas City, Mo.: Test Corporation of America.

Swift, Edgar. 1914. *Learning and Doing*. Indianapolis: Bobbs-Merrill.

———. 1930. *Psychology and the Day's Work: A Study in the Application of Psychology to Daily Life*. New York: Charles Scribner's Sons.

Talen, Mary, and Janeece Warfield. 1997. "Guidelines for Family Wellness Checkups in Primary Health Services." Pp. 311–322 in L. Vandecreek, S. Snapp and T. Jackson (eds.), *Innovations in Clinical Practice: A Source Book*. Sarasota, Fla.: Professional Resource Press.

Tavris, Carol. 1999: "Mozart Isn't the Answer." *New York Times Book Review*, October 17: 14.

Taylor, Charles. 1989. *Sources of the Self: The Making of Modernity Identity*. Cambridge, Mass.: Harvard University Press.

Taylor, Eugene. 1994. "An Epistemological Critique of Experimentalism in Psychology: or, Why G. Stanley Hall Waited until William James Was out of Town to Found the American Psychological Association." Pp. 37–61 in H. Adler and R. Rieber (eds.), *Aspects of the History of Psychology in America: 1892–1992*. New York: New York Academy of Sciences.

———. 1999. *Shadow Culture: Psychology and Spirituality in America*. Washington, D.C.: Counterpoint.

Tead, Ordway. 1933. *Human Nature and Managers*. New York: McGraw-Hill.

Terman, Lewis. 1916. *The Measurement of Intelligence*. Boston: Houghton Mifflin.

———. 1921. "Intelligence and Its Measurement." *Journal of Educational Psychology* 12: 127–133.

———. 1932. "Trails to Psychology." Pp. 297–331 in C. Murchison (ed.), *A History of Psychology in Autobiography*, Vol. 2. Worcester, Mass.: Clark University Press.

———. 1938. *Psychological Factors in Marital Happiness*. New York: McGraw-Hill.

Textor, Martin. 1989. "The 'Healthy' Family." *Journal of Family Therapy* 11: 59–75.

Thoen, Gail. 1985. "Only Qualified Persons Should Be Parents." Pp. 193–211 in H. Feldman and M. Feldman (eds.), *Current Controversies in Marriage and Family*. Beverly Hills, Calif.: Sage.

Thorndike, Edward L. 1906. *The Principles of Teaching Based on Psychology*. New York: A.G. Seiler.

———. 1921. *The New Methods in Arithmetic*. Chicago: Rand McNally.

———. 1962. *Psychology and the Science of Education*. Edited by G. Joncich. New York: Columbia Teachers College Press.

Thornstam, Lars. 1992. "Loneliness in Marriage." *Journal of Social and Personal Relationships* 9: 197–217.

Thumin, F.J., and M. Zebelman. 1967. "Psychology vs. Psychiatry: A Study of Public Image." *American Psychologist* 22: 282–286.

Thurber, James. 1937. *Leave Your Mind Alone*. New York: Harper and Brothers.

Thurstone, L.L., and Thelma Thustone. 1930. "A Neurotic Inventory." *Journal of Social Psychology* 1: 3–30.

Titchener, Edward B. 1898. "A Psychological Laboratory." *Mind* 7: 311–331.

———. 1900. "The Equipment of a Psychological Laboratory." *American Journal of Psychology* 11: 251–265.

———. 1911. "A Note on the Consciousness of Self." *American Journal of Psychology* 22: 540–552.

———. 1971 [1902]. *Experimental Psychology: A Manual of Laboratory Practice*, Vol. 1. New York: Johnson Reprint.

Titchener, J.L., and F. Knapp. 1976. "Family and Character Change at Buffalo Creek." *American Journal of Psychiatry* 133: 295–299.

Tolor, Alexander. 1957. "Self-Perceptions of Neuropsychiatric Patients on the W-A-Y Test." *Journal of Clinical Psychology* 403–406.

Towne, Elizabeth. 1904. *Practical Methods for Self-Development, Spiritual—Mental—Physical*. Holyoke, Mass.: E. Towne.

Trilling, Lionel. 1951. *The Liberal Imagination: Essays on Literature and Society*. New York: Viking Press.

Trine, Ralph Waldo. 1897. *In Tune with the Infinite*. New York: Thomas Y. Crowell.

Tucker, James. 1999. *The Therapeutic Corporation*. New York: Oxford University Press.

Tweney, Ryan, and Cheri Budzynski. 2000. "The Scientific Status of American Psychology in 1900." *American Psychologist* 55: 1014–1017.

VandenBos, G., P. DeLeon and C. Belar. 1991. "How Many Psychological Practitioners Are Needed? It's Too Early to Know." *Professional Psychology: Research and Practice* 22: 441–448.

Vasconcellos, John. 1989. "Preface." Pp. xi–xxi in A. Mecca, N. Smelser and J. Vasconcellos (eds.), *The Social Importance of Self-Esteem*. Berkeley: University of California Press.

Vernon, P.E., and Gordon Allport. 1931. "A Test for Personal Values." *Journal of Abnormal Social Psychology* 26: 231–248.

Veroff, Joseph, Elizabeth Douvan and Richard Kulka. 1981. *The Inner American: A Self-Portrait from 1957–1976*. New York: Basic Books.

Viney, Linda. 1969. "Self: The History of a Concept." *Journal of the History of the Behavioral Sciences* 5: 349–359.

Viney, Wayne, Tom Michaels and Alan Ganong. 1981. "A Note on the History of

Psychology in Magazines." *Journal of the History of the Behavioral Sciences* 17: 270–272.

Volle, Frank. 1953. "Comment." *American Psychologist* 8: 594–595.

Wahler, H.J. 1958. "Social Desirablility and Self-Ratings of Intakes, Patients in Treatment, and Controls." *Journal of Consulting Psychology* 22: 357–363.

Walberg, Herbert, and Geneva Haertel. 1992. "Educational Psychology's First Century." *Journal of Educational Psychology* 84: 6–19.

Walkerdine, Valerie. 1984. "Developmental Psychology and the Child-Centered Pedagogy: The Insertion of Piaget into Early Education." Pp. 153–202 in J. Henriques, W. Hollway, C. Urwin, C. Venn and V. Walkerdine (eds.), *Changing the Subject: Psychology, Social Regulation and Subjectivity*. London: Methuen.

Wallin, J.E.W. 1911. "The New Clinical Psychology and the Psycho-Clinicist." *Journal of Educational Psychology* 2: 121–132, 191–210.

Ward, J. 1893. "'Modern' Psychology: A Reflection." *Mind* 2: 54–82.

Ward, Steven. 1995a. "The Making of Serious Speech: A Social Theory of Professional Discourse." *Current Perspectives in Social Theory* 15: 63–81.

———. 1995b. "The Revenge of the Humanities: Reality, Rhetoric, and the Politics of Postmodernism." *Sociological Perspectives* 38: 109–128.

———. 1996a. "Filling the World with Self-Esteem: A Social History of Truth Making." *Canadian Journal of Sociology* 21: 1–23.

———. 1996b. *Reconfiguring Truth: Postmodernism, Sciences Studies and the Search for a New Model of Knowledge*. Lanham, Md.: Rowman and Littlefield.

———. 1997. "Being Objective about Objectivity: The Ironies of Standpoint Epistemological Critiques of Science." *Sociology* 31: 1–19.

Watson, John B. 1917. "Practical and Theoretical Problems in Instinct and Habit." Pp. 51–99 in H. Jennings, J. Watson, A. Meyer and W. Thomas (eds.), *Suggestions of Modern Science Concerning Education*. New York: Macmillan.

———. 1928. *Psychological Care of Infant and Child*. New York: W.W. Norton.

Weiner, Bernard. 1990. "History of Motivational Research in Education." *Journal of Educational Psychology* 82: 616–622.

Weiss, Nancy. 1977. "Mother, the Invention of Necessity: Dr. Benjamin Spock's Baby and Child Care." *American Quarterly* 29: 519–546.

Weisz, J., B. Weiss and G.R. Donenberg. 1992. "The Lab versus the Clinic: Effects of Child and Adolescent Psychotherapy." *American Psychologist* 47: 1578–1585.

Wells, Edward, and Gerald Marwell. 1976. *Self-Esteem: Its Conceptualization and Measurement*. Beverly Hills, Calif.: Sage.

Welsh, George, and W. Grant Dahlstrom. 1956. "Section IV: New Scales." Pp. 178–180 in G. Welsh and W.G. Dahlstrom (eds.), *Basic Readings on the MMPI in Psychology and Medicine*. Minneapolis: University of Minnesota Press.

Whalen, Matthew. 1981. "Science, the Public and American Culture: A Preface to the Study of Popular Science." *Journal of American Culture* 4: 14–26.

White, Harrison. 1993. *Careers and Creativity: Social Forces in the Arts*. Boulder, Colo.: Westview Press.

White, Mimi. 1992. *Tele-Advising: Therapeutic Discourse in American Television*. Chapel Hill: University of North Carolina Press.

Whitehead, T. North. 1936. *Leadership in a Free Society*. Cambridge: Cambridge University Press.

Whitley, Richard. 1984. *The Intellectual and Social Organization of the Sciences*. Oxford: Clarendon Press.

———. 1985. "Knowledge Producers and Knowledge Acquirers: Popularisation as a Relation between Scientific Fields." Pp. 3–30 in T. Shinn and R. Whitley (eds.), *Expository Science: Forms and Functions of Popularisation*. Dordrecht, Neth.: D. Reidel.

Whyte, William. 1957. *The Organization Man*. Garden City, N.Y.: Doubleday.

Wierzbicki, Michael. 1999. *Introduction to Clinical Psychology: Scientific Foundations to Clinical Practice*. Boston: Allyn and Bacon.

Wiggam, Albert. 1928. *Exploring Your Mind with the Psychologists*. New York: Blue Ribbon Books.

Williams, Raymond. 1978. *Marxism and Literature*. New York: Oxford University Press.

Witmer, Lightner. 1897. "The Organization of Practical Work in Psychology." *Psychological Review* 4: 116–117.

———. 1907. "Clinical Psychology." *Psychological Clinic* 1: 1–9.

———. 1908. "Retrospect and Prospect: An Editorial." *Psychological Clinic* 2: 1–4.

———. 1909. "Review and Criticism: Mental Healing and the Emmanuel Movement." *Psychological Clinic* 3: 239–250.

———. 1996. "Clinical Psychology: Reprint of Witmer's 1907 Article." *American Psychologist* 51: 248–252.

Wittgenstein, Ludwig. 1953. *Philosophical Investigations*. Translated by G.E.M. Anscombe. New York: Macmillan.

Wodak-Engel, Ruth. 1984. "Determination of Guilt: Discourse in the Courtroom." Pp. 89–100 in C. Kramarae, M. Schultz and W. O'Barr (eds.), *Language and Power*. Beverly Hills, Calif.: Sage.

Wood, Henry. 1893. *Ideal Suggestion through Mental Photography: A Restorative System for the Home and Private Use, Preceded by a Study of the Laws of Mental Healing*. Boston: Lee and Shepard.

Wood, Wendy, Melinda Jones and Ludy Benjamin. 1986. "Surveying Psychology's Public Image." *American Psychologist* 41: 947–953.

Woodworth, Robert S. 1917. *Personal Data Sheet*. Chicago: C.H. Stoelting.

Wooldridge, Adrian. 1994. *Measuring the Mind: Education and Psychology in England, c.1860–c.1990*. Cambridge: Cambridge University Press.

Woolgar, Steve (ed.). 1988. *Knowledge and Reflexivity: New Frontiers in the Sociology of Knowledge*. London: Sage.

———. 1992. "Some Remarks about Positionism: A Reply to Collins and Yearley." Pp. 327–342 in A. Pickering (ed.), *Science as Practice and Culture*. Chicago: University of Chicago Press.

———. 1994. "Science and Technology Studies and the Renewal of Social Theory." CRICT Discussion Paper #41. Brunel: The University of West London.

Worcester, Elwood, Samuel McComb and Isador Coriat. 1908. *Religion and Medicine: The Moral Control of Nervous Disorders*. New York: Moffat, Yard.

Worden, J. William. 1982. *Grief Counseling and Grief Therapy: A Handbook for the Mental Health Practitioner*. New York: Springer.

Work in America: A Report of a Special Task Force to the Secretary of Health, Education and Welfare. 1973. Cambridge, Mass.: MIT Press.

Wrightsman, Lawrence. 1999. *Judicial Decision Making: Is Psychology Relevant?* New York: Kluwer Academic/Plenum.

Wundt, Wilhelm. 1969 [1902]. *Principles of Physiological Psychology.* Translated by Edward B. Titchener. New York: Kraus Reprint.

Wylie, Ruth. 1961. *The Self Concept: A Critical Survey of Pertinent Research Literature.* Lincoln: University of Nebraska Press.

Wynne, Brian. 1982. *Rationality and Ritual: The Windscale Inquiry and Nuclear Decision in Britain.* Keele: British Society for the History of Science Monograph.

Yankelovich, Daniel. 1981. *New Rules: Searching for Self-Fulfillment in a World Turned Upside Down.* New York: Random House.

Yates, Dorothy. 1932. *Psychological Racketeers.* Boston: Bruce Humphries.

Yerkes, Robert. 1930. "Scientific Method in Making Laws." *State Government* 3: 3–8.

Zenderland, Leila. 1987. "The Debate over Diagnosis: Henry Herbert Goddard and the Medical Acceptance of Intelligence Testing." Pp. 46–74 in M. Sokal (ed.), *Psychological Testing and American Society, 1890–1930.* New Brunswick, N.J.: Rutgers University Press.

Zimmerman, Jane. 1983. "Psychologists' Multiple Roles in Television Broadcasting." *Professional Psychology: Research and Practice* 14: 256–269.

Zuckerman, Marvin, Marc Baer and Irwin Monashkin. 1956. "Acceptance of Self, Parents and People in Patients and Normals." *Journal of Clinical Psychology* 12: 327–332.

Zuckerman, Marvin, and Irwin Monashkin. 1957. "Self-Acceptance and Psychopathology." *Journal of Consulting Psychology* 21: 145–148.

Index

Abbott, Andrew, 26, 34
Academic disciplines, 25–28, 38, 43, 54, 56, 80
Adams, Grace, 150
Adolescence, 75–76; sexuality in, 87–92
Aesthesiometric compass, 120
Allport, Floyd, and Gordon Allport, 127
American Association of Marriage Counselors (AAMC), 178
American Psychological Association (APA), 35, 42, 43 141; membership criteria, 44, 45, 214 n.4; reaction to outsiders, 46; and school psychologists, 67; and the media, 154, 157–58; reorganization of, 160, 214 n.6; and disaster mental health, 208–9; number of sections, 237 n.2
American Psychological Society, 160
American Society for Psychical Research (ASPR), 43, 143, 194
Association for Media Psychology, 158
AT&T Assessment Centers, 173–74
Attention-deficit/hyperactivity disorder, 4, 29

Bachelard, George, 123
Baldwin, James Mark, 38
Barnes, Barry, 109
Behaviorism, 96
Bernreuter Personality Inventory, 127–28
Binet, Alfred, 70, 138 n.13
Binet-Simon Test of Intelligence, 70, 138 n.13, Stanford revision, 71, 72
Bingham, Walter, 45, 151, 168, 169, 172, 219
Bloor, David, 30
Boring, Edwin, 135
Boulder model, 214 n.6
Boundary objects, 132
Bourdieu, Pierre, 3, 23, 30, 31–32 n.6
Bradshaw, John, 183
Branden, Nathaniel, 102
Briggs, Dorothy, 103
Brothers, Joyce, 155
Bruce, H. Addington, 94–95, 145–46, 195
Bureau of Salesman Research, 168
Burt, Cyril, 111

About the Author

STEVEN C. WARD is Associate Professor of Sociology at Western Connecticut State University. He is the author of *Reconfiguring Truth: Postmodernism, Science Studies and the Search for a New Model of Knowledge* (1996).